FIFTY DEAD
MEN WALKING

FIFTY DEAD MEN WALKING

THE HEROIC TRUE STORY OF A BRITISH
SECRET AGENT INSIDE THE IRA

MARTIN MCGARTLAND

JOHN BLAKE

Published by John Blake Publishing,
The Plaza,
535 Kings Road,
Chelsea Harbour,
London SW10 0SZ

www.johnblakebooks.com

www.facebook.com/johnblakebooks
twitter.com/jblakebooks

First published in hardback in 1997
First published in paperback in 2009
This edition published in 2019

ISBN: 978 1 78946 028 5

British Library Cataloguing-in-Publication Data:

A catalogue record for this book is available from the British Library.

Design by www.envydesign.co.uk

Printed and bound in Great Britain by Clays Ltd, Elcograf S.p.A.

3 5 7 9 10 8 6 4

John Blake Publishing is an imprint of Bonnier Books UK
www.bonnierbooks.co.uk

To my family and friends,
whom I can never see again.

CONTENTS

ACKNOWLEDGEMENTS

THERE ARE TOO MANY PEOPLE for me to thank individually who, in their own way, helped me through those years of my life which are now behind me. There are people to whom, literally, I owe my life during the years I was working under cover. To those people, whose names can never be revealed, I say thank you, for I know that you are still working, against tremendous odds, to save yet more lives.

In particular, I must thank those people who have encouraged me to write this book and who have made publishing possible, despite efforts made to keep the facts secret.

I must also thank my friends at the BBC who gave me support and encouragement, including Producer Nick Catliff, Presenter John Ware and Northern Ireland Reporter Mark Davenport. Thanks are also due to TV Producer Geoffrey Seed and journalists Liam Clarke and John Burns of *The Sunday Times*, whose knowledge and understanding of Northern Ireland affairs has been invaluable.

To writer and journalist Kathy Johnston I owe a great debt of gratitude; her enthusiasm and generosity of spirit encouraged me to sit and write the details of this manuscript.

And thanks to Nicholas Davies, the man without whose help this book would never have been written.

I give special thanks to two courageous community workers, Pastor Jack McKee and Sam Cushnahan of Families Against Intimidation and Terror (FAIT), who continue to risk their lives helping others on both sides of the sectarian divide.

PROLOGUE

I TURNED INSTINCTIVELY, knowing there was someone standing by my car. I saw the gun first of all, pointing directly towards me, and then I heard the thud, followed immediately by a second as two bullets slammed into the side of my body. I had lifted my arm to protect myself and the bullets had ripped into my right side just below my arm.

The power of those bullets threw me across the driver's seat. But I knew I had to do something otherwise I was a dead man.

The Provo gunman leant forward into the car pointing the gun almost at my head. Before he could fire a third time, I grabbed the gun by the barrel and tried to turn it so that if he pulled the trigger again he would shoot himself. He fired and the bullet ripped through my left hand, all but severing my thumb and I felt the bullet pass through my hand and embed itself in my stomach.

For a second or so I managed to cling on to the gun,

but he pulled away wrenching the gun from my grasp. I felt my strength ebbing away and although the adrenaline was pumping I couldn't hold on to the gun. At that moment I believed I was a dead man. I had lost the fight I had to win to stay alive. Now I feared the next bullet would be fatal, but I wasn't finished yet.

Somehow, from deep down, I found the strength to make another lunge towards him, to grab the gun a second time. I was desperately trying to stop him shooting me in the head. As I moved towards him he took a step backwards and fired four more times hitting me in the chest, either side of my heart. The power of those bullets sent me sprawling backwards across the car seats. Two more shots followed, one hitting me in the stomach, the other in the top of the leg. All his shots were more or less at point blank range.

Then the bastard turned and fled.

I realised that grabbing the gun had so disorientated the Provo gunman that he had panicked. I knew the Provo order –always shoot people in the head because then we know they're dead men. And dead men can't talk.

Throughout the shooting, I had felt no pain, only the thudding impact of the bullets each time they hit my body, knocking me backwards, knocking the stuffing out of me, preventing me from lunging at him and getting the gun. I guessed at the time it had to be something like a 9mm automatic.

After the bastard fled I knew I was a mess, but at least I had survived. Despite having been shot six or seven times I was still breathing, though blood was pumping from my chest, my side and my stomach and my thumb looked as though it had been shot away My only fear was that I would lie in that garage and bleed to death. I put my arm across my chest to try to stop the blood gushing out but it was everywhere. I wondered if the

Provo bastard had hit my heart or a main artery and realised that I had to stay conscious. I tried to feel my heart to see if it was OK and felt it pumping away. But I worried in case all the blood was being pumped out of my body rather than round my arteries.

I kept telling myself that whatever happened I must not fall asleep, though I felt like closing my eyes and drifting off into oblivion. I kept talking to myself, saying over and over again, 'If you fall asleep you will never wake again. If you fall unconscious you will simply die. Now for fuck's sake keep awake!'

And then I felt pain. A minute or so must have passed since the Provo bastard ran off, and until that moment I had felt nothing. Now the pain racked my body, my chest, my side, my stomach, my arm, my hand. Shit it hurt. I gritted my teeth to try to quell the pain, but I couldn't. I kept talking to myself, telling myself that I could handle the pain as long as I lived. I tried telling myself that the pain wasn't that bad, but it was getting to me. I just wanted to curl up and sleep.

I also realised that if I didn't get to hospital quickly I would be a goner. I tried to shout for help but the words wouldn't come. Somehow I couldn't find the strength, and only moans came from my throat.

Then I heard voices and looked up through the mist in my eyes and saw my neighbours, the Connon family, who live not far away.

Jesus it was good to see them; I could have cried when I realised they had come to the rescue, had come to help me. I knew the whole family – they were good, honest people and we had become friends. Somewhere in my mind I recalled that their elder son Adam, aged around eighteen, had studied first aid and that his mother, Andrea, was something to do with a hospital.

I heard them asking me questions and I can't recall if I

replied or not. My memory was going and so was my brain. I think I murmured 'fucking Provos'.

'Keep quiet, stay still,' Adam said. 'An ambulance is on the way. Just lie still and you'll be OK.

Adam took off my T-shirt and someone ran off and returned with cling film which he wrapped around my chest and my side in an effort to stem the bleeding. I remember him stuffing socks in my wounds trying to stop the flow of blood that was everywhere. I recall his mother Andrea cradling my head in her arms, talking to me, soothing me, keeping me conscious as we waited for the ambulance. I owe my life to that family and particularly Adam. If it hadn't been for his quick thinking I would be dead.

The next thing I remember was waking in hospital some forty-eight hours later, drifting in and out of consciousness. My mother Kate, sister Lizzie and brother Joseph were there standing around the bed, and I wondered why they were there – it all seemed like a dream. I couldn't understand what they were doing there, standing at the end of my bed looking at me. I asked if I was going to live. They gave me the answer I wanted to hear and I drifted away again into unconsciousness.

Five days after the shooting I was still in intensive care, guarded round-the-clock by seven armed police officers, all wearing body armour. For two years I had pleaded with the Northumbria Police and the Home Secretary Jack Straw to give me some protection but they had always refused saying I was in no danger from the IRA. They even refused to give me any CCTV system to check my house for any suspicious strangers.

And yet my former friends in Northern Ireland's Special Branch knew differently. They knew my life was still under threat even though there was a so-called ceasefire. They knew I was still high on the IRA's death list. But the Northumbria Police and the Home Secretary chose to ignore their advice.

If they had listened I would never have been shot because I would have had some protection. I was never cavalier about my security. I always knew they would have another go at me. And I was fucking determined to make sure they didn't get me.

That Thursday morning – 17 June – I had left my house in Duchess Street, Whitley Bay on Tyneside around 8.45am intending to drive my girlfriend to work. As usual, I checked if there were any suspicious strangers hanging around the lane behind my house. The lane seemed deserted. I had walked to the garage, opened the up-and-over door and checked for UCBTS – Under Car Booby Traps – but there were none. I carried out this routine every single day because I knew in my heart that the Provos would one day track me down, even though I was living under an assumed name at a secret address.

I unlocked the car, sat down in the seat and started the engine when I sensed someone was nearby. It had been nearly eight years since the Provos had first decided to kill me. Now they had returned for another try. Once again my luck had held. The man was tall and dark and wearing glasses. I think he had a goatee beard. I didn't recognise him but I'm sure I will if we ever meet again.

After the Good Friday Peace Agreement was signed in 1998, I had high hopes that one day I would be able to lead a normal, ordinary life once again: get a proper job, enjoy my life a little without the constant worry of waiting for the unexpected, the knock at the door, a bullet in the back or a gunman waiting by the garage to kill me. The longer the peace deal was intact, the more my hopes rose.

Then Eamonn Collins, a self-confessed IRA killer who turned against the terrorist movement, was murdered by the Provos. At the time of his shooting, I made a statement saying, 'Now I feel like I am waiting for someone to come to my house and shoot me.'

I tackled Sinn Fein President Gerry Adams during a radio talk show asking him when Sinn Fein/IRA were going to allow people like me to return in safety to Northern Ireland without fear of reprisal. His answer was evasive. That too made me realise that I had to keep my wits about me.

I heard in May this year that MI5 had warned senior politicians, including several former Northern Ireland Secretaries, to take extra care over security for they feared the Provos were intent on launching a new wave of violence. But no one warned me.

My Ma told me when she saw me lying in the hospital with bullet wounds all over my body, 'Marty, you can't go on like this. You've got to get away. You know the Provos will never give up trying to kill you, peace or no peace.'

I know she's right; my Ma was always right. Now I must persuade the Home Secretary and the Police to listen.

North Tyneside General Hospital
June 1999

GLOSSARY

Agent	An operative tasked to infiltrate an organisation and work undercover.
DMSU	Divisional Mobile Support Unit, used by the RUC as backup.
EO	Explosives Officer in the IRA.
Handle	User ID for CB radio.
Informer	A person who passes information to the police.
INLA	Irish National Liberation Army. A hard-line IRA splinter group formed in the 1970s.
IPLO	Irish People's Liberation Organisation. A small and radical IRA faction.
Loyalist	A Loyalist believes that Northern Ireland should remain part of Great Britain.
Mix	Homemade explosive made from fertiliser.
Oglaigh na hEireann	Irish Republican Army (Gaelic).
Peelers	Police.
PLO	Palestine Liberation Army.
Republican	A Republican believes in a Catholic, united Ireland.

RUC	Royal Ulster Constabulary, the Northern Irish police.
Sangar	Fortified observation post in an RUC base.
Saracen	Armoured vehicle used by the Army.
Sinn Fein	The political wing of the IRA cause, headed by Gerry Adams.
TCG	Tasking Co-ordination Group. A group of senior officers from intelligence and security services.
UDA	Ulster Defence Association. The largest and most organised Loyalist paramilitary group.
UPF	Ulster Freedom Fighters. A Loyalist paramilitary group.
UVF	Ulster Volunteer Force. A Loyalist paramilitary group.

CHAPTER ONE

IN THE BEGINNING THERE WERE THE FIFES AND DRUMS. The noise rose into the sky, over the houses and along the streets to where I was playing with my friends. I heard the high-pitched whistle of the fifes and the incessant roll of the drums and turned towards the noise. Curious, I followed the stream of older boys and girls, and the closer I came to the source of the noise, the more excited I became. Then we were all running down the street, across the patch of dark earth that was our playground and on up the hill eager to be a part of the noise.

It was the first time that I responded to the exhilarating sound of the bands that parade through the towns and villages of Northern Ireland during the summer months.

Throughout my childhood and beyond, I would stop and listen to those bands which, without fail, would awaken historical scars and wounds, instilling fear and hatred in some and a triumphant passion and pride in others.

That first answer to the band's magical call would,

1

however, cause my mother anxiety and consternation. It was July 1974, and I was four years old.

I had been playing with other children in the street when my mother realised I was missing. Other Catholic mothers in the neighbourhood had hurriedly collected their young children and taken them indoors when they first heard the distant sound of the drums. But no one had noticed me run off, following the older children. My mother went from house to house, calling my name, hoping to find me playing with some of the other toddlers. But in vain. Friends and neighbours on the estate joined the search but no one had seen me.

She could hear the loyalist band proudly practising *The Sash My Father Wore*, one of their great traditional tunes, as they marched down the Springmartin Road about 600 yards from our house. She looked across the open spaces but dismissed the idea that her little Marty could be there.

And yet, because there seemed nowhere else to search, she began to walk towards the beating drums, wondering if perhaps her lad could have made his way to the noise, attracted by the music. As she walked briskly towards the crowds gathered either side of the road, cheering and clapping the bandsmen in their grey suits, some with their Orange sashes across their bodies and their campaign medals proudly decorating their chests, a friend ran towards her.

'Kate,' the woman yelled above the noise of the crowd and the bandsmen banging and whistling away, 'have you got Marty with you?'

'No, he's missing,' my mother shouted. 'I can't find him anywhere.'

'I think he might be with the band,' she called back. 'I saw a little lad with red hair marching with them. It could have been your Marty.'

'Please God,' replied my mother, running towards the front of the band now half a mile away.

My mother, Kate McGartland, was well known in the area – a striking, slim, young woman with shoulder-length fair hair, green eyes and a strong personality who was never frightened to speak her mind. She had been brought up in a strong Republican tradition and, as a teenager, took part in civil rights demonstrations during the 1960s. She followed in the footsteps of her mother and become a powerful personality, both inside and outside the home.

As my mother ran along the street, darting among the crowds on the pavement, searching for her son, loyalist women called out, taunting her, 'Keep running, you Finian bitch.' Others shouted 'Papist whore' as my mother scanned the crowds in desperation, ignoring the catcalls.

Years later, my mother would tell me, 'I took no notice of their insults; I hardly noticed their obscenities. All I could think of was you, Marty, and what they might do to you.'

My mother found me happily walking and skipping along with the other children at the head of the band, without a care in the world. She noticed my red hair first and instinctively knew it was me, before she actually saw my proud, smiling face, excited by the music and the adventure.

She scooped me into her arms and cried as she carried me back home, one minute scolding me for running off, threatening to give me a good smacking; another, cradling me in her arms, kissing me, with the tears of relief streaming down her cheeks.

She would tell me all this when, many years later, she talked to me of her life and the hardship generations of her family had known; some moved around Ireland in search of an honest day's work, while others had emigrated to America in search of a new life in a new country.

My parents had met when they were teenagers and their first child, Catherine, was born in 1962. Catherine, however, died at the age of eleven when she fell through a skylight at the local school. The second child, Elizabeth was born in 1963 but my parents separated and my mother never re-married, although she kept her married name of McGartland.

Six months after I was born, we moved from the council flat where we lived in Moyard Crescent to a lovely, three-bedroom council house, with a neat, immaculate little garden, just 200 yards from our block of flats.

At that time, both Catholics and Protestants lived side by side on the Ballymurphy Estate of West Belfast, as they had done for generations. But the Troubles, which had exploded across Northern Ireland in 1969, caused the two communities to become openly suspicious of each other. As demonstrations became more fiercely sectarian and violence erupted on the estate, the Protestant families decided to leave the area and accommodation was found for them elsewhere in Belfast. During one weekend in August 1970, 320 Protestant families were moved from the estate to safer housing.

My mother would tell me, 'We were very lucky. I was a young mother with three children and I had known this lovely Protestant widow who was in her eighties who had lived on the estate for years. When I heard that Protestant families were moving out, I went to see her and asked if I could move into her house if she ever decided to leave. The night before she was due to move, she sent a message to me and I immediately went to see her. She invited me to stay the night, telling me she would leave early the following morning. The next day I helped her pack and made her a cup of tea. We kissed each other goodbye and I thanked her. She told me that she had been very happy in the house and wished me luck. She also asked me to take care of the garden for it had been her pride and joy.'

I would never know my father because he moved away from Ireland and settled in the north of England. For a couple of years after their separation he would return to Belfast to see the family, but his visits became less frequent and, when my mother met another man, he would never come back.

During much of my childhood, however, my mother lived on her own with my two sisters and me in the smart new council house. But, on a number of occasions from 1974 to 1978, we had unwelcome visitors disturbing our sleep and wrecking our home.

The British Army, backed by the Royal Ulster Constabulary, would descend in force on the estate and select a number of houses to search, looking for arms and explosives.

I would often wake to a loud knocking at the front door and my mother shouting, 'I'm coming, I'm coming. Wait a moment; wait a moment.'

Sometimes the soldiers wouldn't wait, though, and I would hear the terrifying banging, then the smashing and splintering of wood as they broke down the front door, forcing their way into the hall. I would lie in bed, hiding under the blankets, too frightened to move and the soldiers with their guns and helmets would crash open my bedroom door and snatch away the bedclothes.

'Get out! Get out!' they would shout at me.

My mother would come in, grabbing hold of me as she shouted abuse at the soldiers who pulled out all the drawers from the chest, opened the wardrobe, tore up the carpet and threw my clothes all over the floor. I would stand holding my mother's hand as she told the soldiers to get out of the house and to stop scaring innocent young children.

Sometimes I would be pulled from the bed, pushed to the other side of the room and told to stand still. Other soldiers would walk into my room, tear off the bedclothes and throw the mattress on to the floor. Sometimes they would turn over the bed, ripping away the carpet, before pulling up some of the floorboards to see whether anything was hidden beneath.

Occasionally they would remain in the house for three or four hours, not letting anyone go back to bed, forbidding us to leave the one room where they had ordered us to remain until they had cleared the entire street.

Usually the soldiers would pile into the house and leave their rifles downstairs, lined up against the wall in the hallway under the guard of one soldier, while the others fanned out searching every nook and cranny. I would hate them for doing that, for making us all cry and hurting my mother, wrecking her house.

Once I retaliated, going up to one of the soldiers and hitting him on his legs as hard as I could. But my mother rushed forward and took me away from him.

After their visits my mother would be angry, cursing the soldiers, as she looked around her home at the wreckage the Army had left behind, which she would have to repair, tidy and clean.

As I grew a little older and began to understand more, I would also become angry with the soldiers waking us at 4.30am, ordering us about and treating us like dirt. Following my mother's example, I, too, would shout 'Go away! Get out of our house!'

Occasionally, some of them would try to scare me, deliberately nudging me as they brushed past, telling me to shut up and mind my own business or threatening me with a clip around the ear.

My mother tried to ease my anger, telling me that it would be OK and that we had nothing to hide from the British soldiers. But I could not be so easily quietened and would constantly follow them around the house, telling them to stop ripping our home apart, cheekily ordering them to put things back as they had found them. Generally, the soldiers simply ignored my demands, which frustrated me and made me even more angry.

I had learned a new word, 'respect', and I would tell them that as soldiers they should 'respect' other peoples' property. They would laugh at me on those occasions and I hated them for treating me like a kid.

During one of their last searches of our house, when I was about eight years old, I picked up a large pot of paint which mother had been using to decorate the sitting-room. As soon as the soldiers had left, I poured the paint into two milk bottles and waited for the Army to drive away in their Saracens and Land Rovers. As they drove past our house, I ran out and threw the milk bottles at the dark green army jeeps, splattering paint over one of them. When I went to school later that day I felt ten feet tall, telling all my pals what I had done to the British Army. For a while, I became a hero. It felt good.

'I just want to grow up quickly,' I would tell my mother, 'so that I can help get rid of the soldiers. I don't like them coming into our house, wrecking the place and making you cry.'

I began to join the older boys in stone-throwing – the 'sport', as we saw it, of tantalising and needling the British Army. More important, though, were the battles we young Catholic lads fought with Protestant boys, mostly teenagers, throwing stones at each other. I don't know if I ever hit anyone, and I don't think anyone ever hit me, but those battles made the adrenalin flow and I could not wait to grow up so that I could become part of the Republican movement.

My mother would tell me that I was hyperactive, unable to sleep more than a few hours a night and, as a result, I would frequently get into mischief.

About this time, I decided it was time to find a job and, as I always woke shortly after dawn, I decided to find a paper round. Leaving home at 6.00am, I would walk to a man's house a few hundred yards from my home and the papers I had to deliver would be piled high in the hall of his house. I would distribute 50 newspapers a day and be back home by 8.00am, in time for my cornflakes before leaving for school. I delivered those papers for 18 months, earning £5 a week – a handsome sum, as far as I was concerned.

Early one summer's morning in 1980, I witnessed, for the first time, a robbery in progress as I was running to fetch my newspapers. I had seen a static mobile shop, which had been parked for years near the New Barnsley RUC station off the Springfield Road. But on this particular day, I saw two teenagers whom I recognised as Catholics from the Ballymurphy estate taking food, confectionery and money out of the mobile shop and putting it in cardboard boxes in full view of the police station. As I walked past the vehicle, one of them called at me to come over.

'What are you doing?' I asked.

'We're just nicking some stuff from this store,' he said. 'Do you want something?'

'No, I don't want anything,' I replied. 'If the RUC found me with stuff, they'll think I broke into the mobile. I don't want nothing to do with it.' And I ran off.

Later that day, the same lad came to see me as I was playing outside our house. He was laughing at me, telling me that my face had gone white when I had realised that the two of them were robbing the mobile.

'Did you do that van?' I asked him.

'Yes, of course we did,' he replied, 'what else do you think we would be doing at six in the morning?'

'Jesus, you could have got me into trouble,' I protested.

'Here you are,' he said, handing me a few bars of chocolate. 'Tell nobody what you've seen.' I didn't want to know if they had come from the robbery and I didn't ask. I was learning.

Confidence in my own ability, however, received a nasty set-back when I decided to change jobs, jacking in the paper round and starting to work for our local milkman, Paddy Brady, a massive man in his thirties who must have weighed over 20 stone. He would sit in the milk float reading a paper, while somehow steering it with his big fat belly and barking his orders at us.

His band of three young helpers, including me, officially earned £20 a week, but Paddy would occasionally decide to pay us nothing, saying that we hadn't worked hard enough. And if we ever misbehaved, Paddy would punish us by inviting the miscreant into the cab of the float and then twisting his arm around the steering wheel, causing severe bruising to the upper arm. He would only stop when the boy screamed. On a number of occasions I went to school with huge blue and yellow bruises on my arm.

But, because the money was good, we stayed with him. Every morning, Paddy would order one of us to find him a newspaper, which meant stealing one from the letterbox of a house. One morning, I had delivered a couple of pints of milk to a house and removed the newspaper when I turned and saw a 20-year-old youth come rushing across the road. I recognised him as working for the paper shop. He grabbed me by the scruff of the neck and began kicking my backside as hard as he could while pushing me down the path.

'Now I know who's been stealing the papers,' he yelled at me. 'Do that again, you little bastard, and I'll break your arms.'

On that occasion, however, Paddy came to my rescue, rushing at the young man and telling him to leave me alone. 'I heard you threaten young Marty,' he said. 'You touch a hair of his head again and I'll kick your head in. Do you understand?' he shouted, pushing the young man away and kicking him hard. 'Now go and get me another paper,' Paddy said, turning to me. 'This one's ruined.' And I had to sneak up to another house and steal a second paper for him.

I sometimes found myself in trouble with Paddy for arriving late for my milk round and he would, of course, usually give me a clip around the ear, a hard clip, for arriving late. I had my reasons, though, but I would never tell Paddy or the other lads for fear they would tease me and make me feel silly.

Early one morning, while running towards the rendezvous where I met Paddy each day, I noticed an old man, a tramp, in dirty old clothes slowly walking out of a derelict cinema off the Falls Road. I saw him again the following day and he looked a pitiful figure. The next week I saw him I stopped to speak to him. 'Are you OK?' I asked. There was no reply; the man just looked blankly at me. 'Are you OK?' I asked, shouting louder this time. 'Where do you live?' He pointed with his blackened, dirty thumb to the picture house behind him. 'You live there!' I said, amazed that anyone could live in such an abandoned, derelict place which had been shut up for decades.

Again I asked him if he was all right and this time he nodded. 'Are you hungry?' I said, realising from his hollow cheeks and filthy appearance that he probably hadn't eaten for days.

'Yes, I'm hungry,' he replied.

'I've nothing with me,' I told him, 'but I'll bring you something tomorrow,' and I ran off.

The following day, I took him a small carton of milk, some biscuits and a sandwich I had made myself with butter and two pieces of ham. He was there waiting for me that day. 'Here you are,' I said, and before I ran off he was already wolfing down the sandwich.

During the following few weeks, we would become friends. Every day I would give him food I had taken from my mother's kitchen; at other times I would buy him food with the money I earned each week from Paddy. And each morning, after handing over the food, we would talk. I found out that his name was Oliver and that he had been living in the picture house for a year or more. He seemed nearly 70 but, in fact, he told he was only 55. I looked at him and wondered if he was telling me the truth, for he seemed so old with his pale, whiskered face, his blackened, broken teeth and his thick, matted hair. He wore a dirty sweater and trousers which were too big for him, held up with two boot laces tied together and, whatever the weather, a dark, bottle-green overcoat with one pocket half ripped off.

'Do you ever have a bath?' I asked him. He shook his head. 'Do you ever wash?' Again he shook his head.

I never asked him whether he drank, though, because he always smelt of alcohol. And although I realised he was an old drunk, I felt sorry for him, wondering how a man could live in those conditions night and day, year in, year out. Sometimes I lay awake at night wondering whether I should bring him back home so that he could sleep and bathe and wash in a house for just one night. But I didn't, because instinct told me that my mother would never permit such a man in her house.

My meetings with Oliver continued for months and I made sure I gave him something to eat every day. Once a week, and sometimes more, I would give him a £1 note – I did so because throughout all the months I knew him, Oliver never asked me for anything.

Then, one day, I ran to see him and he had gone. I looked inside the picture house and saw his filthy old blanket on the floor beside the pathetic remains of a fire he lit each night to keep himself warm. But he had vanished without a word. For weeks I checked each morning but he never returned and I never knew whether Oliver had died in the night and his body had been taken away, or whether he had just moved on without saying a word to me.

I discovered that a woman living a few doors down from us in Moyard Parade kept chickens at the bottom of her garden and I decided that, as my mother liked fresh boiled eggs, I would make it my duty to get up early each day and take one from the neighbour's hens.

Shortly after dawn, I would climb over two sets of fences and sit outside the wooden hutch waiting for the hens to lay. I became so proficient at this that, after a while, I would time my arrival to within a few minutes of the hen laying and I would sometimes actually catch the egg before it hit the ground. However, the treats didn't last long for the hens suddenly stopped laying, no doubt due to my constant visits.

One day, the woman told my mother, 'Those hens of mine are useless. I'm thinking of killing and eating them because they hardly lay any eggs.'

My mother had no idea that I was responsible, neither did I tell her, and shortly after the hens stopped laying I lost interest in the idea. My mother never discovered the truth of my early morning adventures, neither, it seemed, did she ever realise during those weeks that her supply of eggs in the kitchen cupboard never diminished.

I did, however, get into trouble for my next adventure. Once again I would leave the house early before my mother or the neighbours awoke, and set off to the fields leading to the Black Mountains where herds of cattle grazed. Armed with a stick, I would drive half a dozen or more cattle down to the streets below, making sure they ended up in the front gardens of the houses.

They would be driven through the narrow gates into the front gardens and left munching away at the grass, leaving their cow pats all over the lawns. I found this prank so amusing that I repeated it a number of times before one man leaned out of his bedroom window at 6.00am one morning and saw me chasing the cows.

'Martin McGartland,' he yelled at the top of his voice, 'You're the little dickhead causing all this shit. Wait till I get hold of you.'

I did not wait more than a second, however, as he slammed the window shut. I left the cows munching and splattering the gardens and ran home. I didn't risk his wrath again because I feared he would have given me a real hiding. I was also well aware of the possible repercussions from another quarter – my mother.

Although I was prepared to challenge my mother in my early teens, as a child I never dreamed of disobeying her.

My mother had become a single parent, solely responsible for two young sons and a daughter, and she determined that we would learn what the word 'discipline' meant. She had been brought up in a large family of four boys and four girls and her father had been just as strict.

As a child, she earned a reputation for taking on and beating up boys older than herself, and even her own brothers would take care not to upset their wild, strong-willed sister.

I never disobeyed my mother for I had learned at a very young age that the consequences would be severe. Whenever my mother told me to stop doing something, I would stop immediately, not daring to risk the lash of her tongue or the crack of her hand across my head.

When I was 12 years old, I had been recruited by an older teenager to sell cigarettes which I knew had been stolen. I went around the estate and the building sites, selling them to anyone. I made about £30 to £40 a day, an absolute fortune for me.

A few weeks after starting to sell the cigarettes, I was upstairs in my bedroom one Saturday night when I heard the front door bang shut and my mother's voice downstairs. 'Martin!' she yelled. 'Come down here.'

I knew from the tone of her voice that I was in deep trouble and I feared the worst. But I obeyed immediately.

As I stood in the hall, my mother, who was about my height and size at that time, wagged her finger in my face. 'Listen,' she said, a sting in her voice, 'tell me the truth, my boy, or it will be the worse for you. Have you been selling fags?'

'No,' I lied.

I didn't see the punch that cracked me on the jaw, sending me sprawling on the floor.

'You little liar,' she screamed. 'Now tell me again. Have you been selling fags?'

'Yes,' I said, and began to explain that I had never stolen them but was only selling them for a friend to make some pocket money.

Her fist landed on my head as I struggled to my feet and I tried to ward off the barrage as she continued to beat me with her fist around my head and shoulders. She must have hit me a dozen times and then ordered me upstairs to bed. I never forgot my mother's anger, I never sold another stolen cigarette and I vowed always to tell her the truth.

On another occasion, my mates and I were sitting in the ruined fifteenth-century castle nestling in the Black Mountain, all playing truant from school and inhaling glue, passing the bag from one to another. I was out of my mind, hardly aware of what we were doing, when one of the lads said he was hungry. We decided to go to a shop owned by a distant relative on my mother's side. It was closed so we broke in through a rear window and stole cigarettes and chocolates before making our way back to the castle.

A man had followed us back and when he saw all of us sniffing glue and acting as if we were drunk, he decided to return to the estate and inform our mothers. One woman arrived shortly afterwards and I found I could not even speak, so affected was I by the glue. Stumbling about we eventually arrived back at the woman's house and I sat down in a stupour, hardly aware of what was going on around me.

Suddenly, however, I sensed my mother standing over me, her hands on her hips, looking down at me on the floor.

'Get up! Get up!' she ordered, pulling me to my feet, although I could hardly stand. 'Now start running and don't stop till you get home.'

I didn't need any further encouragement and, like

an automaton, I ran the few hundred yards back home while my mother walked briskly behind me. Within seconds of closing the door, my mother started to batter me. I could see the anger in her face and her fists cracking me around the head over and over again. And yet I could feel nothing and I wondered if it was all a bad dream.

She kept yelling at me but I couldn't hear what she was saying, and when the battering was over I went upstairs to bed. I had been lying there only a few minutes when she came into my bedroom, dragged me out of bed and took me to the bathroom. She had filled the bath with cold water and, without ceremony, pushed my head into the bath, holding me with her hands around my neck, forcing my head underwater. I struggled and fought to escape but without success, and the more I struggled the more she kept me under. I thought she was trying to drown me.

When she finally let me up I could barely breathe, gulping madly for air.

She walked out and down the stairs and I went to my bed, still trying to catch my breath. The ducking, however, had done the trick and my head cleared. I suddenly felt hungry and went downstairs for something to eat.

I grabbed a couple of cream crackers and stuffed them into my mouth as I walked into the living-room where my mother was sitting. Our eyes met and I knew I should never have looked at her because the sight of me inflamed her fury once more. She jumped to her feet, took an old First World War sword from the wall where it had been placed as an ornament years before, and began lashing out at my legs, thrashing me over both thighs with all her might.

'Glue, my boy,' she yelled as she hit me, 'I'll fucking glue you.'

I tried to evade the sword, which must have been about two feet long, and ran around the room while she continued to yell and scream at me as she struck out. And the more she yelled and screamed obscenities at me, the more she hit me.

The following morning before dressing, I inspected the damage. It looked as though I had been given a real whipping – my thighs were bruised black and blue, and some of the skin was broken. I thanked God that the sword had been blunt. But I learned my lesson: I would never sniff glue again.

As the Troubles escalated and riots raged between the Republicans and the 'enemy' – the British Army and the RUC – my friends and I enjoyed every moment of the excitement and chaos. Each night seemed to bring new adventures. Our home on the Ballymurphy Estate became the epicentre of the Troubles and the action seemed to continue most nights throughout the spring, summer and autumn.

So many disturbances took place that, most evenings, the local Protestant families from the neighbouring Springmartin Estate would come to the nearest vantage point to watch the action. Barricades would be thrown up and burning buses, lorries, cars and vans would light the night sky, the air filled with sparks and the stench of burning rubber thrown on to the barricades, providing a focus of attention for us and the hundreds who came to watch.

We would learn later that after we had been sent to bed the air would be filled with tear gas from the grenades that the RUC and the Army would rain down on the rioting Republicans. In the morning we raced from our beds back into the streets, sometimes still in pyjamas, to collect the used gas canisters and take them as prized souvenirs to show our friends at school.

Television news teams from around the world would descend on the estate and most days we would be asked to find plastic bullets that the TV crews could take back home as souvenirs. Some would offer as much as US$20 for a bullet but the average was just US$10. It became a lucrative investment for me and my mates and we would carry them home and hide them in our bedrooms, ready to sell to the next TV crew that came along.

Despite the stern warnings and pleading of our parents, we would hide behind walls near the action and rush out to pick up the plastic bullets after the Army had fired each volley.

Most nights, one or two people would be hit by the plastic bullets and when they hit their target, they hurt like hell, half crippling victims for days, at other times breaking and chipping ankle bones which then required hospital treatment. Most victims, however, would refuse to go to hospital for treatment for they knew that they would immediately be picked up by the RUC, arrested and charged with rioting. So most of those hit would retire home and rest for a few days, hoping that the pain would ease and they would be able to walk again.

One young Ballymurphy lad called Mick, who loved to boast that he had no fear of the Army, would dance around provocatively in front of the troops until one night he was hit squarely in the cheek by a bullet, smashing his teeth. He received little sympathy from any of us, however, despite his bravado. From then on he would be called 'Hamburger', because it looked for weeks as though he had a large piece of burger stuffed in his mouth. But the injury cured him of his recklessness for he would never again be seen prancing in front of the British soldiers.

Most of the incidents, however, were no laughing matter but deadly serious affairs. One Ballymurphy man was cheered by the Republicans and acclaimed a hero after he scored a direct hit with a petrol bomb on a police line. The petrol bomber, caught live by a TV cameraman, threw the bomb over the lines of Land Rovers in front of him, the bottle exploding on the roof of a vehicle and splashing the fireball over a policeman's head and face. TV pictures the following night showed other officers trying to beat out the flames, but the officer received serious burns.

During these weeks and months, the IRA became increasingly powerful, claiming a higher profile within the community, dictating tactics, ordering young men around as if they were troops and instilling their own brand of discipline.

In the early hours of most mornings when the rioters turned in for the night, the Army would return equipped with huge cranes and tractors to remove all the burned-out vehicles hijacked and torched the previous night. By dusk, however, more lorries would have been hijacked and brought on to the estate, driven into position by armed IRA members and then torched, providing new barricades for that night's rioting.

My young friends and I would occasionally fall foul of IRA discipline, even though we were not yet ten years old. One evening we decided to raid the back of a refrigerated ice-cream lorry which had been hijacked and had had a petrol bomb thrown into the cab. We opened the back while the lorry blazed and began taking out boxes of ice cream. When the IRA men saw what we were doing they quickly intervened, throwing the boxes back inside the vehicle and giving us a good slap on the head.

'Don't take anything from the back of that van,' one said, 'or you'll get a clip. Now fuck off home.'

Others were more brutal, slapping and kicking the kids who tried to steal from the burning vans. Most of the women, our mothers, were of course on our side and they would berate the IRA hard men. 'Let the kids take the things,' they would shout at the armed men, 'you're only going to burn it.'

Matters came to a head when Republicans began hijacking trucks containing TVs, videos and fridges, for most families on the estate longed for brand new electrical goods. Most of the families, all working class, were renting their TVs for a few pounds a week, a lot of money for people with several children surviving on unemployment benifit. But once again the armed men would have none of it, refusing to listen to the pleas of the womenfolk to permit the goods to be taken out of the vehicles and offered to anyone on the estate.

'That's looting,' the IRA men would argue. 'We are a disciplined military organisation, not a bunch of criminals thieving anything we can lay our hands on.'

The few people who did succeed in looting a TV or video would not get away with their booty for long, for the IRA would go from house to house searching for stolen gear. When they found a stolen machine they would snatch it and throw it out into the street, deliberately smashing it to pieces. I watched all this with a certain envy and admiration, but also with fear. I had no intention of crossing these strong men who would brook no argument, demanding that their orders be obeyed without question.

The army 'snatch squads' would create even more excitement and tension for all of us. The burning barricades kept the Army and police vehicles out of the estate most nights, so the Army changed tactics, sending in heavily armed snatch squads to pick up men they targeted as ring-leaders.

At first, the snatch squads were successful in picking up some men because of the speed of their unexpected raids. But soon after, IRA look-outs, mostly keen young teenagers, would be posted to shout whenever they saw a snatch squad preparing to make a dash against the Republican lines.

'Run, run, the fuckers are coming!' a look-out would scream and the hundreds of people out on the streets would disperse, the IRA men racing away to safety, often sprinting through people's homes whose doors had been deliberately left open for such an eventuality. As soon as the ring-leaders had darted through a house the doors would be closed, the republican leaders would be away and the Army squads thwarted once again. On those occasions, we young lads would simply stand aside and watch as 20 or 30 heavily armed soldiers would rush past us chasing their intended victim. At such times, I wondered if I dared try to trip a soldier, to send him sprawling but, because I feared the repercussions, I could never summon up enough courage to do so.

Sometimes, of course, the deadly serious business of rioting and arson would be tinged with humour, though these occasions were few and far between. Roy, a skinny teenager with freckles, occasionally provided such a release from the intensity of the moment because he suffered from a stammer which became worse the more agitated he became. Without thinking, we gave him the job of look-out, waiting for the Army 'Pigs' (heavily armoured vehicles), to drive through the estate. For sport we would find vantage points where we could not be seen, but were close enough to the road for us to hurl milk bottles filled with white paint, in the hope of smashing them on the camouflaged vehicles. Roy would be stationed 50 yards away around a corner and his task would be to shout 'Saracen' at the top of his voice when he saw a convoy of Pigs driving towards us from the local RUC base.

Thirty minutes later we heard the familiar swoosh of Saracens racing past us at high speed and we had no time to leave our hiding place to throw our bottles. As we looked down at Roy we could see him pointing to the flying Saracens, still desperately trying to stammer out 'Saracens'.

We gave him hell on that occasion for missing a golden opportunity and, for ever after, the wretched Roy was called 'Saracen' by all his school mates. Fifteen years later, his pals still call him Saracen, even though he has completely lost his stammer.

*   *   *

The army Saracens became the focal point of our hate for these powerful vehicles, with strong steel grids on the front, would be used for smashing down road blocks we had built for our own defence. It didn't matter whether these barricades were constructed of burning buses or trucks for the Saracens would crash into them at speed and, more often than not, would succeed in breaking through.

The deadly Saracens, which were invulnerable to the type of attacks the rioters mounted against their formidable armour, did suffer from one weak point: if the rioters could find a way of lifting the driving wheels off the ground, they could be slowed to a halt and become easy targets for republican petrol bombers.

Stopping the Saracens became one of our favourite sports. The stronger boys would steal aluminium beer kegs from the pubs and wait for the Saracens to come through the estate, usually travelling at speeds in excess of 50 miles an hour. The young men would wait on either side of the road, holding the kegs above their heads, ready to hurl them into the path of the oncoming vehicles. When the Saracens were a few yards away, they would all hurl the kegs at the same time.

The kegs would usually bounce off harmlessly, but sometimes the Saracens would be brought to a halt, their driving wheels spinning helplessly in the air. Then, like ants, we would swarm all over them, cheering and shouting, some of us dancing on top of the vehicle, others trying to torch the tyres before reinforcements came to the soldiers' aid. There was no way of getting inside the vehicle as the doors were locked securely from the inside. Stopping a Saracen would be one of the most exhilarating sights for us young lads and would be the talk of the school playground for days.

We only had a few minutes to rejoice before having to scramble from the vehicle and run for our lives when we saw the reinforcements arriving, called up by the Saracen's radio operator. Sometimes the vehicle would turn turtle, hurling the occupants around inside and causing us to cheer even louder at what we saw as a major victory over the hated enemy.

*　　　*　　　*

As I reached double figures and became more adventurous and mischievous, attracting trouble and taking risks would occasionally bring me face to face with various authorities – the Army, the RUC, the IRA and, more importantly, my mother.

Only once did I find myself in trouble with the British Army and that was through no fault of mine. With half a dozen of my friends from on the estate, including my best mates, Sean O'Halloran, Stevie McCann, Micky McMullan and Dee Daley, we would sometimes take long walks across Black Mountain, spending most of the day away from home.

Our house was situated on the edge of the Ballymurphy estate, on one side the drab, grey terraced houses that are forever Belfast; on the other stands the magnificent Black Mountain, a hundred shades of green, touched by the soft rains which fall across the country throughout most of the year, but which through the winter months is lashed by the gales and storms that pelt across the land from the Atlantic.

During one walk we came across an army firing range about seven miles from home, and we began stuffing as many spent rounds as possible into our pockets. At school, the spent bullets had become a symbol of bravery for we would polish them with Brasso, drill a hole through the base of the round and then thread them on to a bootlace, wearing them as a pendant round our necks.

On this occasion, however, unbeknown to us, we had also picked up some live rounds which had been accidentally left behind on the shooting range.

As we returned home, exhausted, we saw some armed soldiers patrolling our estate and we began throwing the rounds at them, teasing them. Suddenly, three soldiers came rushing over to us, grabbing us as one of them shouted into his radio, 'Get the RUC, fast; there's kids here with live rounds.'

We were made to empty our pockets and stand still. Within ten minutes, five or six RUC Land Rovers came racing towards us and the police jumped out of the vehicles. I was frightened, not knowing what we had done wrong, wondering what my mother would say if she found me in trouble.

'We were only throwing bullets at the soldiers for fun,' we protested, 'we didn't mean any trouble.'

'Where did you find these?' one of the senior police officers asked, picking up one of the rounds.

'On the firing range,' we answered in chorus.

'On the firing range?' he asked incredulously. 'That's miles away.'

'We know,' one of us replied, 'we've just walked there and back.'

Then the officer picked up two rounds, showed them to us and explained that they were different; one bullet had been fired, but the other was live and very, very dangerous. We looked blank, not realising the difference, unsure how one could be dangerous and the other of no use whatsoever.

The officers told us to empty our pockets and place everything on the ground. Then they picked up the live rounds and kept asking us, 'Have you any more of these at home? Are you sure?'

We all shook our heads, protesting our innocence. We told the officer that we had never been to the firing range before and the only bullets we had at home were ones we had found on the streets from time to time, which some children had made into pendants to wear round their necks.

As we waited patiently, fearing our mothers would give us hell, other army units arrived and began scouring drains and searching gardens to check if any other live bullets were lying around. Fortunately for us they found none, and 30 minutes later we were allowed to go home. I ran home as fast as possible, fearful that my mother might catch me and give me a hiding for stealing the bullets. She never knew of that incident until I confessed many years later and, by then, she could enjoy the joke.

CHAPTER TWO

As EACH YEAR PASSED, I began to realise that the Troubles were no longer fun but deadly serious. I began taking an interest in the early evening news bulletins, even though I was little more than ten years old. One of the effects of the the Troubles would be to make young people like me grow up before our time.

I would watch television pictures of the devastation caused by explosives and bombings which wrecked the centre of Belfast and other towns and villages; I would see the remains of dead bodies, barely covered by blankets, as soldiers and police officers scoured the area fearing booby-trap devices; and I would see fires raging as hijacked cars, buses and lorries were torched.

On other occasions, I would see Catholics and Protestants at loggerheads, building burning barricades, throwing stones, bricks and petrol bombs at each other, and I would notice the ferocity of their anger and the hatred in their eyes. Some of these TV pictures would capture my imagination and I would become mesmerised, desperate to understand what was happening and why.

But much of what I saw on television passed way over my head. I understood the action and the violence which gripped my attention but had no idea whatsoever of the political arguments which bored me. My innocence, however, would not last long.

*   *   *

I was an ambitious young lad and I wanted to earn better money than I ever could slaving away on Paddy Brady's milkround all year. In 1981, however, at the age of 11, fate intervened and I began earning really good money. My sister's husband, Joseph Lindsay, a happy-go-lucky, good-natured young man who drifted into petty crime because he couldn't find a regular job, asked me if I wanted to go into business with him, legitimate business. Twenty-one-year-old 'Jo-Jo', as we called him, and my sister, Elizabeth, who was 17, had been dating for a year.

Jo-Jo would go to a Belfast wholesale store and buy £200 worth of household goods which I would sell door to door. We would make a quick, small profit and divide the proceeds. I generally earnt between £30 and £40 a time and we would repeat the operation perhaps twice a week. I felt like a millionaire!

But Jo-Jo wanted to earn more, so he began stealing pairs of jeans from shops all over Belfast and selling them door to door. He was earning a small fortune, but his luck would not continue. In Belfast at around this time, the local IRA commanders wanted to show the entire Catholic population that they not only organised the lives of the people and protected them from loyalist mobs, but also took over the role of local policing from the RUC. They heard about Jo-Jo's maverick escapades and decided to make an example of him.

One night, as he walked along the Falls Road, an

IRA punishment gang wearing balaclavas waylaid him, took him into a back street and kneecapped him, shooting him with a single bullet from a handgun. It smashed his kneecap, and left him writhing in pain. After a couple of months, Jo-Jo recovered the use of his leg and his good nature but he would never walk again without a slight limp.

Jo-Jo's kneecapping was allegedly carried out as an example to others thinking of becoming involved in petty crime, but such a cowardly attack not only frightened me but angered me as well. I would go and visit Jo-Jo in the Royal Hospital while he was recovering and would see him in great pain. I would never forget what the IRA did to him, nor would I forgive.

I respected Jo-Jo because he would talk to me like a grown-up and explain that he stole things from shops to make some money for Elizabeth and the kids. 'If I could find a job,' he would say, 'I would work as hard as the next man. But if I can't get a job I'll steal things, because your sister and the boys are more important.'

I loved visiting Jo-Jo and Elizabeth at their home and felt happy for them and their two young sons, Joseph and Barry, when they moved to a brand new council house in the Turf Lodge district of Belfast in the spring of 1983. Within weeks, Elizabeth announced that she was pregnant once more but, soon after, their happiness would be brutally shattered.

Out drinking one night in August 1983, Jo-Jo was persuaded by some mates to join them in a break-in somewhere in Belfast's city centre. Jo-Jo had never been involved in such serious criminal activity before, but, with a skinful of beer, he went along with their plan. As they walked across a roof together he lost his footing, fell 40 feet to the ground and died from his injuries. He was 23.

The violence of Belfast would touch my life again 15 months later. My first employer, the milkman Paddy Brady, was shot dead in cold blood by an assassination squad of the loyalist Ulster Freedom Fighters as he parked his car outside Kennedy's Dairies early one morning. What I had not known, however, was that Paddy had been a member of Sinn Fein for many years, carrying out menial tasks for the organisation.

Like every young Catholic boy, I had edged towards total support of the IRA during the hunger-strikes of the late 1970s and 1980s when Republican prisoners demanded the status of prisoners of war rather than ordinary criminals, as had been the case before 1976. In those days, Republican prisoners had been permitted to wear their own uniforms. The policy had been changed, much to the anger and annoyance of genuine Republicans and two years later, IRA prisoners began their 'dirty protest', refusing to wear regulation clothing, wrapping themselves in blankets instead.

Throughout their campaign for the return of political status and privileges, hundreds of Republicans chose to stay in their cells, covering the walls with their own excreta. The willingness of prisoners to subject themselves to these conditions 24 hours a day caught the attention of the world's media and triggered an emotional upsurge throughout the Catholic community.

In 1981, a new hunger-strike began, led by Bobby Sands, who had become the leader of the prisoners in the 'H'-block. Every few days, more prisoners joined him, so that the authorities would be faced by a stream of prisoners nearing death, one after another.

In March 1981, the Member of Parliament for Fermanagh and South Tyrone died and Bobby Sands was entered as a candidate. Sands won a narrow victory after an 87 per cent poll in what was seen as a massive boost for the hunger-strike campaign.

I was awoken in the early hours of 5 May, 1981, by the most fearful noise – the banging of dustbin lids and the constant blasting of car horns. I ran down stairs and the entire street was crowded with people; virtually every resident, including most of the children, were shouting and banging anything that would make a noise.

'What's happened?' I asked my mum.

'Bobby Sands has died,' she shouted back above the din.

Anger, fury and frustration gripped the whole estate that night. I watched in awe, desperate to help, as people began ripping up paving stones with their bare hands to build barricades; others collected bottles from around the estate, while teenagers went from car to car syphoning fuel to make the petrol bombs. To cheers from the residents, young men would return in triumph to our streets driving diggers and JCBs stolen from around Belfast, and they knocked down lampposts and dug up roads in a desperate effort to secure the barricades against the expected attack from the Army and the police.

The entire street would erupt in cheers and clapping and the residents would resume banging their dustbin lids whenever a Belfast bus was driven on to the estate to form part of a barricade before being torched, all in a bid to keep the Army away from the Catholic Ballymurphy estate.

During the following few nights in that early May of 1981, riots and bombings would spread across the north with major disturbances in Londonderry and Belfast and riots in Dublin. I felt excited by all the violence and action I had witnessed first-hand and on the television news, and I wanted to be a part of it. A few nights later, I witnessed an IRA Active Service Unit in action and felt thrilled by their courage and daring.

At about 5.00pm all the boys and a few girls from the estate were in the streets watching what was going on, waiting with excitement and anticipation for dusk to fall and the rioting and petrol bombing to begin. To us, at that age, it all seemed like a game, but I was beginning to realise that there was also something serious happening.

We were hiding behind barricades of burned-out buses, dodging the rubber bullets that were being fired towards us by 'peelers' sheltering behind their RUC Land Rovers. The vehicles were parked side-on as the officers would use them as barricades to protect themselves from the bombs and stones we were throwing. Suddenly, I noticed everyone moving back.

'Come back, Marty,' someone yelled at me and I looked to see that I was standing almost alone by the barricade. I obeyed and withdrew and, within a few minutes, we heard the rattle of machine-gun fire coming from our side. We realised that the IRA was retaliating, firing machine-gun bullets at the Land Rovers in a bid to force the RUC to withdraw. We screamed with delight, cheering like any football crowd whose side had just scored a goal.

I was too young to understand fully, but the anger throughout the community was almost tangible. With the death of Bobby Sands, the Irish people's respect for martyrdom had been resurrected, so passionate and bitter had people become about the hunger strikers. Bobby Sands, however, would not be the only man to die. In the following four months, nine more hunger-strikers would die and tens of thousands of people would attend their funerals. Finally, in October 1981 the British Government relented, permitting prisoners to wear their own clothes. Ten Republicans had died in jail, but in the streets a total of 61 people had been killed in retaliation, including 30 members of the security forces.

I watched the funerals on TV, as well as the riots that flared across the north after every single hunger-striker died. I felt for all of them, as did all the young boys I knew. I had become confused, knowing I totally supported the men who died in prison for their beliefs, but realising that other Catholics who supported the hunger-strikers could also become brutal and violent, kneecapping innocent Catholics like Jo-Jo, for no reason at all.

*   *   *

At the age of 11, I had left primary school and moved to St Thomas's Secondary School on the Whiterock Road, a 15-minute walk from home. I never liked school and never wanted to study, but I would never play truant like most of my friends, because I was always fearful of what my mother would do if ever she found out that I had skipped lessons.

But that fear didn't stop me spending most of the lessons fooling around, doing as little work as possible and frequently being cheeky to teachers. Sometimes, however, I overstepped the mark. Angry at being given a public ticking-off for messing around in class, I decided to seek revenge, so during one lunch break I nipped back into the classroom and set light to the curtains. As the flames leapt up the curtains I fled from the scene, realising that I had gone too far this time. There was an inquest and the headmaster was determined to discover the culprit, but I said nothing, feigning innocence. I was never caught, and I never repeated the offence.

One of the few thrills at St Thomas's during the early

1980s was watching the teenagers who had stolen cars from all over the city, practise their driving skills on the school football pitch. We would run out of lessons to watch them racing around the pitch, skidding and sliding the vehicles, ramming the goal posts, racing each other before fleeing the area as soon as the RUC arrived. But it was always good fun. I couldn't wait until I was old enough to drive stolen cars. I knew for certain that I would not wait until the statutory age of 17 and vowed to have a go when I was tall enough to sit in the driving seat and reach the pedals.

In fact I was 13 when I first drove a car, a maroon Vauxhall Cavalier that a friend of mine had stolen. I begged him to let me have a drive. I had a rough idea what to do, knowing I had to push the clutch down before changing gear. The accelerator and the brake were straightforward, but I still managed to crash the Cavalier after driving around a field for only five minutes.

I had been trying to be too smart. I had watched, mesmerised, as other, older teenagers with some experience had driven the cars fast, making hand-brake turns, swinging the cars 180 degrees by snatching at the hand-brake while suddenly turning the wheel. I drove to the edge of the field and accelerated hard, pulled on the hand-brake and immediately lost control, the car hitting a rut in the field and flipping over a number of times before coming to rest upside-down against some railings. I clambered out, my head fuzzy, and saw the car wheels still spinning madly.

The lads who had let me drive had all run away, afraid that I had seriously injured myself or even died in the crash, and they feared that they would be in trouble for permitting a youngster to drive the stolen vehicle.

Sometime later, when I asked the lad who had let me

drive the car why he had run off, he replied, 'I wasn't frightened of the RUC, Marty, it was your mam that terrified me!'

That night I had learned a lesson. I had terrified myself and resolved never to steal a car. I never did.

But that didn't mean I never broke the law – far from it.

During the summer holidays of 1984, a school pal, Pat, and I were idly walking near our former school, the Vere Foster Primary School, when we found two recorders lying on the ground. I had learned the recorder at school but I never took much interest in music. That day we walked along playing the only tune I had learned well, *Three Blind Mice*, when two RUC officers, who were patrolling in our estate with half a dozen soldiers, walked up to us.

'Where did you get those?' one asked, pointing at the recorders.

'We found them,' I said.

'What do you mean, you found them?' he said, as if not believing a word we had said.

'We found them near the school fence just a few minutes ago,' I said.

'You two had better come to the station with us,' he said, and we were bundled into an RUC Land Rover and driven off.

We were taken to the RUC station and made to wait in a room before being asked the same questions by another officer. We told him the same story and after a matter of minutes we were taken back home. But they kept the recorders.

Only later would we hear that the previous night the school had been broken into and along with the recorders, thousands of pounds worth of equipment including TVs, videos, film projectors and musical instruments had been stolen. The recorders had apparently been dropped as the thieves made their escape.

Back home, however, the interrogation from my mother was much tougher as she insisted on hearing every tiny piece of information about the recorders, exactly where we had found them and why we had kept them. She wanted to know why we hadn't taken them immediately to the police rather than kept them for ourselves. On that occasion I escaped without a good hiding, but it had been close.

*   *   *

My first serious brush with the IRA occurred about this time and I had never felt more scared in my young life.

Johnny McGinty was a strong, well-built, stocky man in his early 30s, a stalwart Republican with a friendly, fun-loving nature, who hated both the RUC and the British Army with a passion. He would openly flout their orders and, if stopped and questioned at a road block, would leap from his car, fists flying as he waded into the nearest RUC officer or soldier without a care for himself.

He soon earned a reputation as a wild man, whom both the RUC and the Army realised needed to be handled with kid gloves. On some occasions, however, they would set out to provoke him deliberately so that he would throw punches and they would then arrest him and throw him in jail to cool off.

In the mid-1980s, the IRA decided to get tough with the joy-riders who would steal cars from the centre of Belfast and often leave them on the Ballymurphy Estate. The IRA did not want to draw the attention of the authorities to the estate, which had become one of the organisation's best recruiting areas in Belfast. So they decided to issue warnings to joy-riders to stop their activities or face the consequences.

Two Republicans ordered to police the estate and crack down on the joy-riders were Johnny McGinty and an IRA sympathiser, Marty Morris. They would walk around the estate at night watching for the young teenagers who loved to steal cars, rip out the radios and then show off, performing hand-brake turns to the cheers of other youths. The daring teenagers would also deliberately set out to provoke the RUC in their slow, lumbering Land Rovers, which the young drivers could easily out-perform. When warned by the IRA enforcers, most youths would stop for a while and then continue at a later date.

Paul McFadden, a slim, innocent-looking young teenager with a pale, angelic face under a black thatch of hair, became one of my best mates. Sometimes he would find himself picked on unfairly. One hot summer's evening, along with other teenage boys from the estate, we ran out to watch the joy-riders after hearing the accelerating cars and screeching tyres.

As the old Ford Cortina was being thrown around by the two teenage occupants, half a dozen hard-looking men came out of the nearby licenced club and walked over to the makeshift race track.

'You little hoods,' one yelled to a couple of my mates, 'you little bastards have been told to stop this.' He grabbed hold of a kid and hit him repeatedly on the head with a snooker cue, while a tough-looking man with a beer belly grabbed hold of another young kid and began kicking him.

Realising what was happening, the boys in the car braked hard, stopped and ran for safety, abandoning the vehicle. Then one of the men, whom I recognised as Johnny McGinty, and another well-built man with a shaven head, grabbed my friend Paul, one taking his arms, the other his legs. Before he realised what was happening, they picked him up and hurled him bodily through the windscreen of the car. Every kid scattered but the men managed to grab one or two more, thumping and kicking them, telling them to 'get off home'.

On that occasion I managed to escape without a beating, but the next time I met Johnny McGinty I thought he was about to kill me.

Occasionally, a friend of the family would ask me to babysit and I would happily agree, even though I knew nothing whatsoever about caring for babies. This particular night, when I was perhaps 14, I was hurrying along in drenching rain to the woman's house when I met a friend of mine, a boy everyone nicknamed 'Mackers'. He was standing under cover, drinking a bottle of strong cider.

'What you doing?' I asked.

'Nothing; drinking,' he replied.

'Aren't you cold?' I asked him.

'Of course,' he said, 'I'm freezing my bollocks off standing here.'

I told him where I was going and invited him along. In our innocence, what neither Mackers nor myself understood at that time was that Johnny McGinty was having an affair with the woman I had been asked to babysit for. Shortly after midnight there was a tapping at the window and we looked out to see a man with a balaclava rolled up on top of his head and wearing a long, black military-style overcoat. At first we ignored the tapping, but it continued and we realised we would have to answer it.

I gingerly opened the door.

'Is Maria in?' he asked.

'No, she's out,' I replied. 'We're babysitting.'

The man pushed the door open and walked in, uninvited, removing the balaclava and shaking off the rain. My mouth went dry as I recognised Johnny McGinty. As I followed him into the room I saw Mackers's face as he also registered McGinty. He went white, almost choking on a bottle of cider.

He jumped to his feet. 'Hi, Johnny, how are you?' he asked, pretending to be a great mate. Johnny said nothing but sat down on a chair to watch the film on television.

Mackers and I exchanged worried glances, wondering why Johnny McGinty had walked into this house at this time when only we two youngsters were there. We wondered if he was going to give us a kicking for something or other. We sat still, hardly daring to breath.

After about half an hour, when Mackers and I had begun to relax a little, McGinty got to his feet and I heaved a sigh of relief, believing he was about to leave.

He put his hand down the front of his trousers and took out a hand-gun.

'Shit,' I thought. 'Please God let nothing happen.'

At that time in my young life, guns spelt danger and possible death. We had always seen the Army and police walking around the streets with their rifles and hand-guns; a number of my friends had been injured by plastic bullets and I had seen an increasing number of Republicans walking around at night with their AK-47s. And I had also heard and seen the effects of the IRA's favourite act of terror, the well-documented kneecapping.

'Do you know what this is?' Johnny asked, pointing the weapon at Mackers.

'Y-y-y-yeah', he stammered, looking ill. 'It's a gun.'

'I know that, you little cunt,' said McGinty. 'What type of gun?'

'I don't know,' he said, shaking his head.

'Do *you* know?' he asked, turning to me.

'No idea,' I replied, not wanting to say any more in case I annoyed him with the answer.

'It's a Luger, a 9mm German Luger,' he replied. 'Do you know anything about these guns?'

Both Mackers and I shook our heads.

He knelt down with one knee on the ground, put his hand down the front of his trousers again and took out a handkerchief, spreading the contents on the carpet beside the gun. There must have been a dozen or so bullets there. He looked at both of us and then slowly began filling the magazine, putting about six in the Luger, before carefully wrapping the rest in his handkerchief and putting them back into his trousers.

'Come with me,' he ordered and walked into the hall, through the kitchen and out of the back door into the small back garden of the terraced house.

I had never been so frightened in my life. I was praying for Maria to return, to save us, for I was convinced that McGinty was about to kneecap or shoot us. I couldn't think why he would want to shoot us, but the fact that our lives at that time were preoccupied day and night with killings and beatings had obviously taken its toll.

'Watch this,' he said and took the gun, knelt down on the ground and, placing the barrel on the grass, pulled the trigger. The noise of the shot seemed to reverberate around the neighbourhood and I prayed someone would hear and come to investigate. At that age I didn't realise that during that phase of the Troubles, people never investigated the sound of gunfire in Belfast, for fear of getting involved, and perhaps shot, for their curiosity.

McGinty got up and walked over to where the metal dustbin stood in the corner of the garden. He adjusted it slightly, stepped back three feet and fired again into the bin. The noise was even louder this time and I wondered where all this would lead, convinced he was only showing off before turning the gun on us.

'Your turn,' he said to Mackers, handing him the gun.

Gingerly, Mackers took the Luger and fired a single shot at the bin, before quickly handing the gun back to McGinty.

'Now your turn,' he said to me.

I took the gun, unsure what to do because I knew McGinty to be a hard man, one of those boastful bigheads who liked to pretend he was an important part of the IRA. Others knew him to be a wild man, unafraid of anything and capable of carrying out any atrocity.

I pointed the gun at the dustbin, shut my eyes and squeezed the trigger tight with both hands. Nothing happened. It seemed I hadn't the strength to pull the trigger hard enough.

'Pull the trigger!' he shouted. 'Pull the fucking trigger!'

But I didn't. I was frightened something might go wrong; that the gun might backfire or that the bullet would ricochet and kill me or Mackers.

'If you don't fucking fire that gun I'll shoot you in the kneecap,' he yelled.

That did it. I closed my eyes tight and pulled the trigger as hard as I could. The gun jumped and the bullet missed the bin and went into the garden wall.

'I told you there's nothing to it,' he said, taking the gun from me.

He fired two more rounds and I suddenly realised that all the bullets had been fired. Although my heart was still thumping, I began to relax a little.

'Inside,' he said, nodding his head towards the kitchen.

Once inside, he stripped down the gun, washed it in the sink with washing-up liquid and hot water and dried it with a tea towel. I thought that it was an odd thing to do to a gun but I said nothing. Then he put it back together again, stuffed it down his trousers and walked out, leaving Mackers and myself literally shaking with shock.

'We must tell no one about this,' I said to Mackers when he had left, 'for if he finds out we've been telling stories about him he'll kill us.'

When Maria returned some 30 minutes later, she asked us if everything had been all right.

'Fine, not a squeak,' I replied, and before she had taken off her coat, Mackers and I were outside the house, running back to the safety of our homes as quickly as possible.

From that time on, I would always say 'hello' to Johnny McGinty whenever I saw him and, in turn, he would shout to me in a loud voice, 'Shoot the bins, Marty, shoot the bins!' and laugh as he passed by. I felt it would be wise for me to have McGinty as a friend rather than an enemy and I would always stop and chat to him.

One Sunday afternoon, I was at home and heard shouting outside. When I went to investigate I saw an army foot patrol had stopped a taxi in which was Johnny McGinty and one of his best friends, Geordie. The Army had ordered the men out of the vehicle and a very drunk McGinty had half-fallen out. As I walked towards the group, McGinty suddenly went berserk, flailing away with his fists, trying to make contact with the officers who had stopped him. His pal joined in and together they tried to punch their way free but they were far too drunk. Within seconds of the first punch being thrown, the eight soldiers joined in, punching the hell out of the two men who were in no fit state to defend themselves.

I thought it was my duty to rescue poor McGinty and I ran towards the mêlée in the middle of the street. As I neared the fight, a soldier stepped in front of me, blocking my path. I turned and punched the soldier in a bid to escape and, as he tried to evade my fist, he tripped and fell over a small garden wall.

I ran on towards McGinty shouting at the soldiers, 'Get off them! Leave them alone! Leave them alone!'

As I reached the skirmish, the soldiers had managed to grab McGinty and Geordie, pinning their arms behind them, but some of the soldiers had taken some punches and I could see bruising and marks on their faces.

Hearing the noise and the shouting, other people had come out of their houses to see what was happening and I heard my mother shouting at me at the top of her voice, 'Get down here, you mad bastard, come here at once.'

But I ignored her orders as I wanted to make sure that the soldiers would not start hitting the two men again. My mother walked briskly towards us but when she realised the ruckus was over she went back home, allowing me to remain at the scene.

*　　　　*　　　　*

I became involved with a crowd of young men, all in their 20s, who never had jobs and never wanted to work. They did, however, become professional shoplifters, driving all over the Province, hitting different towns, somehow managing to keep one step ahead of the law. They all lived on the estate and I ran errands for them.

At first, I had no idea that the goods they were selling had been stolen, but I didn't remain innocent for long. They would ask me to call at the house where two of them lived and take away a bag, a black plastic dustbin liner full of merchandise, and they would tell me how much to charge. Very quickly I learned the ropes – if an item was marked at £60, then they would demand £20 and I was allowed to keep £10 for myself.

Of course, many of the items were only marked at £20, so I would receive just £2, but I would usually sell 10 to 20 items a day, perhaps two or three times a week. I felt loaded.

I also had some narrow escapes. On one occasion, when I was nearly 16, two of the young men gave me £10 to go and collect a car they had parked a mile from home.

'Why don't *you* go?' I asked.

'We're too tired,' one of them replied.

'Is it full of stuff?' I asked.

'Maybe,' he replied, 'but I'll give you a tenner if you pick it up.'

I thought about it for a split second. 'Give me the key,' I said. 'I'll get it.'

I took the £10 and went to find the car, parked as they had told me on a hill a mile away. I could see nothing inside but presumed the boot to be full of stolen gear. No sooner had I opened the door, started the engine and driven gingerly away than I looked in the rear-view mirror to see two RUC Land Rovers bearing down on me, their blue lights flashing. As I went round corners I could see the Land Rovers leaning over wildly, their tyres screeching as they raced after me.

'The bastards,' I thought, referring to the friends that had happily put me in such danger for a miserly £10. I realised that the RUC 'jeeps' were much slower than the vehicle I was driving, so I drove as fast as I could around the streets where I lived and which I knew well. I lost them, turned into a road and then into a friend's drive. I slammed on the brakes and leapt from the car, running like hell across the gardens, fearful I would be caught.

'You bastards,' I screamed at my mates when I finally found them. 'You knew the car was being watched.'

If I had been a little older, I would have hit one of them when he turned to me and demanded back the £10.

'Fuck off,' I said and ran off as they laughed at me.

My reputation for providing stolen jeans, suits, expensive china ornaments and light electrical goods spread widely and people began asking me for individual items: anoraks for kids, electric shavers for young teenagers and videos and TVs which I never dealt in. Some adults began calling me 'Arthur', after the TV character Arthur Daley. I hated that because it made me feel like an old man.

My budding reputation also got me into trouble with the police because they had heard of this young teenager, Kate McGartland's lad, who always seemed to have lots of money. They began stopping and searching me whenever I was walking around the streets. Those who knew me well would stop and search me, asking for my full name and address which they already knew by heart. I knew they were trying to rile me, and would make me stand and wait while they questioned me.

On one occasion, an officer was searching me and began to probe, frequently and forcibly, between my legs.

'What do you think you're doing?' I shouted and pulled myself away.

'I'm just searching you,' he replied.

'Well keep your hands to yourself, you're hurting me,' I said.

'Stand still and shut up,' he said, 'otherwise you'll be down the station. Now let me search you.'

'OK,' I replied. I loosened my belt and, in the middle of the street, dropped my trousers to my ankles.

'You perverts!' shouted some women who were

walking past at the time, making the officer look uncomfortable.

'Leave him alone,' shouted others who were gathering to see what was going on.

'Satisfied now?' I said and I could see the other RUC officers looking surprised and not a little embarrassed at what was going on.

'On your way,' he said, and I realised he was feeling guilty at having given me a hard time.

My life of crime, however, ended when all the lads who had been shoplifting were caught and put away. I had been working with them for nearly a year, sometimes making £200 a week, but I had nothing to show for my ill-gotten gains. I had squandered the lot on clothes, chocolate and amusement arcades.

I had also received a visit from an IRA disciplinary squad.

CHAPTER THREE

T<small>HEY CAME TO MY MOTHER'S HOUSE</small> at around 3.00pm one day during the winter of 1985. The two men were in their 20s – one was generally known by the nickname 'Andy', and the other was called Martin Morris.

'Where's Marty?' they asked my mother.

'What do you want him for?' she replied.

'We want to talk to him,' one said.

'What about?' my mother asked in her belligerent tone.

'We've been told he's been running about selling blocks of cheese.'

'Blocks of cheese!' she exclaimed. 'What are you talking about?'

'Can we come in?' one asked.

'No, you can't,' she replied. 'I'll find out if he's been selling cheese and I'll deal with him in my own way.'

The two men began arguing with her, demanding that they be permitted to search the house, telling her that she must hand me over to them for questioning. My mother knew that they were IRA and also that if she did hand me over then I would be punished. That punishment could entail anything from a heavy thumping with sticks and baseball bats to a kneecapping. My mother would hear none of their demands.

'Just take yourselves off, the pair of you, and I'll deal with him. Do you hear me?'

Kate McGartland's fearsome reputation was legendary on the Ballymurphy Estate and there were few men who had the courage to take her on; her tongue was fast and venomous; her strength of character was challenged only by the strongest or the most foolhardy of men. The two IRA men looked at each other and left.

When I returned that evening my mother was waiting with that look on her face – the one that spelt trouble.

'Have you been stealing cheese?' she asked.

'No,' I replied honestly. 'I've been selling cheese, but I never stole any.'

'Are you sure?' she asked, challenging me.

'It's true, Ma, I swear it.'

On this occasion, my mother believed me and she would later give the two IRA men a dressing down for spreading false rumours. But it was not the end of the matter.

A few weeks later, I and five teenage mates from the estate left the Matt Talbot Youth Club where we had spent the evening playing pool. We were standing around chatting when we saw a group of ten young men, all wearing masks, running towards us waving baseball bats and hammers. At first we thought it was just some friends having a joke, but we quickly realised that these men meant business.

'Get the little bastards,' one shouted, and the others began yelling at us. The group of men were only about 20 yards away when we realised what was going on. Someone shouted, 'Run, run for it, it's the fucking IRA!'

We all turned and fled down the street as fast as we could, as we knew full well that if we were caught we would have been subjected to a hell of a beating. We had all seen victims battered black and blue by IRA punishment squads, some with broken bones, others with their heads cracked open.

Behind us, the mob yelled at us to stop, screaming abuse, effing and blinding. I turned for an instant and saw them swinging their baseball bats and hammers and I could feel my heart thumping as they seemed to be getting closer. I was convinced that I would stumble and fall and concentrated on keeping my footing as I ran faster than I had ever run in my life.

Suddenly, the yelling stopped and the noise of running feet faded. I looked round. There was no one there. We had run more than half a mile but the IRA gang had given up the chase. Then we realised that one of us, Patrick, a slim lad with a fierce temper and remarkable courage, had disappeared.

We decided to investigate, to see if the IRA had captured him. Gingerly, we walked back, suspecting that the gang may have laid a trap. As we rounded a corner we saw Patrick standing on the pavement repeatedly hitting one of the IRA men in the face with his fists, giving him a real pasting. Later, Patrick told us what had happened.

After a few hundred yards, Patrick said he felt exhausted, unable to continue running. As he stopped and turned to face his attackers he realised that most of them had stopped and only three were still in the chase. He had grabbed the first one who was wielding a hammer, disarmed him, threw away the hammer and then belted him around the head and body with his fists. The other two wanted none of the fight and fled, leaving their mate to take a hiding.

'Jesus, Patrick,' I said when the man had run off, 'they'll fucking kill us for beating one of them. What the hell did you do that for?'

'What the fuck did you think I was going to do?' he said. 'Let them beat me with hammers and stuff? I'll not give in to those bastards.'

We would never discover what that IRA punishment gang wanted that night. They had all been masked so we had no idea who they were or where they lived. But the fright I received that night made me realise that I would have to tread carefully, keep out of the limelight, and make sure that the IRA had no idea of any of my money-making schemes.

Later, I discovered that the IRA had only authorised two men, Andy and Martin, the men who had come searching for me, as the disciplinary squad in the Ballymurphy area. Their job would be to speak to people whom the IRA considered to be law-breakers, youngsters like me and my mates who were trying to earn a few pounds, as well as the thieves, muggers and shoplifters who were acting without the authority of the IRA.

From the late 1970s, the IRA had appealed to all Catholics to report civil offences to Sinn Fein centres dotted around Belfast, rather than go to the RUC. And I knew that over the years more and more Catholics had turned to Sinn Fein, knowing the matter would be passed to the IRA to take whatever action they deemed necessary. Of course, I understood that part of the reason was to convince all Catholics that Sinn Fein had both the power and authority to protect them, thus gaining the community's support for their political activities. And the IRA took advantage of the situation to stamp their authority in all Republican areas. Indeed, the IRA did become the community's police force for many years, using their terror tactics to control the Catholic population.

I learnt of many occasions when Catholics turned to Sinn Fein – when their cars had been stolen, for example, and the wrecked car had been found abandoned with the radio, the wheels and most of the interior ripped out. Most Catholics knew that reporting the matter to the RUC would achieve little or nothing, so they began reporting such instances to Sinn Fein.

If Sinn Fein discovered who had stolen the vehicle, the thief would be taken away and interrogated by an IRA punishment squad and the man would be left shaking with fear, having been ordered to repay the cost of the car or face the consequences. Everyone knew that meant two possibilities: a punishment beating with iron bars or a kneecapping.

It was through one of my close friends, Ricky McNally, a boy with a natural talent for football, that I witnessed the viciousness of the IRA. Ricky's elder brother Martin had been targeted by an IRA punishment squad on a number of occasions for allegedly stealing cars and joy-riding around Belfast. Three times he was picked up by a squad, taken away and given a fearful beating, before being left unable to walk. On each occasion he needed hospital treatment for broken bones and dreadful bruising.

The IRA, however, believed their beatings did not stop young Martin McNally from stealing more cars. They returned and took him away again, but this time one of the punishment squad produced a powerful Magnum hand-gun and shot him in the ankles, leaving him on the ground, writhing in agony. It would be months before he regained the use of his legs and he would never be able to walk properly again.

After he had been shot, I went to visit Martin in the

City Hospital. I saw him lying there on his bed, pale and obviously under sedation. But I could see pain in his eyes and a sense of hopelessness in the way he spoke. I looked at Martin and a feeling of disgust came over me; that the IRA, the so-called protectors and friends of the Northern Irish Catholics could treat one of their own in such a way

Millen, a distant cousin of mine and a good friend, was also targeted by the IRA for what the punishment squad described as 'anti-social behaviour'. They gave no other reason.

I was passing Millen's house on the estate one night and I heard him shouting from a bedroom window. 'Marty, call the peelers, for fuck sake, call the peelers. I think I'm going to be targeted.'

'Don't be stupid,' I told him, 'I can't call the peelers. If I did, the IRA would shoot me dead.' And I walked on down the street.

Later that night, I heard that poor Millen had indeed been taken away and badly beaten. I felt awful that I had not done something to try and save him. Yet I knew that if I had called the RUC I would probably have been shot dead by the IRA. Betraying the 'cause' would certainly have earned me a kneecapping, for the act of calling the police would have been seen as treachery.

But Millen refused to go to hospital and lay for days on the settee at his mother's home. I called in to see him on a few occasions and felt angry that the IRA needed to stoop to such repulsive violence against young teenage boys.

During the following 18 months, I would be warned on a dozen occasions or more by various IRA members. They would call at my house or stop me in the street, ask me questions, grill me and pretend they knew more about my activities than they in fact did. I would deny everything, never revealing that I was ever involved in buying or selling stolen goods. Some were Sinn Fein officers, others junior members of the IRA trying to make a name for themselves within the organisation. There were others, though, whom I knew to have been fully fledged members of criminal organisations prior to joining the IRA. Sometimes I would be warned for no reason whatsoever, but the fact that I always had money to spend made them suspicious. I had continued to sell goods that other people provided, taking my cut and handing over the rest to my suppliers.

In some ways I brought attention to myself, for I would always gave small amounts of money away to kids whose parents I knew were having a tough time, without work and trying to survive on the dole. It was around this time that I earned the nickname 'Money Bags', and the kids would run after me in the street shouting my nickname and begging for money. That worried me and so I scaled down my generosity, only giving money away to young kids whose parents really needed it.

I knew that my buying and selling activities were illegal; I knew in my heart that the vast amount of goods I was selling around the estate had been stolen, mostly from shoplifting expeditions. But I also knew that the great majority of the people I sold the goods to were on the dole, many with large families to care for. Nearly all were living a hand-to-mouth existence and I provided them with goods at half price or less. I felt it was worth the risk and it made me feel good. It also earned me good money.

*   *   *

It wasn't only the IRA who troubled us. My pals and I also had to make sure we kept one step ahead of the RUC and the Army.

One summer's evening, my mother and a few of her friends went to consult a fortune teller called May, renowned as being one of the great professional fortune tellers of Belfast. She agreed to spend a few hours at a house in our street reading tarot cards and telling fortunes. She knew that my mother and her friends would cross her palm most generously for an evening's work.

May was, in fact, a Protestant from the Donegall Road, a strong Loyalist area of Belfast, but she was perfectly happy crossing the line to tell fortunes in the Catholic areas. That night, a dozen women crowded into my Aunt Agnes's home waiting for their cards to be read.

As they sat waiting for May to arrive, an RUC foot patrol, backed by the Army, was seen in the street. The squad stopped a man, searched him, questioned him and gave him a hard time.

'Leave him alone, you bastards,' one of my mates shouted. 'He's done nothing wrong.'

'Shut up,' shouted the officers, but we had no intention of keeping quiet.

'Leave him alone, let him go,' we all shouted.

At that, one RUC officer ran across the street and grabbed one of us. The officer took hold of the lad and began to drag him towards the squad across the street. But the RUC man had misjudged our mood and our courage. There were perhaps 12 to 15 teenagers on the street that night and we were not prepared to see one of our own lads taken away by the police for simply shouting abuse at their rough treatment.

A friend of mine, Dave, grabbed the RUC officer by the arm forcing him to release his grip on the lad. As he did so, the other members of the foot patrol, 15 in all, raced across the street towards us. Within seconds there was a general mêlée with all of us trading punches. I hit one soldier on the chin and other friends of mine connected as well. But we also took some stick.

Suddenly I heard a shout and looked up to see another dozen or more peelers and soldiers running up the street to join in the fray.

'Run for it! Run for it!' we all shouted, knowing full well that if we were caught and taken away we would all face serious charges for assaulting the officers.

As we broke off, a woman began screaming at the soldiers 'Let them go, you bullies, let them go.'

At that, a soldier turned, took aim with his rifle and fired a plastic bullet at the woman who was standing only three feet away. The bullet hit the poor woman full in the chest, knocking her to the ground.

As we fled, the sound of the fracas and the shot had brought scores more people, mainly women, out on to the streets. At least half a dozen had witnessed the woman collapse in a heap, felled by the plastic bullet.

'She's dead! She's dead!' one yelled. 'They've killed her! They've shot her dead!'

Within seconds, word had spread that the Army had killed a woman. My mates and I returned to the attack, now supported by others who took up rocks and began hurling them at the foot patrols. I saw one soldier kneeling, his rifle in the firing position, aiming at a group of women a few yards away. I was convinced he was about to kill another women so I grabbed a wooden stake, ran up behind him and smashed the piece of wood across the back of his neck, sending him sprawling unconscious.

At least a dozen separate fights had broken out across the street but once again we could see reinforcements, Land Rovers this time, racing up the road towards us, their blue lights flashing.

'Run for it!' people screamed, for we knew we faced

arrest. As we ran towards the houses the soldiers pursued us, determined to catch up and take us away. I followed four lads to my Aunt Agnes's house, running through the open front door into the hall, but as I turned to shut the door, a soldier put his boot in the way and I could not hold it.

The house was full of people trying to escape out of the back door, as well as the fortune teller and a dozen of my mother's friends who had been sitting and standing around in the kitchen. I realised that the soldier at the front door would soon smash his way in, so I fled to the back door through the kitchen. As I ran through the group of women, I could see the fortune teller hiding under the kitchen table.

I escaped into the back garden and ran like hell with the others across a number of gardens and over innumerable fences before finally reaching safety. That night, the crack troops, members of the Divisional Mobile Support Unit, were called in but not one of us was arrested. We hid in a number of homes until the police and the Army had left the area. That was the closest I came to getting into serious trouble with the RUC or the Army.

Later I heard that as the soldiers burst into my aunt's house, desperate to catch us, she collapsed with a heart attack in the hallway and had to be rushed to hospital.

Neither my mother nor her friends ever invited the fortune teller back again. 'If she had been any good at predicting the future,' my mother would say when recounting the story, 'she would have known the Army and the police were about to invade the house and warned us.'

And she would roar with laughter.

*   *   *

Despite the attentions of the RUC and the Army, as well as the ever-present IRA, I continued making money selling stolen goods throughout the neighbourhood and beyond. But I didn't want money simply to enjoy life. Now I *needed* the money.

I had become addicted to CB radio. From the age of 14 I had dabbled with a friend's CB and when I bought my own radio, and stuck a 20-foot-high aerial on top of my mother's house, I discovered a new set of friends. I would stay awake half the night chatting to my new-found friends throughout the Province.

One night, when 15, I heard a young woman chatting on the CB whose 'handle' (call-sign) was 'White Suspenders, Shankill'. Understandably, the girl and particularly her handle, interested my burgeoning sexual awareness, and from that moment White Suspenders and myself would talk to each other for three or four hours a night, usually signing off, tired and half asleep at around 4am.

Being from the Shankill, of course, I realised that White Suspenders was probably a Protestant girl, but that never bothered me. Through my CB I had made friends with a number of Protestants also addicted to CB. Many of us CB freaks would meet outside Boots the Chemist in the centre of Belfast every Saturday morning and we would chat and drink coffee for a few hours. Some of those I met, from both the Protestant and Catholic communities, became good friends.

One evening, a CB friend drove to my home and hooted the horn for me to go out and see him. Sitting next to him was a lovely girl I had never seen before.

'Do you know who this is?' my pal asked me, pointing to the girl in the car, a good-looking tall blond with a good figure. She was wearing jeans and a short, white cotton bolero top.

'No,' I said, my pulse racing, hoping the girl was White Suspenders.

'This is Liz.'

By this time, of course, I knew that Liz and White Suspenders were one and the same.

'Hi,' I said, surprised and a little embarrassed that I was finally face to face with White Suspenders. And I was standing there dressed in nothing but a pair of jeans.

'Are you coming for a spin?' he asked.

'Hold on,' I said, 'I'll be right with you,' and I ran inside, grabbed a shirt, looked at myself in the mirror and dashed back to the car.

Within a few weeks Liz and I would become lovers, much to the consternation of my mother. It wasn't that she thought we were too young, but that Liz was a Protestant from the hard-line Loyalist Shankill area.

Throughout the mid-1980s, particularly in Belfast and 'Derry, sectarian killings by both sides became an everyday occurrence with taxi drivers, in particular, being killed nearly every week.

My mother feared what would happen to either Lizzie or myself if the sectarian hardliners on either side discovered we were dating. She would occasionally allow Lizzie to stay at our house but she could never relax.

'You know what the IRA will do with that girl if they find she's staying here, don't you?' my mother would ask. And without waiting for a reply, my mother continue, 'They'll kill her. Do you realise that?'

I discussed the situation with Liz but we were young and in love and believed nothing could touch us. I would occasionally stay at her house in the Shankill and, before going to bed, I would push the settee against the front door in case of possible intruders. I believed that with the settee against the door I would have a few seconds or more to make good my escape through the back door and over the garden wall.

Most evenings we would spend some time together and then Liz would take a taxi back home at around midnight. For the next few hours we would chat on the CB, lovers talking about our future together, our love life and sometimes the intimate details of our new-found sex life.

Seven months later, while chatting late at night on the CB, Liz told me she was pregnant.

There was no way that Liz and I could stay together unless we decided to leave Northern Ireland and live somewhere else in the United Kingdom. Once, and once only, we discussed that possibility but we were both so young, without jobs and with virtually no money between us. We agreed that the idea would be impractical, if not impossible, and we never discussed the matter again.

My mother took the news of the pregnancy remarkably well, but she never mentioned the possibility that Liz and I should marry or live together because she knew that both those options would be impossible. She knew, better than Liz or me, what would happen if the hard men on either side of the sectarian divide heard that we were living together and proposing to bring up a family.

Liz and I would see each other throughout her pregnancy and we swore undying love. But in our hearts we knew that we would not, we could not, stay together. After baby Martine was born in January 1987, I tried to be a good father and bought a pram, baby clothes and everything that Liz would need to care for our baby. We continued to see each other but even meeting was fraught with difficulties as the sectarian violence increased and the hatred between the two communities intensified. When Liz became pregnant we had stopped our nightly chats on the CB and a few weeks after Martine was born it became obvious that the relationship could not continue.

One night, Liz and I were walking from the Catholic area towards the Shankill because she needed to be back home to look after Martine. We came across a friend of mine, who had obviously been drinking, and who had met Liz on a few occasions. He had always been polite and pleasant, but drunk he was a different man.

'Fuck off, you Shankill slag,' he shouted at her. 'Go and get fucked by one of your own.'

'Shut up,' I told him, threatening to hit him if he didn't.

'You should know better, Marty,' he scoffed. 'You should never fuck a Prod – they're all on the game.'

Liz was on the brink of tears and we walked quickly away. But the incident would never be forgotten for it made Liz realise that we could never build a life together.

Meeting had become extremely difficult, exposing both of us to physical danger. The IRA and Loyalist patrols were becoming more vigilant, and passing between the Catholic and Protestant areas meant risking exposure and punishment every time either of us made the trip. Neither my mother nor Lizzie's parents ever suggested that we should live together, because they knew that one day we would be discovered and our lives would be at risk. Within a matter of months the relationship faded and died.

*　　　　*　　　　*

I was 16 and, during the first few months of 1987, I found that I was being stopped and questioned at regular intervals by one particular RUC officer, a friendly, middle-aged, stout man with a bushy moustache. As usual, he asked for my name, address and date of birth, where I was going, and why.

The following week he stopped me again and asked me the same questions in a similarly friendly manner. This happened a third time the following week. I didn't like the attention because Republicans were suspicious of any Catholics who were seen talking regularly to RUC officers.

'Why do you keep stopping me and asking me the same questions?' I asked. 'You should know me by now.'

'No reason,' he smiled. 'Just doing my job.'

But the officer, who told me his name was Billy, continued to stop and question me for no apparent reason and I wondered why. He would even shout after me in the street while dealing with another matter, and drop everything to come over and chat to me.

A month or so later, Officer Billy stopped me again.

'Now what do you want?' I remonstrated, annoyed and worried in case any IRA men were watching.

'I hear you're taking driving lessons,' he said.

'That's right,' I said, somewhat startled, wondering how on earth he knew I was taking lessons.

'When you're ready to take your test, let me know,' he said, ' because I have a couple of mates who might be able to help.'

There was nothing I wanted more than to pass my driving test, buy a car and start to enjoy life. It had been my ambition since childhood and the thought of being assisted to pass my test seemed like a dream.

The next time we met, Officer Billy told me to go to Grosvenor Road RUC base, close to the Republican Falls Road, and someone would be there to see me. No names were mentioned. I was intrigued, wondering how calling at the RUC base would secure me a driving licence.

The following evening, on Officer Billy's instructions, a taxi dropped me off a couple of miles from the RUC base, and I completed my journey on foot. I wondered if I was out of my mind as a dozen or more RUC Land Rovers passed by on their way to and from the base.

As soon as I arrived at the base it was clear that the RUC officers on duty had been forewarned. As I approached the heavily-fortified steel gates, I was amazed that they glided open – no one had challenged me or asked my identity. I suspected a trap.

I waited inside the gate and stood motionless expecting someone to challenge me. For a full minute I stood still, watching the officer inside the sangar, expecting him to question me and ask me to explain the reason for my presence. But he ignored me.

After a minute or so I decided to walk across the square to an office with 'Reception' on the door. I walked slowly, deliberately keeping my hands by my side so that no one would think I was about to throw a grenade or go for a gun. I still believed I might be entering a trap, but there was no turning back.

I walked warily into the reception room and saw another officer sitting in an adjoining room. He looked at me and then turned away, as though I wasn't there. He didn't say a word either, so I sat down and waited, wondering why no one had spoken to me.

Five long minutes later a door at the side of the room opened and a tall, well-built man in his 50s, called across to me. 'Marty,' he said in a friendly voice, 'come on in.'

At that moment I had no idea what the future would hold – I later discovered that I was about to start my career as an agent working for the Special Branch.

CHAPTER FOUR

I WALKED INTO THE TINY, BARE, WINDOWLESS ROOM, not more than seven feet by seven feet, furnished with a small table and wooden chairs. The man who greeted me shook me by the hand – his grip firm and strong, his hand seemingly twice the size of mine. The other man in the room, also powerfully built and more than six-feet tall, spoke with a strong Belfast accent.

'Sit down, Marty,' the first man said, trying to put me at ease, 'Did Billy explain to you why we wanted to see you?'

'No,' I said, 'he just mentioned something about a driving licence.'

'Listen,' said the first man, 'I want to be straight with you, Marty. We will be able to help you obtain a licence but it will take some time. I'm sure we'll be able to sort something out for you. We just want you to do some work for us, to keep an eye on some people. We're the Special Branch and it's our job to keep an eye on trouble-makers. From time to time we need help from local people. We thought you might be interested in helping. If, on the other hand, you don't want to work for us, we will understand. You can just leave here and go home and you will hear nothing more.'

Number Two added, 'If you decide to walk away you can be sure you won't hear any more from Officer Billy either.' With a laugh, he said, 'Has he been giving you a hard time?'

'A hard time!' I replied. 'He's been chasing me up and down the street wanting to talk to me.'

'Listen,' said Number One, laughing, 'Billy is a good man at heart. He won't do you any harm, I promise you.'

The two men sitting in front of me, dressed in light-coloured anoraks, sweaters and grey trousers, intrigued me. They seemed like ordinary blokes I saw everyday in Belfast and nothing like what I expected Special Branch officers to look like. I had only ever heard about the mysterious, legendary Special Branch but, to my knowledge, had never seen or met one of them before.

'What would you want me to do?' I asked.

Number One replied, 'All we would want you to do is keep an eye on some people in your area.'

'Who are you talking about?' I asked, somewhat mystified. 'Who are these people?'

He replied, 'These will be people who we will identify to you and then you can keep an eye on them for us.'

Number Two intervened. 'We will show you pictures of them; they all live in your area and ask you to keep an eye on them.'

'Who are these people?' I asked again.

'We will let you know,' said Number One. 'Could you meet us in a couple of days?'

'Sure I could, where?' I asked.

'Somewhere near your area,' said Number Two, 'We could meet you in the Turf Lodge ...'

Before he could finish the sentence I exploded, 'Turf Lodge! Turf Lodge! Do you think I'm fucking mad? If I'm seen there meeting you two I'll get killed, you know that?'

They both laughed at my outburst. 'Calm down, Marty, don't worry; we go in there all the time.'

Then I think my mouth dropped open in disbelief, for I would never have imagined plain-clothes Special Branch officers daring to enter the tough Republican Turf Lodge area which the IRA controlled and where RUC officers only ventured in armoured Land Rovers.

'Listen, said Number One, 'walk through Turf Lodge towards Kennedy Way and we will pick you up in a car. Don't worry. We will check you're not being followed.'

I looked from one to the other and they could see I was still undecided, fearing that they could never guarantee my safety.

'We will meet you at 7.00pm,' Number two said, 'so it will be dark by then. No one will see you.'

Excited by the prospect, I replied, 'OK then, I'll give it a go.'

We chatted for about five minutes and they asked me whether I had a job and what I did with myself during the day. I wasn't going to tell them about my money-earning activities and must have blushed. I noticed they looked at each other and both laughed. 'We don't want to know anything about your private life, Marty, don't worry,' said Number One.

That reassured me. I began to relax and to believe that I had not entered a trap.

'We'll see you then. Seven o'clock down Kennedy Way. OK?'

It was time to go. I got to my feet and shook hands with them, once again noting the size of their hands. I knew I would never mix it with either of them.

As I walked back home that evening, I vowed never to tell anyone of my meeting with the Special Branch. I was learning.

Two days later, as I walked the mile-and-a-half to the appointed rendezvous, I kept glancing at the passing cars to see whether I recognised any of the vehicles. If I had recognised a friend's car I would probably have turned round and walked straight home; but I saw no one I knew.

I had no idea what to expect when, as if from nowhere, a silver, four-door saloon pulled up in front of me and stopped. As the rear passenger door opened I saw another car across the road with two men inside. That scared me.

I could feel my heart thumping as I climbed inside. 'Shit,' I said, hardly able to string two words together, 'I've just been spotted ... there's two men in a car over there ... they saw me get in.'

The Special Branch men could see I was nervous. 'Don't worry,' one of the officers said, 'it's one of ours.'

Number One, who was in the front passenger seat, picked up a walkie-talkie radio, and after giving a call sign, said, 'Everything's OK on our side; you can return to base.'

We drove to Musgrave Park Hospital in Balmoral and stopped in the visitor's car park, which was nearly full at that time of night.

'We'll be safe here,' said Number Two. 'There's no need to worry.'

'We're going to give you a telephone number where you can contact us 24 hours a day,' said Number One, 'and we're going to give you a code name, too. Alright?'

'Yeah,' I nodded.

'You can't write down this number, you must memorise it'.

They gave me a Belfast number and told me to repeat it over and over again until I knew it by heart.

'Right,' said Number Two, 'now we're going to give you a code name. It's Bonzo.'

'Bonzo,' I said, repeating the word. 'What's that mean? It sounds like a dog.'

It was at this point that the two officers introduced themselves. Number One said, 'My name's Dean and his name's Jimmy. Have you got that?'

'Yes,' I replied. 'You're Dean and he's Jimmy.'

'Good.'

'And what's the telephone number?'

I stumbled and made a mistake.

'No, listen again,' said Dean, and he repeated the number slowly.

'Now, what's your code name?'

'That's easy,' I replied. 'Bonzo.'

'Good. Now give me the number again.'

This time I got it right. At this point Dean lent over and handed me four £10 notes.

'What's this for?' I asked, surprised, but taking the money.

'That's for you.'

Never in my life had I ever been given money for doing nothing and these two were giving me £40 for just walking a mile or so for a meeting.

'I'll meet you tomorrow night if you give me another forty quid,' I said, laughing.

They liked that. 'Take the forty quid,' said Jimmy, 'but don't come tomorrow night and we'll call it quits.'

Dean then told me. 'This is what you must do. If you need to contact us you must phone the number and ask for Bonzo. Do nothing else. Then you will be put through to either Jimmy or me. Got it?'

'Got it,' I said.

'We'll drop you where we picked you up. OK?'

'Fine,' I said.

'But first tell me, what's the phone number?'

I got it right.

Before I left, Dean said, 'Phone us sometime during the next few days and we'll arrange another meeting, OK?'

'OK,' I said.

That night I could hardly sleep, excited by the new life that I believed lay ahead. I had made £40 and two new friends whom I felt I could trust. They had also made me feel important, a real man. I had no idea at this stage what they wanted me to do, but believed Dean and Jimmy were probably involved in catching big-time criminals, robbers and people involved in organised crime. I knew they were important because they were Special Branch, not ordinary peelers.

A few days later, I phoned the number from a telephone box a long way from my home.

A voice said, 'Hello.'

And I said, 'Can I speak to Bonzo?'

'Wait one moment,' said the voice.

Seconds later, Jimmy came on the phone. 'How are you Bonzo?'

'I'm OK. I'm phoning you because you told me to call.'

'That's good. Will you be able to come and see us in a day or two?'

'That's no problem,' I replied.

'We'll meet you on the same road as before but further down. Is that OK?'

'That's fine.'

Three days later, I met Dean and Jimmy at the rendezvous again, only this time they were in a different car. As I got in, Dean told me to lie down on the back seat. We parked in a street behind King's Hall near Balmoral Golf Course.

Once again we chatted for about 30 minutes before we returned and they dropped me off. That arrangement continued for more than a month. I would phone once a week, we would arrange a meet, and sit and chat for 30 minutes or so. Each time we went to different locations and never once did they use the same car. I began to wonder what they wanted.

During the fourth chat Dean said to me, 'We're going to put you on the pay-roll. We're going to pay you £100 a week.'

'What!' I exclaimed. 'A hundred pound a week. What for?'

'You're working for us now,' Dean replied.

He went on, 'While you're working for us you'll be paid £100 a week and we will give you the money once a month, in cash. Is that OK?'

'Fucking right that's OK,' I said, hardly able to believe my luck earning that sort of money.

As I walked back home that night, I felt elated. I would be earning £400 a month tax free from the Special Branch on top of my dole money. And I was still dealing in stolen goods, earning between £100 and £200 a week. And I wasn't yet 18!

The following week, Dean produced a large A4 sheet of paper covered with perhaps thirty photographs, all of different men. I glanced through them but didn't recognise anyone.

Dean said, 'Take a good look at these photographs. Tell me if you recognise anyone.'

I checked the sheet of paper again. 'No, no one,' I said.

'That's OK,' he said, and took back the sheet of paper.

Then he produced a detailed map showing the individual houses in a block of streets, giving the numbers of the houses and the names of the people who lived in some of them. He then showed me five photographs and told me where each man lived, giving me the exact address and the number of the house.

'Keep an eye open for any of these, will you?' he asked. 'And next time we meet let me know if you've seen any of them.'

I had no idea at this stage who these men were, whether they were criminals or gangsters. The thought that they were active members of the IRA or any other paramilitary organisation hadn't crossed my mind.

During the following week, I made sure that I walked down the various streets where the five men lived in the hope of seeing them. I would glance at the houses as I passed and sometimes fool around in the streets with my mates, while keeping an eye open in case they showed up. During the first few weeks I never recognised a soul.

Each week I reported back to Dean and Jimmy, feeling that I had let them down, that I was taking money for doing nothing and wondering how long they would go on paying me if I never identified anyone from the photos they showed me. Each week they told me not to worry but to keep my eyes open.

Then one day, outside Raffo's chip shop in Whiterock, I saw a man I recognised from the five pictures. He was with two other men whom I couldn't identify and all three were getting into a silver Nissan saloon before driving off. I wrote down the registration number.

Thrilled at finally identifying one of the men I went to a telephone box, called my number and asked for Bonzo as usual. I told Jimmy what had happened and gave him the car's number.

'Good man.' he said. 'Well done.'

The next time we met Dean produced a photograph of a man. 'Is that one of the men you saw?'

'Yes,' I said, 'he was the driver of the car.'

A few weeks later, after I had successfully identified another three men, I was sitting in the car talking to Dean and Jimmy when I finally learned of the work I had, in fact, been doing.

'Listen Marty,' Dean said, 'these men that you have been asked to identify are the hard men of the IRA and the INLA. These are the men that are deeply involved with killing and maiming Protestants. But remember they also deal in the same way with any Catholics that cross them. They are highly dangerous men.'

Since the start of 1987, the two factions of the INLA had been carrying out an internecine feud in Republican areas of Belfast. A breakaway group, the IPLO believed that every type of criminal activity, including organising the drugs trade, was permissable in building funds to buy more sophisticated arms to tackle the British Army and the RUC. The INLA leadership thought that they should have nothing whatsoever to do with crime or drugs. One reason for this was that they were convinced that the IPLO leaders were using the money from crime to line their own pockets.

In the first few months of 1987, a dozen members of the two factions were shot dead in gun battles and assasinations as the feud raged across the Republican areas where I lived. Barely a week would pass without another body being discovered. Most were killed as they returned home, shot down by their rivals who were lying in wait.

Some time later, when the leaders of the IPLO thought they had become so strong they were untouchable, they were taught a harsh lesson by the IRA. A dozen IPLO members, whom the IRA believed were involved in serious criminal activity, including drug-running, were kneecapped by IRA punishment squads. Eventually the IPLO capitulated and disbanded.

Throughout the summer and autumn of 1987, I continued to supply the Special Branch with information they requested, identifying the hard men and reporting their movements. Once a week I would meet my two controllers, changing the places we met and, once a month, they would hand over £400 in cash which I would stuff into my trouser pocket before walking home.

One evening, I jumped into the back of the car as usual to find a strange face in the driver's seat.

'Marty,' said Dean, 'I want you to meet Coco. He will be joining our team because Jimmy has been detailed to work somewhere else.'

I was sorry that Jimmy had been taken off my case because I had come to respect and, more importantly, to trust him.

Coco, too, was a tall, well-built man but younger, in his late 30s, and he also looked capable of taking care of himself. Later, when alone with Dean, I asked why the new man was named 'Coco'.

Dean laughed. 'It goes back a few years,' he said. 'He had been away on holiday overseas and returned as brown as a berry and wearing the most garish, wild-coloured shirt imaginable. When he walked into the office that first day back he almost blinded people with the colours. Someone walked in and said, "My God, I didn't know Coco the Clown's joined the outfit!" From that day he has been called Coco.'

Dean and Coco continued to show me photographs of various men they wanted me to look out for and, sometimes, I would see them and phone, informing my handlers – my Special Branch bosses – whom I had seen, where I had seen them and what had happened. I sometimes wondered what use my information was to the SB, but Dean kept telling me that I was doing a 'great job'.

FIFTY DEAD MEN WALKING

Nearly every time we met, Dean would tell me, 'Marty, you don't fully understand everything yet but you are doing vital work. One day I will explain everything but for now, keep up the good work.'

To me, a teenager with little prospects of finding a proper job, the work offered good pay and excitement; it was more fun than selling stolen goods around the estate. But I would continue those activities because it gave me a reason to be out and about the entire Ballymurphy and Turf Lodge estates, keeping my eyes open for the men they wanted me to spot.

One night in the autumn of 1987, I was walking along Moyard Parade in Ballymurphy when I saw a young man whom my controllers had asked me to look out for. He was standing on his own on the corner of the street smoking a cigarette, a boxer dog sitting at his feet. I wondered why he would be there alone.

The following night I walked along the same street and again I saw the same man, at the same spot, this time sitting on the garden wall. Again he was alone but without the dog. Instinctively I knew he was up to something, either working as a lookout or waiting for someone else to join him. I walked on and decided I should keep an eye on him. Further down the road I saw an opportunity to duck down behind a wall, where I could watch him without being seen.

I stayed in that position for about an hour, the adrenalin flowing, thinking that I was now working as a proper agent, checking and watching dangerous men. Suddenly, as if from nowhere, another man appeared. I realised he must have used the short-cut from the Catholic Church nearby, from an area called 'The Farm' because many years ago it had in fact been a small farm. I also recognised the second man for he was a well-known trouble-maker on the estate. I knew he had once been kneecapped by the IRA for selling fake charity tickets and keeping the money. Extraordinary as it may seem, however, many young men who had fallen foul of the IRA disciplinarians and had been punished would later join the organisation, some becoming its most fervent members.

The second man disappeared back into The Farm while the first stayed sitting on the garden wall, obviously keeping lookout. I became convinced that something was about to happen but I had no idea what. I knew I should tell my controllers and walked nearly three miles to find a public phone box that worked. There was another reason I walked well away from the area. If I had been seen making calls from a public phone box in the area where I lived, people would have become deeply suspicious.

'Can I speak to Bonzo,' I said, when the voice answered the phone.

'Wait a minute,' he replied.

After perhaps 60 seconds or more, far longer than I usually had to wait, the voice came back, 'There's no one here. Is it urgent? Can I take a message?'

'Yes,' I said, 'it's urgent.'

'Give me the number of your phone box and someone will call you straight back.'

Within 15 seconds the phone rang. Immediately, I recognised Dean's voice. 'What's up?'

I told him everything I had seen that night and the previous evening.

'Listen,' he said. 'Go straight home and don't return to that place. Leave everything to us. I know what they're planning. They're going to lay a trap, a bomb for an RUC foot patrol.'

Dean told me that he would now phone the RUC telling them to put the area out of bounds to patrols until further notice. 'We'll check it out tomorrow. Well done.'

I was flattered that Dean should have taken me into his confidence, telling me everything that would happen as a result of my intelligence work. As I walked back home I also hoped that I may have helped to save the lives of two or more innocent peelers and their army escorts.

The following morning there were far more police and army personnel in the area than usual and later I would see army disposal teams searching The Farm. Later that day, I heard on the news that a command wire more than 400 yards long had been discovered, buried in the earth and hidden from view. I phoned Dean.

'You've done a real good job,' he said, sounding very happy. 'You were right. An IRA active service unit was planning to plant a bomb at that point to catch a police and army foot patrol as they walked through the short cut. Your work last night may well have saved some lives.'

Encouraged with that success, I re-doubled my efforts, spending more time on the streets, watching everything that moved at the same time as keeping an eye open for the men whose photographs Dean and Coco showed me at our weekly meetings.

Some time later I was walking my new girlfriend Carol back home late one night when I noticed three or four suspicious looking characters carrying bags and holdalls from a car into a nearby house. After leaving my girlfriend at her home I retraced my steps and recognised two of them as men the SB had asked me to look out for.

The following morning I phoned, spoke to Coco, and gave him all the details I could remember including the names of the two men, the exact address and details of the car.

'Well done,' he said. 'Leave it to us.'

Within minutes of returning home, I heard a number of Land Rovers, vehicles belonging to the DMSUs, as well as army Land Rovers, racing up the street. I wondered what was going on and went out to investigate. When I saw all the vehicles come to a screeching halt outside the house I had targeted, I was surprised that the SB had acted so fast.

I walked to a cousin's house directly opposite where the police and Army had stopped and watched, fascinated.

My cousin had come out and we were standing on the pavement, chatting, while watching the activity across the road. 'What's happening?' I asked, as though totally unaware of what was going on.

'God knows,' he said. 'The peelers have just kicked that door in and loads of them have piled in.'

Thirty minutes later we were still watching and having a drink of tea, when an RUC man came over to us. 'What are you doing, lads?'

'Just talking,' I replied.

'What's your name?' he said.

'What do you want my name for?' I replied.

He asked for my name again, and this time I told him. He asked where I lived and told him I lived down the street.

'You're going to have to move on,' the officer said

'I'm not going to move anywhere,' I told him. 'This is my cousin's house and we're talking.'

The officer decided not to press the matter and walked back to his vehicle. I smiled as he walked away. I wondered how he would have behaved towards me if he had any idea that the peelers were searching the house because I had provided the intelligence. Later, Dean told me that the police had discovered a sawn-off shotgun and arrested a man, a known terrorist, who would later be jailed for possession.

On another occasion, I was walking to the local chippy when I noticed a man I recognised from the SB files. He was walking out of a house where I knew a man with a drink problem lived alone. I phoned Dean and told him that I thought it was suspicious that this particular man would be walking away from that house.

The following morning the house was raided and police discovered a high-powered rifle with a telescopic sight hidden in the roof space above the bedrooms. Later, Dean told me that after interviewing this man, they learned that his house had been used regularly as a secret arms dump by the INLA.

The INLA was formed in 1974, becoming the military wing of the Irish Republican Socialist Party, an organisation whose members included disenchanted Republicans and socialists allied to the official IRA. The founder of the INLA was Seamus Costello, a committed Republican, who had joined the IRA as a teenager and fought in the campaign of the 1950s earning for himself the nickname 'The Boy General'. Three years later, however, Costello would be shot dead during internecine strife which racked the INLA during its formative years.

But Costello left a valuable legacy, having established a link with the PLO, whose leaders were happy to provide low-cost weapons and explosives to a socialist revolutionary army like the INLA.

The INLA exploded on to the stage of international terror in March 1979, when it assassinated Airey Neave MP, the Conservative spokesman on Northern Ireland and a close friend and political adviser to Margaret Thatcher.

But Airey Neave had been only one name, just

another murder, that I had heard of as I was growing up. To me, his death seemed less dramatic, less important than the killings and beatings in Belfast. As far as I was concerned, there were many more atrocities, which had occurred closer to home and which had meant far more.

*   *   *

I had grown up in a staunch Republican, Catholic family on a strong Republican estate in Belfast and my teenage years had been spent taunting the RUC and the British Army as they stamped their presence and their brutal authority on the Catholic families of Belfast.

I supported the IRA in their efforts to defend the Catholic community against the hardline Loyalists, the UVF and the UFF, who would terrorised Republican areas, killing innocent people at random, many of whom had no involvement with the IRA.

And yet I could not understand why it was necessary for the IRA, who protested that they were the guardians of the Catholic community, to use such strong-arm tactics against their own people through their disciplinary committees, their anonymous punishment gangs and their penchant for kneecapping young, so-called 'hoods'.

The slaughter of 11 innocent people at Eniskillin on Sunday, 8 November 1987, when 63 other men, women and children were injured, shattered my faith in the IRA once and for all. Without warning and for no reason whatsoever, the IRA triggered a bomb during the Remembrance Day parade that Sunday.

The television film of that bombing as the Cenotaph collapsed, bringing tons of rubble down on the 70 people attending the Poppy Day parade, and the words of Gordon Wilson, the father of Marie, one of the victims', have become one of my lasting memories of the Troubles.

Marie Wilson, 20, a student nurse in her third year at the Royal Victoria Hospital, Belfast, played the violin, sang in the hospital choir and was known as a keen horsewoman who enjoyed badminton, squash and tennis.

Buried in rubble, Marie clung to the hand of her father for 15 minutes as she fought her losing battle for life. Later, in an unforgettable interview, Gordon Wilson, 60, spoke of those minutes as he held his daughter's hand.

'All through the noise that followed the blast there were these urgent questions racing through my mind – Where's Marie?... Is she hurt?... Is she trapped?... Is she alive?

'Then, almost by magic, I found my hand being squeezed and I knew it was Marie. She asked, "Is that you, Dad?"

'I shouted, "How are you, Marie?" She replied, "I'm fine." But then, suddenly and terribly, she screamed. Again I asked her, "Are you alright?" And again she replied, "Yes." But there seemed a little hesitation.

'A little later she shouted to me, "Dad, let's get out of here." I replied, but then she screamed again. It must have been four or five times I shouted, asking if she was alright. But then, suddenly, her voice changed. She held my hand tightly and gripped as hard as she could. She said, "Daddy, I love you very much." After that her hand slipped away.'

Marie Wilson died nine hours later in hospital after undergoing surgery to her brain and pelvis, which had been crushed when the bomb ripped through the Cenotaph.

Stunned by the worldwide outcry to the Remembrance Day bombing the IRA issued an official statement saying that the leadership 'deeply regretted the catastrophic consequences' of the bombing and claimed that there had been a deadly blunder. The IRA statement declared that one of their units had planted the bomb which was targeting Crown Forces rather than civilians. It could also have been detonated early by army experts trying to block the terrorists' remote-controlled attack. They claimed that the bomb blew up without being triggered by the IRA's radio signal. No one believed the IRA's version of events.

Gordon Wilson's emotive description of the blast and his daughter's death would never be forgotten. He publicly forgave the IRA for murdering his daughter. He became a campaigner for peace and later a Senator of the Irish Parliament in Dublin. A Methodist who spoke with a soft, gentle voice, Gordon Wilson went from being a small-town draper to an international speaker, telling the world in simple language why the fighting in Northern Ireland had to stop. He died in June 1995, aged 67.

That single bombing ended any doubts that I had experienced over my intelligence work and re-doubled my resolve to do everything possible to end the sectarian violence and save innocent people's lives. It also removed, at a stroke, any fear I had felt for my own safety.

CHAPTER FIVE

THREE DAYS AFTER THE ENNISKILLEN BOMBING, I met Dean and Coco as usual by appointment in Belfast, but on this occasion they drove me to a Special Branch safe house in the north of the City.

While fixing the meeting on the phone earlier, Dean had said, 'What do you like to eat?'

'What do you mean?' I replied. 'Why do you want to know that?'

'Because we're going for a bite to eat,' he replied.

'Steak and chips, if you really want to know,' I said.

'And what do you drink?' he asked.

'Diet Coke.'

'Alright.'

'And make sure it's Coca-Cola,' I said. 'I hate Pepsi.'

'Fuck off,' he said, laughing. 'I'll get what I can.'

After driving for 20 minutes or more in a blacked-out van, we stopped and the side door was opened. 'We're here,' Dean said as I walked the two steps from the van into the house.

'Sorry about the cloak and dagger business,' Dean said when we finally walked into a room down the corridor. The carpeted room was sparsely furnished with an old brown sofa, two easy chairs and a couple of wooden upright dining chairs. The heavy curtains were drawn shut.

'This is one of our safe houses,' he explained, 'where we can sit and chat in comfort and safety. Don't worry while you're here, it's well guarded by our lads.'

Soon, Coco walked into the room with two plates and handed one to me, the other to Dean. I looked in surprise at the steak and chips on the plate as I had forgotten about the earlier phone conversation.

As Coco left the room to bring in his meal, Dean shouted, 'Don't forget the Diet Coke,' emphasising the word 'Coke'. He had remembered. It was proper Coke.

I was amazed at the speed Dean ate. I had only taken a few chips when I realised that he had eaten his entire meal and put down his knife and fork.

'Do you always eat that quickly?' I asked.

'No,' he replied. 'I ate slowly today to keep pace with you.' And he laughed.

'We thought it about time that we regularised everything, Marty,' Dean began. 'Everyone is really impressed with the work you've been doing and we hope you want to continue.'

'I do,' I replied, 'and I'll tell you why.'

'Why?' he asked.

'Enniskillen,' I said. 'I can't be putting up with that.'

'Good,' he replied. 'I feel the same way.'

'Are you happy with the way things are going?' Dean asked.

'Yes, I think so,' I replied. 'Why do you ask?'

'Because we want to use you more than we have up till now,' he said. 'So far, everything has gone like clockwork and we believe that you are a valuable addition to our intelligence network.'

'Aye, thanks,' I said.

'But I've really asked you here today to explain a few things to you.'

'Like what?' I asked.

'Well,' he began, coughing a couple of times before starting his speech, 'you do realise that working as an undercover agent like this can be dangerous.'

'To me?' I asked, which must have seemed most naïve.

'Yes, to you,' he answered, laughing.

'Yeah,' I said.

'Do you realise what would happen if the IRA ever discovered you were working for us?'

'Yeah,' I said again.

'Listen, Marty,' he said. 'If they ever catch you, if the IRA ever discover that you are working for us, they'll kill you. They'll take you away for weeks if they need to and they will interrogate you. They'll beat you, torture you and do anything to try and get you to confess.

'There have been some poor bastards that have never had anything to do with Special Branch, the police or the security forces, who have been found dead with marks on their bodies showing they have been tortured, burned and beaten before being killed. It always ends up the same way. The bodies are found shot dead with one or two high-velocity bullets in the back of the head.'

Dean looked at me wondering what my reaction to such gruesome detail would be. He may have noticed that I had stopped eating my steak and chips, though my meal was only half finished.

I respected Dean for telling me the truth, for pulling no punches about my fate if I should ever be taken prisoner by the IRA.

'I understand,' I replied. But I felt nervous at the thought of what could happen to me.

I pushed away the plate, my appetite gone. I felt like concentrating on the conversation rather than eating. I told him about various reports I had read when the IRA had issued statements claiming they had executed people for allegedly 'informing or collaborating' with the RUC.

'So, are you happy to continue?' he asked.

'Aye,' I replied.

'Good,' Dean said. 'We will do all we can to protect you. You can rest assured that we will never put you in jeopardy and, if we hear anything about you from any IRA source we will take you out immediately. I can promise you we will never put you in any danger.'

'Thanks,' I said, and laughed, but the sound of my laughter was hollow.

Only months before, I had read in the newspapers that the Special Branch's most senior IRA double agent, a high-ranking member of the IRA's Brigade Staff, had been pulled out of Northern Ireland. It was claimed that his information had been responsible for half a dozen IRA deaths and more than 20 arrests. He was given a new identity and settled in England. The very fact that the Special Branch had managed to rescue one of their top men when he came under suspicion gave me some confidence. But not much.

'I'm glad you understand the score,' Dean said, 'because I don't want you to think this job is just a picnic, a little bit of fun to earn a few pounds. This is deadly serious. I want you to know that a number of my close friends have been killed by the IRA since the Troubles began. And some of those were true professionals.'

Dean always showed respect for the IRA. He would

never bad-mouth them, insult their intelligence or, more importantly, never underestimate their capabilities to bomb targets, murder people and, when necessary, terrorise the community.

He told me that he wanted me to concentrate more and more on identifying known suspects whose photographs he would continue to show me on a weekly basis.

Before leaving, Dean said, 'You are becoming more important than you realise, Marty. Keep up the good work and remember, above all, take care.'

A few weeks after my *tête-á-tête* in the Special Branch safe house, Dean asked me to keep a look-out for a dangerous IRA bomber who was setting off massive 500lb and 1,000lb bombs in Belfast City Centre.

'What's his name?' I asked.

'Harry Fitzsimmons,' Dean replied.

'Do you have a photo of him?' I asked.

'Yes,' Dean replied, 'here it is.'

'What!' I exclaimed. 'Bullshit. He's been a mate of mine for years. We were at the same school. He's never IRA.'

I must have sounded convinced for Dean simply shook his head and waited for me to quieten down before continuing.

'Listen to me, Marty,' Dean said. 'I can tell you that this young man is working for a highly active bombing team. And let me tell you the head of the bombing team is a very well-known IRA member.'

'Shit!' I exclaimed. 'Are you *really* sure?'

'Yes, we're positive.'

I had known Harry Fitzsimmons since childhood. We had grown up on the same street, spent time in each other's homes and had gone out roaming the Black Mountain together during summer holidays. I knew that

Harry had become involved in petty crime, as I was, but I never imagined that he had become an active member of an IRA bomb squad.

I told Dean that I would keep a close eye on Harry and report back, but I was still not convinced that he was an IRA member. Harry had married his teenage sweetheart Charlene and they lived together in a new house round the corner from me. I often saw them going out together in the evening.

From then on I sometimes stopped Harry and Charlene as they were walking down the street and chatted to them about nothing in particular. Over a period of a few weeks, I noticed that Harry was always wearing different baseball caps, with the peak concealing his face as much as possible. This made me suspicious. After some time I noticed that three or four men would occasionally call at Harry's home, park their new Nissan car and go inside for an hour or more. I reported all this to Dean who told me later that the four men were all part of the same IRA bombing team.

I felt awkward telling Dean about Harry, identifying him every month or so. Harry, despite being three years older than me, had been a mate and I wished that Dean had never asked me to target him. I kept having to tell myself that if Dean was certain that Harry was an IRA member, then the probability was that he was correct. Nevertheless, it still troubled me.

Years later, Dean informed me that Harry's team was behind the bombing of the law courts in Chichester Street on Saturday, 9 January 1988, causing extensive damage. They had planted the bomb which ripped apart Belfast City Centre on Tuesday, 23 August 1988. And they had taken part in one of the IRA's biggest explosions on Monday, 31 July 1989, when a laundry van, packed with a 1,000lb bomb, was triggered after being allowed entry into the precincts of the High Court in Belfast. Together, all three bombs had caused millions of pounds' worth of damage.

The successful bombing of the High Court happened by chance. For months, the IRA had been trying to find a way of bombing the building, seen as a symbol of British authority in the Province. One day, one of the IRA bomb team was surveying the courts when he noticed a laundry van driving through the tight security cordon and into the courts. More importantly, the man recognised the driver as a lad who lived on the Ballymurphy Estate. The lad was then visited by the gang and forced to drive the vehicle, packed with explosives, into the courts.

Harry Fitzsimmon's successful career as a member of the gang continued for at least two years until the IRA decided, in late 1989, that the squad should be split up.

Throughout the time that I was watching Harry, Dean encouraged me to become more friendly with my old mate and, if possible, meet the friends who continued to visit his house from time to time.

'Why do you want me to do that?' I asked him.

'It could be very useful, very useful indeed,' he said.

I had not the slightest idea at that time how close I would become to senior members of the IRA. At the height of my career as a British agent, I was in daily contact with the men who organised and controlled the bombings and shootings throughout Northern Ireland.

I had also struck up a relationship with a middle-aged man named Danny, a down-and-out who spent his time hanging around pubs and betting shops in Belfast and for whom I felt some compassion. I had noticed him hanging around, running errands for anybody and everybody, and in return he would be handed a few cigarettes or a couple of quid. Few people bothered to speak to him and most treated him like dirt. I felt sorry for him and began to stop and chat whenever I saw him in the street. Poor Danny had terrible dermatitis on his hands and face and children would run away from him as though he was a leper.

Danny was dirty, unshaven and always smelt of alcohol and I never saw him, even on the hottest summer's day, without his big, black overcoat wrapped around him. He told me that he had never had a job and survived on hand-outs from people. I would usually buy him food, sandwiches and burgers, and gave him the odd £5, though I knew he would spend it on drink or the horses. I even lent him money from time to time and, to my surprise, he always repaid it on the dot. He would tell me, 'Marty, you've no need to worry in life because I'll look out for you. I'll watch your back.'

I always wondered if, by taking some time to talk to him and buying him the odd snack, it would bring me luck, but I didn't care for him for that reason. I simply felt sorry for someone who seemed unable to care for himself.

All of a sudden, however, I began giving less thought to both Dean and poor Danny for I had become far more interested in someone else – a beautiful, dark-haired, 17-year-old girl by the name of Angela Crane.

I met Angela one afternoon when I went with a friend to the YTP in Kennedy Way where she was training to become a hairdresser. I saw two girls walking along the street and the one that attracted my attention was only 5' 5" tall with shoulder-length, curly hair, a pretty smile and engaging eyes.

As she walked towards us, however, I could hardly take my eyes off her beautiful, slim legs for the mini-skirt she wore that day was very, very short.

As we drove the girls home, I chatted to Angela

and I felt captivated. Angela was the first girl I had become interested in since I had started working with the Special Branch 18 months earlier. During that time, I had become so involved with my own secret world, watching people, earning money selling stolen goods and keeping myself to myself, that I had had no time for girlfriends. Angela changed all that.

After dropping off the girls I said nothing to my pal, but I knew that I wanted to see her again. Four days later a friend of mine persuaded me to go with him to a party on the Ballymurphy Estate. I never smoked, drank or took drugs, so attending parties had never been of great interest to me. I quickly became bored and wanted to leave. Friends often tried to persuade me to get drunk, go to pubs, attend parties or clubs, but I was never very interested.

I had been born in the Troubles and had grown up in the most violent environment. Facing RUC truncheons, Army plastic bullets, raids on our streets and houses by the Army and the RUC, nightly riots, sectarian hatred and the noise of IRA bombs tearing the city apart made me grow up fast. To many of us, parties and getting drunk seemed frivolous, even silly, for there were more important things in life. It seemed that we enjoyed our carefree fifteenth birthdays like schoolboys the world over and then, suddenly, grew beyond our years and began behaving with the maturity and seriousness of 25-year-olds.

Whenever I went out with my mates to a pub or a party, I usually made an excuse and returned home early. On this particular night, for some unknown reason, I decided to go along.

Only eight people were present when we walked into the house, the music blaring. And to my absolute surprise and delight, sitting on the sofa was Angela, once again wearing a tiny mini-skirt and a white baggy shirt. She looked gorgeous.

After chatting for an hour or so I told her that I was going to the local shop for some cans of Diet Coke.

'I'll come with you,' she said enthusiastically, and ran to join me as I walked out of the house.

As we walked down the street, chatting, we exchanged phone numbers.

'Are you going to call me?' she asked.

'Of course I am,' I said.

As we walked back again I felt a new man, for I knew that there was a certain chemistry between us. I thought that Angie seemed genuinely interested in me. As we talked we discovered that her elder brother, Tommy, had been at school with me and we had been good friends.

I phoned Angie the following evening and we met an hour later. I told my sister Lizzie about her and asked to borrow the key to the house she was renovating up the street from my mother's. I grabbed some tapes and walked the two miles to Falls Park where we had arranged to meet. For several hours we sat, kissed and cuddled in my sister's house while listening to tapes. We got on really well.

From that night on we became inseparable. We would see each other most evenings and in no time we had become lovers, wanting to spend as much time together as possible, making love at every opportunity. And Angie had a heart of gold, buying me presents every week, despite the fact that she had little money.

She took a part-time job in a fish and chip shop on the Falls Road and would work Thursday, Friday and Saturday afternoons. I would meet her at 7.00pm and we often babysat for her mother, looking after Sam and Louise, or spent the evening at my mother's or sister's houses.

My mother took to Angie. She treated her as another daughter and they would sometimes go shopping together. I often found them chatting together in the kitchen over a cup of tea as though they had known each other for years.

'I don't know how you put up with my son,' my mother would tell Angie. 'He's such a head case. You must be some girl to cope with him.' And she would laugh.

After dating Angie for a few months, a mate of mine, Joe Ward, a married man five years older than me, asked me whether I wanted to work with him. I had admired Joe all my life as he had always showed me kindness and generosity when he had lived next door. I respected the fact that when I was growing up he would treat me more as an adult than a child.

On this occasion, Joe told me that he had taken a contract with the Housing Executive and needed a partner to help erect fencing on the Ballymurphy estate. Joe had a reputation for being a competent and fast worker and many men would not work alongside him because his work-rate was so exhausting.

I was only too happy to join him and make some honest money, enough to finish my career selling stolen goods. I also respected and trusted Joe for he had proved a good friend. Once, about a year earlier, Joe had saved me from being arrested by the RUC after we had become embroiled in a fight near Queen's University in the centre of Belfast. We had been surrounded by a group of half a dozen young men who had obviously been drinking, and they began pushing and shoving us. After Joe had asked them to stop a number of times he grabbed hold of a couple of them and gave them a few good punches. When one of them jumped on Joe's back I joined in, pulled the man off Joe and started punching him. Seconds later we heard a yell and saw another six or seven of their mates running towards us.

At the same time we heard police sirens and could see a number of police cars, their blue lights flashing, bearing down on us.

'Joe,' I shouted, 'let's go.'

He gave one of the troublemakers two more hefty punches and shouted, 'Right, Marty, run for it.'

We took off, and after running a few hundred yards, another police car came round the corner, saw us running and stopped. The occupants leapt out of their car and took up the chase. Joe and I ran down a side road and into a cul-de-sac. Ahead of us was a ten-foot brick wall. Joe, short, strong and athletic, scrambled to the top of the wall, but I didn't make it. I jumped but couldn't reach the top.

'Jump again, Marty, jump,' Joe shouted. I looked behind and saw two police officers only yards away. I gave one final leap and, as I did so, Joe leaned down from the top of the wall, grabbed my shoulder and heaved me on to the top of the wall. For a few moments, one officer was hanging on to my foot, trying to pull me down, while Joe was trying to heave me over the wall. I lashed out at the officer with my other foot and he released his grip. Joe heaved me over and we dropped down the other side and ran like hell. From that moment, I knew Joe to be a genuine friend and anything he asked me to do I would happily agree to.

Erecting fences was tough work but good fun. I fetched the pallets of fencing and brought them to Joe who would nail them into place. The work lasted us about seven months, but the Housing Executive had reckoned that the contract would take us eighteen months to complete. They were amazed, believing we had employed others to help. But we hadn't, as Joe needed the money.

A few days before the job was finished, one of the officers came down to inspect the work.

'Do you two want another job?' he said.

'Depends,' replied Joe.

'Now you've put the fences up so quickly, do you want the contract to paint them?'

'Depends on the money,' said Joe.

They quickly agreed a price. When the officer left, Joe looked at me and winked, 'I would have done it for half the money,' he laughed, 'we've got a great deal.'

'So you've done it again, have you, Golden Balls?' I said.

'What do you mean, you cheeky bastard?' he asked.

'Every time you do something, Joe, you end up getting a good deal.'

Joe looked at me. 'It's not luck, Marty, it's hard work,' he said. And I knew he was giving me some sound advice.

Angie would occasionally come and visit me while I was fencing. I used to stop to chat to her but Joe would soon put an end to that. 'Angela,' he would shout, 'can you not leave this lad alone; you'll see him tonight. I need him to do some work here, you know, he's not on holiday.' And he would laugh.

'OK, slave driver,' Angie would say, and she would quickly kiss me and leave. I liked Angie popping round to see me at work. It made me feel good, gave me a lift and made me feel I was lucky to have such a lovely, beautiful girl in love with me.

Dean and Coco, however, were not happy that I had taken a job erecting fencing. They preferred me to be out selling stolen goods, moving about the area, using my eyes and ears, providing useful intelligence, rather than staying in one spot putting up fencing day in, day out.

'Do you ever visit Republican clubs?' Dean asked me during one of our weekly chats.

'No, never,' I replied honestly.

'Have you ever been inside any of them?'

'No, never,' I said. 'Remember, I don't drink.'

'It might be an idea if you started to pop into one or two,' Dean explained. 'Many of the people we have given you to ID spend their time in those clubs. That's where the IRA recruits many of its members.'

'OK,' I replied.

'Do you think you could face going into some of these clubs, letting us know some of the people that frequent them?'

'I suppose I could,' I replied but, privately, I didn't relish the prospect of bumping into people I had known for years, suspecting they were all IRA men.

'Good,' Dean said.

He didn't actually put me under any pressure, nor did he order me to frequent the clubs looking for suspects. Yet the way he asked me to start visiting the clubs left me with little scope but to go along with his plan. I could not forget the fact that, in many respects, he was my boss, the man who paid me £400 a month.

*   *   *

Near the Whiterock shops, where I used to go to buy food for my mother, a group of young men would laze around day and night asking people for money. In particular, they would try to 'tap' pensioners and single mothers as they came out of the Post Office with their weekly allowance. Their victims complained to the local Sinn Fein office and the IRA decided to move them on.

One day I noticed a local man I knew as Micky, a stocky man in his 30s, with dark hair and a moustache, telling the lads to move away from the area or face the consequences. I decided to strike up a relationship with him, figuring that he had to know loads of IRA people in the area.

Some weeks later, after many conversations with him, Micky asked me to accompany him to a new building site in Moyard Crescent where the Northern Ireland Housing Executive planned to build a dozen new homes.

'Are you Jim?' Micky said as he approached a tall, slim man in his 50s.

'Aye,' he replied.

Micky took the man by the arm a few yards away from me so I couldn't overhear the conversation. A few minutes later they returned to me and Mickey said, 'This is Marty; he's your new security guard.'

Until that moment I had no idea that I was to be the security guard for the building site. Micky had mentioned nothing whatsoever to me about the job.

The man said, 'How much do you want?'

Before I could reply, he continued, 'You won't have to do too much. Just keep an eye on the place and tell your people if you see anyone suspicious hanging around.'

Before I could answer, Micky butted in, 'One hundred pounds a week, OK?'

'No problem,' the man replied. Turning to me, he said, 'I'll come and pay you cash every week. Alright?'

'Fine,' I replied, flabbergasted at the prospect of my new job.

As I walked back with Micky I realised that I was now working on behalf of the IRA, employed as a member of the IRA's protection racket. I was also employed by the Special Branch as a British agent. I was 18 years old.

CHAPTER SIX

'Brilliant, fucking brilliant!' Dean shouted and punched the air with sheer delight when I told him that I had just been taken on as a security officer with an IRA protection racket.

'How the fuck did you do it?' he asked. 'Tell me, tell me everything, Marty. I want to hear every word of what happened.'

I told Dean exactly what had happened and he seemed surprised that a member of the IRA had taken me on as a security officer when I was not, in fact, a member of the organisation.

'Do you think that's suspicious?' I asked Dean.

'No,' he replied, 'I don't think so, not from what you've told us about Micky. He probably did it off his own bat, without thinking. He probably thought he was just doing a good turn for an unemployed lad from the estate.'

Every day I would walk down to the building site about 200 yards from my home shortly after five o'clock in the evening, just as the workers were knocking off for the day. I would walk around the site, nodding to a few of the workers who would give me odd looks, suspicious of me, not knowing exactly who I was or what job I did. But they were also respectful because they knew that the IRA would have demanded protection money for permitting the firm to build in the heart of such a strong Republican housing estate.

And every Friday at about five o'clock my man would arrive in his brand new Audi saloon and hand me the promised £100.

'Everything alright?' he would ask each week.

'Aye,' I would reply, 'everything's fine.'

'Any trouble?'

'No, of course not. What did you think?' I would tell him.

'That's good,' he would say and, having looked briefly around the site, he would climb back into his car and drive away.

One night just before midnight, I returned to check on the building site and noticed a hole had been cut in the perimeter fencing. I looked around and realised that about 20 bags of cement had been stolen. I quickly looked around the immediate vicinity but could see no sign of the missing bags. I wondered what the boss and Micky would say about the missing cement as it was my responsibility to keep a check on the site.

At that moment, a young teenager on his bike came up to me. 'Hey, Mister,' he said, 'are you looking for cement?'

'Aye, I am,' I said. 'Did you see it go?'

'Yes,' he replied, 'I'll show you,' and I followed him to a house not more than 100 yards from the site. There, in the back garden under some plastic sheeting, were the missing bags. I gave the lad a pound and breathed a sigh of relief.

That night I searched everywhere for Micky but to no avail. Finally, I left a message with his mother asking him to come immediately to the building site as something had been stolen. Then I returned to the site and stayed there till the workers arrived some time after 7.00am.

An hour later, Micky arrived with a young man I had never seen before. I told him everything that had happened and took him to where the cement had been hidden.

'Leave this to us,' he said to me and as I walked away I heard them banging the front door of the house. Ten minutes later I saw two men walking towards the site with bags of cement on their shoulders. For the next 40 minutes, the two went back and forth until every single bag had been safely returned.

'You'll get no more trouble,' Micky said later. 'They didn't know the IRA were looking after this site. Now they know they'll be no further trouble.'

After that I hardly ever guarded the site, for now that it was public knowledge that the IRA were 'protecting' the plot, no one dared steal anything. I would simply open up the gates in the morning and be there at five o'clock to shut them. And each week I received my £100.

In the evening, I would often go and find Micky in one of the Republican clubs and buy him a couple of pints of lager while I kept to my Diet Coke. We would chat for a while and he would introduce me to everyone who came up to speak to him. Over the four months I guarded the site, I got to know many IRA members and would report back to Dean each and every week. Many of the names I gave them were people they had been targeting for months.

But many of the friends with whom I had grown up were surprised to hear that I had joined the IRA. I had attended school with them, played truant with them, mucked around with them. They were trying to lead decent, straightforward lives, working at honest jobs or, more usually, looking for jobs, and having nothing whatsoever to do with the IRA. They knew that in my youth I had been wild, had challenged the RUC, thrown paint at their vehicles and fought with the Army in the streets, but they were surprised that I had become such a staunch Republican, prepared to carry out operations on behalf of the IRA.

One afternoon, however, not far from home, it became obvious to everyone in the area that I had become committed to the IRA. I was walking home helping a neighbour, carrying her little girl on my shoulders, when a British soldier on foot patrol made a remark as I passed by.

'What did you say?' I asked pleasantly.

'Nothing,' he replied, and I walked on.

Seconds later I felt a pain shoot through my body and realised that the soldier had taken a flying kick at me, hitting me with his boot in the small of the back. The force of the kick nearly knocked me over and I struggled to hold on to the child, fearing I might drop her in the road which was full of traffic. Somehow, I managed to stay on my feet.

I saw red. I handed the little girl to her mother who was walking next to me and turned on the soldier, who was standing with his rifle aimed at me about six feet away. I lunged at him and smashed him with my fist as hard as I could on the side of his face. He went down on his back and as he tried to struggle to his feet I threw myself on top of him, determined to smash his face to a pulp. I must have thrown 20 punches, hitting him in the face and on the chest with all the strength I could muster.

As I heard Army Land Rovers screech to a halt nearby I jumped up, leaving the soldier to struggle to his feet, my anger assuaged by the beating I had given him. He knew he had been wrong to kick me, because after he had struggled to his feet he made no attempt to apprehend or attack me but, instead, moved away, keeping his eye on me in case I attacked again. Two officers approached the soldier and two others came over to me. I stood my ground, still pumped with adrenalin. Fortunately, the young mother whose baby I had been holding and who had witnessed the entire fracas, told the NCO in charge exactly what had happened.

Two RUC vehicles and another army Land Rover arrived quickly and again the woman explained what had happened, her voice trembling with anger and emotion at the actions of the soldier. I, too, told the police exactly what had happened, but I was still a very angry man, angry that a soldier should have risked injuring an innocent kid by kicking me so hard in the back, and for no reason whatsoever.

After listening to my story, the RUC man went over to the soldier. One side of the soldier's face had blown up into a large bruise and his entire face was battered, bruised and bloodied, as though he had been in a fight with a dozen men.

'Did he do that to you?' the officer asked the soldier, pointing over to me. The soldier nodded.

The RUC man returned to me. 'We are arresting you for assaulting a member of the armed forces,' he said. 'Come with us'.

At that moment my mother, who was in a shop across the road, appeared on the scene. Someone had told her that her son had been fighting with the Army. As she ran across the road, the woman told her exactly what had happened.

'What are you doing with that boy?' she shouted at the RUC men.

'Who are you?' the officer in charge asked her.

'I'm his fucking mother!' she yelled at him, 'And this soldier kicked him and the baby.'

'Please,' said the officer, 'he has assaulted a soldier. We will have to take him down to the station, take evidence from some witnesses and then see what's going to happen. Have you seen the soldier?'

'Serves the bastard right,' she said, 'for what he did to the baby.'

I was put in the back of the Land Rover and taken to Grosvenor Road Police Station, put in a cell and made to wait for more than an hour before being taken to a room to be interviewed. Some time later, an officer came into the cell and said, 'Marty, you're free to go.'

When I walked into the house, my mother's first words to me were, 'What the fuck did you do that for?'

I tried to explain what had happened, but she would hear none of it. 'I know what happened, I've been told,' she said. 'But if you go on fucking about like that you'll end up in jail, or something worse. If you're not careful they'll get you one dark night and give you a fucking good hiding. Have you no sense in your head?'

I knew there was no point in arguing with my mother for she would win every argument she ever started, whether she was right or wrong. But that day I had flown into one of the worst rages of my life for, in the instant before I hit him, I imagined what might have happened to the child if I had fallen into the road.

I knew that my mother had been right to warn me against picking fights with the Army, but I also knew in my heart that on this occasion I had every right to thump the bastard who had kicked me. I had felt good, and there was a certain satisfaction in thumping the soldier and getting away with it.

*   *   *

For months I had been saving hard because I wanted to buy a second-hand car. Now, because of my involvement with Angie, I was keener than ever to buy a car so that we could go out together wherever and whenever we wanted.

My first car was a four-year-old, red Vauxhall Cavalier hatchback with 50,000 miles on the clock. I told Dean one day that I had saved up the money, £1,600, and was going to buy the car the following week.

'Don't waste your money,' Dean said. 'How much did you say it would cost?'

I told him.

'I'll give you the money,' he said. 'We always promised you we would arrange a driving licence for you but you've gone and passed the test without our help, so we'll buy you the car instead.'

'Fuck me, will you really?' I asked, somewhat taken aback.

'Yes,' he said, 'that's a deal. You'll have the money next week.'

And the next week he handed over the £1,600 in £20 notes. I immediately went to the man who was selling the car and handed over the cash. That night, I took Angie for a drive in my new car, to a lonely spot at Craigavon and we made love in the back while the radio blared sweet music. As we drove back home later, I felt great.

I became so keen on driving that I decided to jack in my job as a security officer and drive taxis instead. I told

Micky I no longer wanted the job because I was going to drive full-time. He understood.

I went to the first taxi firm in Ballymurphy and asked if they needed drivers.

'Yes,' the man said. 'Have you got a car?' I nodded. 'The depot money is £35 a week. £30 goes to the owner and £5 pounds to the IRA.'

I decided to take a day shift, working as a 'pirate driver'. That meant I was not officially licensed and, if stopped by police, the people in my taxi would say that I was a relative giving them a lift. Probably half the taxi drivers in Belfast worked the same routine. But I enjoyed my new life, driving around the city all day and taking home around £150 a week, tax free.

Dean was also happy with my new job because it gave me a greater chance to watch people and move around the city without anyone suspecting I was working with the Special Branch.

Within a few weeks, however, I was asked to drive IRA punishment squads around the area. It was 8.00pm when I drove up to the tiny brick building that was the office. Three young men who had lived in the Ballymurphy area all their lives walked up to my car and got in.

'Hi, Marty,' said their boss, Martin, an overweight man in his 30s with short dark hair and a strong Belfast accent. 'We're on a job.'

One of the men, called 'Fra' (short for Francis), talked openly. 'I hope we get this little fucker tonight,' he said, 'he keeps giving us the slip. The other night, I got one of his young mates and after we dragged him out of the club, I got a milk crate and put his leg across it. We began to smash the leg with the iron bar and he was screaming for mercy.'

I tried not to listen but, as Fra continued, he began

laughing so much that he was hardly able to finish the story. 'Suddenly we saw a piece of his bone sticking out the side of his leg,' he said. 'God, it looked funny, and we were pissing ourselves laughing and he was screaming blue fuckin' murder. It was one of the best ones we ever did.'

Fra was a skinny, young-looking man in his early 30s, a coward who would run from any fight, but who acted brave as part of a gang. The other man, Joe, was in his late 20s, a very skinny man with carrot hair. They were all IRA sympathisers who would swagger around Ballymurphy wearing black gloves, scarves covering the lower part of their faces and baseball caps. They hoped one day to become members of the IRA, and to that end they were happy to throw their weight around and to carry out the IRA's dirty work, not caring about the poor, defenceless young men they would pick up and beat with their baseball bats and iron bars.

Martin told me to drive to the Whiterock Road and stay in the car. Soon, they returned carrying a holdall. I wondered whether it contained the dreaded tools of torture or guns.

'Drive to the Rossa Bar on the Falls Road,' Joe said as I started the engine.

They told me to park around the corner and wait for them. I knew what would happen next, because I had heard about it so many times.

They would walk into the bar, their balaclavas pulled over their faces so they could not be identified. One would go the the DJ and tell him to stop the music and turn the lights on. The boss would stay by the door in case anyone tried to make a run for it, while the other two would walk together around the room, searching for the intended victim. When they found him, they would pounce, pin his arms behind him and frog-march him out of the club. Sometimes they would beat the poor man there and then, at other times put him into their car and take him away to some isolated spot where they would hang him on a fence and then belt him with their staves and their iron bars. Usually, the beatings continued until the thugs tired, and they would usually leave the man, who would be unable to walk or even crawl, until some passer-by heard his cries for help.

That night, I sat in the car shaking with rage, frustration and humiliation, not knowing what to do, hoping and praying that the poor bastard wouldn't be found. Within minutes they were back.

'Little fucker fucked off,' Fra said as he got into the car. 'Just wait till I get my hands on the little cunt.'

As I drove them back, I was relieved that their intended victim had not been found, but I feared what would happen to him when they eventually caught up with him. I vowed that night that I would never take another punishment squad in my taxi.

I told Dean about the incident and he urged me to continue working as a taxi driver because it was a wonderful cover for someone in my situation, becoming more involved with the IRA and being led from one to another, learning of their arms dumps and their meeting houses, their members and, occasionally, their targets.

Quite often during the following few weeks, the same three men would call me and tell me that they had a job. I knew that all they did was carry out punishment beatings and so I devised a plan. I would tell them to meet me in an IRA bar and when I arrived I would insist on buying them all a pint of lager. When they had downed the first, I would buy them another. After two or more pints, it seemed that their urge to smash the hell out of someone had passed and I would tell them that I had to go on to another job.

But I knew that, one day, I would be forced to drive them on one of their operations and I wanted no part of their nauseating business.

*   *   *

I had always been violently opposed to punishment squads, both IRA and Loyalist, because they were cruel, unfair and unjust. I knew of several occasions when totally innocent people were beaten, paralysed and sometimes crippled for life for absolutely no reason. Others were 'punished' because someone had a personal vendetta they wanted to pursue. I wasn't prepared to help these bastards carry out their evil work so I quit my job and moved to another taxi firm.

I joined another depot on the Falls Road which I knew paid no protection money to the IRA. I worked for this firm for almost a year, earning around £200 a week tax free for a five day week.

Dean and Coco were happy with me working for the taxi firms because they realised it gave me a great opportunity to ID far more people than I had done in the past. Now, I was driving across all Republican areas and would report back to them whenever I managed to identify a targeted suspect.

Dean encouraged me to continue my friendships with both Micky and Harry Fitzsimmons. My handlers had taken my Vauxhall into one of their high security SB garages and fitted it with a tracker device so they could pinpoint the whereabouts of the car 24 hours a day. At the same time, they handed me a radio to keep at home. It appeared to be an ordinary AM/ FM radio but it concealed a device which alerted my SB controllers that I needed to meet them urgently. Whenever I pressed the secret, silent alarm it meant that I would meet them in exactly one hour's time at a pre-arranged rendezvous.

One evening, in the summer of 1989, I answered a knock at the door of my mother's house and a woman was standing there.

'May I speak to Martin McGartland?' she asked.

'I'm Martin McGartland,' I said. 'What do you want?'

'I've got good news for you,' she said. 'I'm from the Northern Ireland Housing Executive. I've found a flat for you that may suit: a nice, one-bedroom flat in Beechmount Pass.'

'What?' I said, 'A flat, for me?' I must have sounded incredulous.

'Yes,' she said, unfazed by my apparent ignorance, 'if you would like to go over and see the place we could go now.'

As she spoke, I suddenly realised that this must have been organised behind the scenes by the SB. I had never applied for a flat for I had always been happy staying at home, being looked after by my mother, yet enjoying total freedom to come and go whenever I wanted.

I arranged to see the woman an hour later at the address and went to collect Angie.

'I've got a surprise for you,' I told her, 'I'm getting a flat.'

'What do you mean?' she said. 'Are you daft, or something? You never told me anything about a flat. Tell me, is this flat for you or for us?'

'It's for us, of course!' I told her, knowing I was telling a white lie. 'I arranged it as a surprise.'

Angie threw her arms around my neck and gave me a hug and a kiss. I felt a bit of a fraud, but it was great news.

I could not, of course, tell Angie that the flat had come as a total surprise to me. She knew nothing of my work for the Special Branch. She believed I earned all my money from driving taxis. And there was something else. Angie had always been a staunch Republican and whenever we talked of the Troubles she made it plain to me that she had often considered joining the IRA.

Angie and I met the woman at Beechmount Pass and looked around the flat in a four-storey block. It needed some decorating but was clean, and I realised that by living here Angie and I could spend as much time as we wanted together. The location was also handy for Angie as she was studying at another YTP only half-a-mile away.

'I'll take it,' I said. 'When can I move in?'

'Now,' she said, handing me the keys with a smile.

During the next two weeks, we painted and decorated and bought the bare necessities we needed for the flat. My sister gave me a settee and I bought a new carpet and a bed.

Days later, Angie told me, 'Ever since we met we have had nothing but surprises, and I've got another one.'

'What's that?' I said, only half thinking what she was saying as we lay together naked on the bed, cuddling each other.

'I'm pregnant', she said, looking intently at me, watching for my reaction.

'Shit!' I thought instantly, but I said nothing. My mind raced as I thought of my life. I was now a fully-fledged British agent who had almost succeeded in infiltrating the IRA. I had no idea what was going to happen to me or where my life would lead over the next few months, let alone the next few years. The last thing I needed at that moment was a woman and baby to become totally dependent on me.

Now, it was too late; too late to back out of my involvement with the IRA and too late to tell Angie anything of the work that I was doing with the Branch.

Slowly, I raised myself on one elbow and kissed her on the lips, slowly and passionately, as my mind raced, wondering what I should say to her when the kissing stopped.

'That's wonderful,' I lied to her. 'Finding this flat at this time was perfect.'

'Are you sure you're pleased?' she asked, seeking reassurance.

'Of course I am. Have you told your ma?' I asked.

'No,' she said, 'I'm too frightened. I don't know how she will react.'

'Are you sure you're pregnant?' I asked.

'Yes, I am,' she said. 'I did one of those home tests and that showed positive so I went to the hospital. They confirmed it.'

Two days later, Angie came bursting into the flat a great smile on her face.

'What's up?' I asked her.

'I told my Ma and she was brilliant,' Angie said. 'She didn't have a go at me or anything. She just asked me if you were the father and if I was alright. And do you know what? Before I came here tonight she kissed me. Isn't that wonderful?'

I was happy for Angie, who seemed to think that everything was going brilliantly for us. We had met, fallen in love, found a flat and now were living happily together, waiting for the birth of a little baby. I, on the other hand, had become deeply concerned at the sudden turn of events, though I tried not to show it.

Some weeks before, I had read of the murder of Joe Fenton, a 35-year-old father of four, an estate agent who lived in Republican West Belfast. He had been found shot dead, with four bullets in his head, in an alley not far from his home.

Within hours of his death, the IRA said it had carried

out the killing, claiming that the dead man had been a 'British agent'.

Generally, it is suggested that a murdered man might not have been an agent, but on this occasion Fenton's father said that he had been provided with evidence by the IRA and 'accepted' that his son had been working for the Special Branch.

The day before his funeral, the IRA issued a lengthy media statement detailing Joe Fenton's alleged work for the Special Branch based, it seems, on a lengthy interrogation carried out by his captors. Though unstated, most people fully realised that Joe Fenton's interrogation would also have included prolonged and appalling torture.

As a result of such incidents, I believed in my heart that I would never survive beyond the age of 25 and yet I was about to become a father, involved with a girl whom I loved but who could not hear anything about my secret life. I also kicked myself for falling in love with Angie, because I realised how unfair it would be on her and her child if I should die at such a young age. I tried to put such thoughts behind me, as I remembered the advice Dean had given me during one of my briefings.

'Marty,' he had told me, 'there is one important lesson you must learn. Whatever happens, you must remember: never, but never, look back. Always look forward. That way you will survive much longer in this business. Some people worry about what has happened. That is silly because it's history, it's over. Only look forward, always plan ahead. It is probably the best piece of advice I can offer you.'

Soon, it became common knowledge in the IRA clubs that Marty, the taxi driver, would be prepared to lend his car to friends. I would phone Dean or Coco and inform them who was borrowing it and when they were using the vehicle. Usually, of course, I had no idea why they wanted to borrow the car nor where they were planning to drive. But I knew that my handlers would be able to track precisely the whereabouts of the vehicle at any time. Dean was very happy with the plan and encouraged me to lend the vehicle to my new friends.

One day, in the summer of 1989, Harry Fitzsimmons asked me if he could borrow the car and I readily agreed, informing my controllers exactly what was happening. As 'Fitzy' borrowed my car more frequently we became mates, and on many occasions he would ask me to drive him, visiting different places around Belfast. I suspected that he was viewing potential bombing targets and I would tell Dean which buildings and places he was checking out.

At one of my SB briefings, Dean and Coco told me that they had tracked Fitzy when he was using my car and discovered that each time he was driving to Comber in County Down. They believed he was planning an operation and they wanted me to find out anything I could. They suggested that I should propose to Fitzy that he and I should buy an old car together from the weekly car auction that took place at Carryduff, not far from Comber, spend some money tarting it up and then sell it, sharing the profit. They hoped that during journeys to and from Carryduff, Fitzy would want to take the opportunity to check out the unknown target.

Fitzy and I went to the auction and bought an old Mark V Ford Cortina for £200. On the return journey, Fitzy did not head straight back to Belfast but made a detour to Comber. I followed in my car and opposite a large house in the town he stopped and spent perhaps 30 seconds surveying the building before continuing the journey home. The following day, I phoned Dean and told him the news.

'I knew you were in Comber last night,' he told me, 'because we tracked you. Did you see anything?'

'Well, he stopped outside a large house there.'

'Did you get the address?' he asked.

'Not exactly,' I replied, 'because it was too dark. But I could take you there.'

'Can we meet you in an hour?' he asked.

'Aye,' I replied, and we arranged a meeting.

An hour later, we were parked outside the house in Comber, in the van that the SB used for secret surveillance purposes.

'Is this it?' he asked.

'I think so,' I replied, 'but it looks different in daylight.'

'Not to worry.' Dean got out of the van and walked round the corner. Five minutes later he returned to Coco and me with a piece of paper in his hand. We drove back to Belfast.

Nearly a week later, Dean told me that the house in Comber was home to one of the Blues – a police officer – and his wife who was an RUC woman who worked in West Belfast, perfect targets for an IRA bomb squad.

I noted that on most occasions, whenever he asked to be driven somewhere, Fitzy would take plastic supermarket shopping bags with him, and I informed Dean that I believed the bags probably contained bomb-making equipment. I would make a note of the houses he visited, memorise the addresses and inform Dean the following day.

But Dean and Coco began asking non-stop questions about Fitzy, asking me to keep tabs on his exact whereabouts at all times of the day. I felt that Dean and Coco were trying to lay a trap for Fitzy and I didn't like that. Fitzy had been a pal of mine for most of my life and I believed that he would never intend to kill innocent people, either Catholics or Protestants, not even Loyalists unless they were actively involved in trying to kill him and his IRA mates.

Dean and Coco had always told me that my principle role would be to save innocent lives, that the information I gave them would be used to save lives. I decided tochallenge them.

'Why do you keep on about Harry Fitzsimmons?' I asked them one day.

'What do you mean?' Dean replied.

'You know what I mean. Every time we meet lately all you ask me about is Fitzy. Where he goes. Who he meets. What he does.' Warming to my argument, I continued, 'You know what I think. I think that you're planning to trap him, take him out, and I don't like that.'

'What do you mean?' Dean asked, wanting me to spell out my thoughts.

'Dean, you're smart, you know exactly what I mean. I'm not prepared to put myself in a position where I am responsible for Fitzy going to jail, or maybe for his death, unless I believe he really is a man prepared to kill innocent people. And I know he's not that sort of person.'

'So,' said Dean, 'what are you saying?'

'I'm telling you that I'm not going to give you any more information about Fitzy unless you promise he will not be targeted, or arrested, or whatever.'

'So you don't want to work for us anymore?' he asked in a challenging voice.

'I didn't say that,' I protested. 'I'm saying that I am one hundred per cent *with* you, but I believe that my role is to save people's lives – not to lay traps for you to arrest or kill people who I believe are involved in the IRA for all the wrong reasons.'

Dean stared blankly at me.

'I think that people like Fitzy, who have a wife and kids, are often involved with the IRA for other reasons. Sometimes it's to be macho, but deep down you must know that many people in the area where I live look to the IRA for security and protection when they need it. Many people living in Republican areas have no faith in the system or the police or the Army. They have grown up seeing them as the enemy and the IRA are the only people who will protect them.'

But Dean didn't seem to want to hear my argument. He responded, a hardness I had not heard before entering his voice. 'Listen, Marty,' he said, 'Harry Fitzsimmons is a member of a highly professional, devious bombing team who will stop at nothing to destroy this city and sometimes take the lives of innocent people. These people must be stopped.

'And I'll tell you something else. If it wasn't for the good work of the RUC and the British Army one hell of a lot of innocent people would have been killed or maimed in these bombings. It's as a result of their work, risking their lives on occasions, moving people out of these targeted areas, that lives have been saved, not the bombers taking precautions. And if you don't like doing this job trying to stop the bombers then you can leave at any time.'

Dean's reaction upset and angered me. It seemed that he could not understand what I had been saying. But I was convinced I was telling him the facts of life which faced hundreds of young men like Fitzy, but he didn't want to put those facts into the equation. I walked out without saying another word.

For the following four weeks I never used the car that the SB had fitted with the tracking device. Though I continued to work part-time for the second taxi firm,

I deliberately took not the slightest notice of any IRA suspects. I also stopped visiting Republican clubs but continued to lend Fitzy another cheap, old banger I had bought as a runabout.

I took the opportunity to spend as much time as possible with Angie and we had great times together. Angie had quit the YTP and her job in the chip shop and the two of us were really happy together in our little flat. I was also happy for Angie, for not only was her pregnancy going well but her mother visited her most days, bringing her presents, and helping to furnish the flat.

One day on the Springfield Road, I was walking to the shops when I noticed a face I recognised under his flat police hat. It was Officer Billy on foot patrol with an army unit.

I looked the other way and tried to sneak past Billy as he was checking a vehicle that had been stopped at the check point. 'Yo,' I heard and instantly knew it was Billy calling for me to stop.

'Come here,' he said and, as though he had no idea of my identity, said, 'What's your name?'

'You know what my fucking name is,' I replied, irritated that Billy was playing games with me.

'You don't seem in a very good mood today,' he replied, walking over to me. 'Did you get out of bed the wrong side, or something?'

'What do you want?' I asked, annoyed that he had stopped me.

'I've got a note for you, from Dean. He wants you to call him on this number,' and he handed me a small piece of paper with a number I did not recognise.

I thought long and hard about phoning Dean. I was in two minds, not sure what I should do. I needed to be alone to think and I walked to the Black Mountain and sat for several hours deciding which path I should take.

I realised that I had every reason to forget about the Special Branch, turn my back on the whole business, get a decent job and settle down. I had my beautiful Angie, the first girl in my life that I had ever really loved. I was convinced, too, that she felt the same. Every day Angie would tell me how happy she was and how much she loved me. And, even more important perhaps, was the fact that in a matter of months I would be a father. I recalled that I had never known my father because my parents had separated when I was a child. I was determined to try and be a good father to my unborn baby.

And at the back of my mind I could never forget the stories I had heard of British agents who had been discovered, dead, often after days and weeks of the most horrendous torture. I had no wish to end my life like that.

My heart and my head told me to stop working for both the Special Branch and the IRA, to walk away from the whole awful, messy business. And yet I felt that if I took that course of action I would be walking away from reality, that I would be turning my back on my responsibilities. I knew that the Special Branch were trying to stop the killings and the bombings; I knew in my heart that the IRA were wrong to use the bomb and the bullet to pursue their political aim of a united Ireland, instead of persuading the people to vote for their policies like any democratic party should.

I also believed that if I didn't continue working for the SB, who were trying to bring peace to Ireland, then I would regret my decision for the rest of my life. I wondered as I sat in solitude on the mountain whether had been selected to play this role, working for both the IRA and the Special Branch because I could be of some use.

Then I realised that all I was thinking was nothing but a load of crap. I wanted to go back to the SB because of the excitement and because Dean and the others treated me with respect. They didn't treat me like the IRA did, using their people as pawns in their great big scheme of things, not caring who got shot or killed, as long as those at the top remained out of reach of the security forces.

As I walked back down the mountain and saw the housing estate in the distance, I realised how insignificant I really was: a young, Catholic kid living in a run-down, working-class area of Belfast who would never make anything of his life. But I had been given a chance to save people's lives and I was determined that I would not turn my back on them. I couldn't.

I went to the nearest phone box and dialled the number Officer Billy had given me. Within seconds I recognised Dean's voice.

'How are you then, Marty?' he said, a warmth and an enthusiasm in his voice. 'Good to hear your voice again. How have you been?'

'I'm alright,' I replied, not wanting to sound too keen.

'Any chance of you popping down to see us?' he asked.

'When do you suggest?' I asked.

'Could you pop down tonight, around eight o'clock?'

'Aye,' I replied. 'Shall I meet you at the usual place?'

'Perfect,' said Dean, 'look forward to seeing you.'

Two hours later I was sitting in Dean's car off the Cregagh Road. Again, there was a new man sitting in the driving seat.

'Meet Mo,' Dean said, 'he's taking over from Coco.'

'Sorry about that spot of bother we had,' Dean said. 'I don't like falling out with anyone, especially someone who has been so good at his job. It's silly.'

I was determined, however, to have my say. 'Listen, Dean,' I began, 'you must remember that I have been friends with some of these lads all my life. Most of them aren't bad lads at all; they've been caught up in the drama of the whole business and they can't see the wood for the trees.'

'But you've got to understand, Marty', Dean said, 'that this is no game. These people bomb and kill, and they must be stopped. You can help save people's lives by the work you're doing with us. You do understand that, don't you?'

'Aye,' I said. 'I believe in what you're doing, trying to put a stop to all this killing, but you must sometimes put yourself in my shoes.'

'Let's you and I have a deal,' he suggested. 'We'll still have to target Fitzsimmons but we'll only keep him under surveillance. I promise you we won't arrest him, if you'll come back to work with us.'

'OK' I said, 'that's a deal.'

The following day, I was back working again as I had done in the past. I would drive around in my Vauxhall, the car fitted with the tracker device, and I would lend it to Fitzy whenever he wanted to borrow it.

One day, Fitzy asked me if I would take him to the DHSS office on the Falls Road so he could collect his Giro cheque. His baby daughter was with us in the car. After collecting the cheque we were driving back home when a DMSU Land Rover overtook our car and pulled in, forcing us to stop. The DMSU were feared by the IRA for their task was to know every 'player' – every IRA member – in their particular area. They also searched local Republican clubs looking for familiar faces and IRA men whom the Special Branch wanted to question. All day they would tour the streets, stopping and searching individuals they believed to be IRA suspects or sympathisers.

I immediately jumped out of the car while Fitzy remained in the passenger seat with his daughter on his knee. I gave the officers my name and address and Fitzy gave the name of my pal Joseph Ward, as well as Joe's date of birth and correct home address. As the officer was writing down these details, Fitzy slowly took his Giro cheque, on which was written his real name, from his pocket and slipped it into his daughter's knickers, fearing he was about to be searched.

I noticed another officer staring at Fitzy. After a few moments, he walked over to him.

'What did you say your name was again?' he asked.

'Joseph Ward,' Fitzy replied.

After taking down all the details, including details of the car, the officers let us go. But it had been a close shave for I knew that one of Fitzy's IRA bomb team had been arrested and the IRA had immediately informed the other squad members to lie low in case he had been 'persuaded' to reveal the identities of the team.

'Fuck me!' Fitzy said, 'I thought that peeler recognised me.'

Shortly after this scare, Fitzy asked me whether I wanted to meet a good friend of his, a senior member of the IRA by the name of Adams, Davy Adams. I could hardly contain my surprise for this meant that I was to be introduced to one of the most powerful IRA leaders in West Belfast. I knew that his uncle was Gerry Adams, the President of Sinn Fein, the man at the very pinnacle of the Sinn Fein/IRA organisation, and the man who had been the Commanding Officer of the Belfast Brigade of the IRA in the 1970s.

I met Davy one afternoon a few days later outside the Whiterock Leisure Centre. He was an athletic man of medium height, with a full beard and dark hair and wearing a simple sweat shirt and new jeans and trainers.

He looked smart in his casual gear. Davy Adams simply nodded as I walked up to him.

'Are you OK?' were the first words he said to me.

'Great,' I replied.

'Shall we take a walk?' he asked, and motioned me to follow him. We walked into the Roman Catholic City Cemetery which adjoined the Leisure Centre, and for the next 30 minutes we walked around the thousands of graves, chatting about the weather and nothing in particular. As we walked I kept thinking that if this man Adams knew I worked for the Special Branch, it would be only a matter of days before I, too, would be incarcerated in one of the graves.

From the moment we began talking, I realised that Davy Adams was nobody's fool but a well-educated, articulate man who had considerable knowledge of the IRA, its background and its position in Ireland's political history. I knew he had also served at least one jail sentence for his commitment to the IRA cause.

He told me that Harry Fitzsimmons had been talking to him about me and how I would drive him around Belfast, knowing that he was moving bomb-making equipment around the city.

'Are you happy doing that, Martin?' he asked.

'Aye,' I said, 'I don't mind helping Harry.'

'Would you like to join the IRA?' he said.

'Yes, I would,' I said, trying to conceal my excitement and apprehension for this was the opportunity that the Special Branch had been guiding me towards for the past 12 months.

'I could speak to someone,' Davy Adams said, 'if you would like to join?'

'I would,' I said. 'Will you arrange it?'

'In the meantime, I want you to keep away from Harry Fitzsimmons. I want you to contact me direct and

I'll give you my numbers. If you want, you can do some work for me, but it will still mean you're working for the IRA. Is that OK?'

'No problem,' I told him.

He told me to see him at his home in Springhill, in the Ballymurphy Estate, the area known locally as 'Beirut' because of the amount of rioting and IRA activity. The Beirut area was full of well-known IRA members, called 'Red Lights' by the IRA because these were the people who could not travel outside the area for fear of being immediately picked up by the RUC, suspected of being on IRA business and taken in for close questioning which could last hours or days. Most of the time, the 'Red Lights' would sit around the IRA clubs openly talking and discussing past and present IRA operations, believing they were totally safe amongst sympathisers and active supporters.

Within minutes of leaving Davy Adams, I went home, collected my car and drove out of the area to a phone box.

'Dean, listen,' I said when I had been put through to him, 'you're never going to believe this. This afternoon I spent half an hour with Davy Adams, *the* Davy Adams. He's asked me to join the IRA.'

'Are you telling me porkies?' he asked, half jokingly.

'No I'm not. I'm deadly serious, honest,' I replied.

'Marty,' he said, 'tell me: how the fuck did you meet Davy Adams?'

'Through Harry.'

'Harry who?' he said. 'Who the fuck's Harry?'

'You remember, Harry Fitzsimmons, the lad from the IRA bomb team.'

'What are you telling me, Marty?' he asked. 'What has Harry to do with Davy Adams?'

'How the fuck am I supposed to know? Harry just asked me if I wanted to meet him and I did what you wanted me to do, go and meet IRA people.'

Dean was not yet certain that I was talking about the real Davy Adams. 'Tell me Marty, what did he look like? Describe him.'

I told him exactly what the man looked like, down to the last detail.

'Hold on,' he said and he put down the phone. A minute later he came back and asked where I was speaking from. When I told him he asked me if I could see him in the usual meeting place in 20 minutes. Before I could reply, he hung up.

As I jumped into his parked car 20 minutes later, Dean turned round and handed me a file. 'Look at these photos,' he said. 'Is that your man?'

'Yes,' I said, as I instantly recognised the face of Davy Adams, 'that's him.'

For a full five minutes Dean said nothing, wondering why someone as senior as Davy Adams would be interviewing me, asking me whether I wanted to join the IRA. To Dean it seemed incomprehensible, and he was searching for possible reasons. I sat still and waited.

'Are you going to meet him again?' he asked finally.

'Yes, in two nights' time.'

'Good,' Dean said, 'go along, see what he's got to say and phone me immediately.'

'OK, I'll be in touch.' I left and returned to my car.

Two nights later I stood outside Davy Adams' house in Springhill, knowing that my life would change once I had summoned up the courage to knock at the door. I put such thoughts to the back of my mind and banged twice on the door.

A young girl, whom I guessed was Davy Adams' daughter, answered the door.

'Is your dad in?' I asked.

'Who shall I say wants him?' she asked with a smile.

'Tell him my name's Martin.'

She walked to the bottom of the stairs. 'Daddy,' she shouted, 'you're wanted.'

'Who is it?' he called from upstairs.

'His name's Martin.'

'Oohh, good!' I heard. 'Tell him to come upstairs.'

I noticed at the bottom of the stairs a barred, steel door which, when closed, would probably have been impregnable. In the following couple of years I would see many such doors at the bottom of the stairs in the homes of a number of senior IRA members. I also noted that behind the front door were two steel drop bars, preventing anyone from breaking down the door. Many IRA and Sinn Fein members had been killed by Loyalist paramilitary gangs breaking into their homes at night and shooting them as they lay in their beds. Now they took no chances.

'In here, Marty,' I heard Davy say, and I walked into the back bedroom which he had turned into a study with a desk and a chair, the walls covered with books. Also on the walls were photographs of former IRA heroes.

'Give me a minute or so,' he said, 'I must finish reading something.'

It was only when we went downstairs and into the garden that he mentioned the IRA. He said nothing but it was obvious that he believed his home was bugged by the security forces.

'I have a little job for you to do,' he said. 'I want you to go and check a house belonging to a member of the UVF.'

I knew the Ulster Volunteer Force to be one of the Loyalists' most violent paramilitary organisations which regularly targeted and murdered IRA members and sympathisers.

He explained that the house was in Arosa Parade near The Grove playing fields, in the heart of Loyalist territory, and gave me the man's name who lived there. He told me that the Loyalist had been responsible for a number of attempted assassinations of IRA and Sinn Fein men. He gave me a brief description of the man and his car, but told me that the man was very cautious.

'You will have to be very careful,' he warned.

Before I left he gave me £10 in cash. 'That's petrol money,' he said. 'If you need any more, just ask.'

I phoned Dean the following morning and told him of the task I had been set by Davy Adams.

'Go through with it and do what he asked you. They might be watching you. We'll try to look after you at the other end, but be careful; if the Prod's catch you in that area they'll kill you.'

I knew Dean was speaking the truth and vowed to be as careful as possible. On some occasions, strangers driving through those Loyalist areas had been stopped and someone had leapt into the car with a hand-gun or baseball bat to check the reason the stranger was in the area.

I drove over to the house at around 10.00pm the following night when I knew there would be little traffic about. If by chance someone tried to stop me, I knew I had a chance of escaping by simply putting my foot on the accelerator and speeding away. During the day, with far more traffic on the roads, there was always the danger you could be blocked accidentally by other vehicles.

And Dean had given me one piece of advice that I did not forget: 'If anyone tries to stop your vehicle by standing in the way, just put your foot down and drive straight through them. If you stop, you're a dead man.'

The following day, I reported back to Davy and told

him that I had visited the street twice and seen nothing; even the lights were out although it was only 10.00pm.

'Don't worry about that,' he said, 'the chances of seeing him straight away aren't very high because he usually walks everywhere. Continue to check out the place from time to time and when you see something report straight to me. If you need more money for petrol just let me know.'

'I don't want any of your money,' I said, 'don't worry about that.'

'It's not my money,' he explained, 'it comes from the IRA.'

Before I left, he said, 'By the way, Martin, you have a meeting with a lad who is going to swear you in as an IRA volunteer. Are you sure you want to go through with it?'

'Yes,' I replied, ' I want to become a full member.'

Three days later, I went to the house in Andersonstown and knocked at the door. A medium-built, scruffy-looking man in his 30s invited me in.

'I know why you're here,' he said. 'Listen to me, carefully. I want you to be sure about what you're getting involved in. There are lots of people who have joined the IRA for all the wrong reasons. Some have been caught while on active service and have been sentenced to long jail terms of up to 25 years.'

I nodded and let him continue, 'After they've been sentenced they have complained they didn't know what they were getting into, and my job is to make sure you don't make the same mistake. If you want to join Oglaigh na hEireann [Gaelic for the Irish Republican Army], you have to promise to promote the objects of the organisation and obey all orders and regulations issued by the Army and its officers.'

He then told me to go home. 'Go to bed tonight and

think hard,' he said. 'No one is forcing you to do this, but you must remember you could be killed by the SAS while on active service or be arrested and sentenced to a long jail term. If you don't come back tomorrow, no one will blame you because we have many young men wanting to join the organisation. But if you do come back tomorrow, you will then become an official IRA volunteer.'

As I walked back home that night, I wondered if I was doing the right thing. I was now within 24 hours of finding myself between a rock and a hard place – the SB and the IRA – and I feared that I would end up as mincemeat. That night I hardly slept a wink, looking at Angie lying beside me, knowing that I would go back to the house the next day in the knowledge that I was making the biggest mistake of my life.

During the oath-taking ceremony, I not only had to swear allegiance to the IRA, but the man would also take me through a number of the army orders contained in the IRA 'Green Book'.

I listened with a sinking heart to three particular pledges the man read out:

> '1. No volunteer should succumb to approaches or overtures, blackmail or bribery attempts, made by the enemy and should report such approaches as soon as possible.
> '2. Volunteers who engage in loose talk shall be dismissed.
> '3. Volunteers found guilty of treason face the death penalty.'

The moment I returned to my flat, I went to the bedroom and pressed the button on the front of the little white radio the SB had given me.

'I have to go out,' I said to Angie. 'I'll see you later.'

I met Dean who was alone in his car, the first time I ever met him on his own.

'Brilliant, wonderful,' he said. 'Marty, you're a professional.'

Within days I thought my career as a British agent was over. I was sitting in a Republican club on the estate when four mean-looking young men approached me. One grabbed me by the shoulder.

'Upstairs,' he said, his voice and his manner menacing.

I am sure that at that moment my face turned white and I felt my mouth go dry. I went with the four men who surrounded me as though trying to stop any thought I might have had of making a run for freedom.

Upstairs, the room, which was used as a disco, was blacked out, the only lights coming from a bar at the far end.

'Keep yourself out of IRA business,' one said, digging me in the chest.

'What are you talking about?' I asked.

'Your friend Paul smashed into a taxi and has refused to pay up. And you went to see the taxi driver to tell him he would not be getting a penny because it was totally his fault.'

'Well ...' I began.

But they refused to listen, ordering me to shut up and mind my own business. I didn't mind what they said; I hardly heard the words, as a wonderful sense of relief washed over me. All they were bothered about was some petty matter over a minor car crash. I thought they had discovered I was a British agent.

I shut up and said nothing, happy to agree with whatever they said. I went home feeling wonderful. But there would be other, more sinister incidents to come.

CHAPTER SEVEN

Soon after taking the oath of allegiance, my cell commander ordered me to attend a meeting at a house in the Turf Lodge area of Belfast where I would meet a man they called 'The Interrogator'. I was suspicious at first and asked Dean for advice.

'I think you should attend,' he said. 'Do as they say and show that you are a committed member of the organisation. I am sure that whatever you learn will be useful, really useful. Remember, Marty, the more we know about the IRA, the better equipped we are to stop their bombings and shootings.'

One evening, a few days later, I made my way to the house in Turf Lodge not knowing what to expect. When I knocked at the door, a balding man in his forties asked me my name before inviting me inside. He was about 5' 8" tall with bright, intelligent eyes.

'Pleased to meet you, Marty,' he said, obviously trying to put me at my ease. 'I'm here to help you in case you ever get picked up by the RUC. My job is to prepare all volunteers in case they get interrogated. You will come and see me a few times and we will go over everything just so that you know exactly what to say and what to do if the RUC ever pick you up and take you to Castlereagh for questioning.'

'Aye,' I replied, knowing that I would have to concentrate and remember everything he was telling me so that I could repeat it to Dean later.

Speaking slowly to make sure that I understood everything, the Interrogator told me that if I was ever suspected of being involved in any IRA activities the RUC could arrest me and hold me for seven days before being charged or released. He added, 'Throughout those seven days and nights the CID will question you, taking it in turns to wear you down, trying to catch you out so they can break you.

'Their intention will be to break your spirit so that you will tell them everything they want to know; details of operations, of bombings and shootings; the names of other members of your cell; names of any other IRA members, even the names of friends and relations of yours.'

'Aye, I know,' I said.

'But it will be your duty to tell them nothing, absolutely nothing,' he said, 'and I'm going to tell you how to do that. That's why it is very important that you attend these anti-interrogation lectures.'

He continued, 'Now, listen very carefully. If you are arrested, you will say absolutely nothing and you will never answer any question the CID asks you. The only time you will speak is when in front of the Custody Sergeant.

'When he asks you any questions, tell him this: "When interviewed I will refuse to co-operate but this does not mean that I am guilty. I want Madden & Finucane to represent me."'

I nodded, for I knew that the highly regarded firm of solicitors represented, among their many clients, Republicans and Catholics.

'Have you got that?' he asked and I nodded again and repeated the words to him.

'Good,' he said. 'Now tell me again to make sure.'

I did and he smiled. 'Good. The IRA is a very strong, determined army. The British Government, the security forces and the RUC have realised that they can never destroy the IRA but, over the years, the IRA leadership has learned that our army has one weakness: the interrogation of our members by the RUC. We have many details of IRA members who have broken under strong police questioning.'

Later, the Interrogator told me that the IRA Army Council had been warned of the danger of untrained members being broken during police interviews and, as a result, had decided to introduce the anti-interrogation lectures.

He added, 'If we can improve the resolve, the will-power of members to resist intensive interrogation by CID officers, then the organisation of the IRA will be that much stronger.'

The Interrogator repeated time and again that under no circumstances must I ever answer any of the questions put to me during any interviews by CID or RUC officers. He instructed me to ask for a solicitor only from the Belfast firm of Madden & Finucane and refuse any other solicitor they might suggest.

During another interrogation lesson, I was told what to expect should I ever be arrested.

'They will usually come for you early in the morning while you're still asleep, some time around five o'clock. They will bang at your door and invade your house making a lot of noise. They will try to confuse you, order you to dress quickly, and come with them immediately.

'But you must refuse to do that. You must tell them that you have the right, as you do, to make yourself respectable. Take your time; go to the bathroom and wash and shave, clean your teeth, comb your hair, even splash on some after-shave if you have any. Dress properly in a clean shirt and wear a jacket and a smart pair of trousers. They won't like it, but fuck them. Take no notice when they try to hurry you. Do you understand?'

'Aye,' I replied, 'I'll do that.'

The Interrogator continued, 'Then the RUC will take you to Castlereagh and put you in a cell. They will leave you there for a few hours before the interrogation officers come to see you. The officers will have known the night before that they are going to interview you and will have had a good breakfast, a shower and a shave and will want to make you seem second-rate compared to them. But, because you will have followed this advice, you will look as smart as they do. They won't like that. They hope that when they enter your interview room you will be pathetic, unshaven, scruffy, putting you at an immediate disadvantage.'

I listened intently, determined to remember it all.

"Tell them nothing. Never answer one of their questions, no matter how many times they ask you. Don't look down at the floor and never appear nervous or frightened. Always remember to keep your head up and look them straight in the eye as though remembering their exact identity.'

'Why should I do that?' I asked.

'Because they will hate that. They will fear that you are trying to remember their faces, seal their identities in your memory so that, one day, you will be able to target them and kill them. They fear you will never forget their faces and that scares the fuck out of them and puts you at an advantage.'

'OK,' I said.

The Interrogator told me what to do in my cell during the hours that I wasn't being interviewed by the police. 'Exercise, keep fit, walk up and down the cell or the room and keep alert the entire time. Sleep and eat at every opportunity. Whatever food you're offered, sit down and eat it and try to enjoy it. It will help sustain your energy, help you to resist the bastards' questions. Some IRA people have refused to eat their food, but that's stupid, because without food you become weak and vulnerable to their questions. You must never appear tired or sleepy, but always look alert. Never let them see you might be weakening or vulnerable, but show you have a resolve like steel.

'Before any interview starts, take the opportunity of going to the toilet. After they begin to interview you, they will refuse to let you go to the loo because they know that when someone wants to go desperately they will say almost anything just so they can go. They also realise that when anyone wants to have a shit desperately enough the concentration goes. That's when you're vulnerable and they know that. If they refuse to let you go and have a shit then you must take action. Simply take down your strides and shit there and then on the floor in front of them. It will be their fault and they will know it. They hate that.'

'Really,' I said, roaring with laughter, 'shit in front of them?'

'Yes,' he replied, 'right there and then in the interview room. Remember, next time you ask to go to the toilet they won't say "no".'

During another lesson, the Interrogator told me what

I should do if the police or Special Branch ever started to beat me up while being interviewed.

'Hit back,' he said. 'Give them everything; smash the fuck out of them. Don't be frightened to hit back, and the harder they hit you, the harder you hit the bastards back again. They know they shouldn't hit you but they will, especially the nasty bastards, the hard men who are determined to break you.

'And if they begin to smack you around while another officer holds you then curl up into a ball on the floor if you can and try to protect your head and face. They'll probably kick the fuck out of you but then you've got them. As soon as they stop, demand to see your own doctor. Tell them you refuse to see any other doctor and, if one comes in, tell him that you demand to see your own doctor. Make sure you give his name and address and keep demanding it. It's your right to have your own doctor, so keep demanding it. That will scare the fucking shit out of them because your doctor will note any marks and injuries you have suffered. That will cause the RUC problems.'

The Interrogator also told me to expect the 'good cop, bad cop' routine that I had heard about before. 'The "good cop" will be your friend, call you "Marty", tell you that if you answer the questions he will make sure you never have any trouble and that the IRA will never know you said a word. The "bad cop" will shout and swear and threaten and probably hit you, and you must never show that bastard that you are the least bit frightened of him. If you do show weakness, he will realise it and know that in a few days' time he will break you.'

I was also told that the quickest way to be freed was to say fuck all. The Interrogator insisted that if I kept quiet, resisted everything and never answered a single question, then the interviews would only last a few days and the police would free a man far sooner than if they felt they were on the verge of breaking someone. Then the odds would be on being detained for the full seven days.

He added, looking me straight in the eye, 'Marty, remember: seven days or seven fucking years.'

I passed every detail of the four sessions I had in the Interrogator's expert hands on to Dean as soon as possible.

'Tell me everything, Marty, every tiny detail,' he said, 'because this is really important. The more we know about their techniques, the more chance there is of getting round them and the less chance there is of innocent people getting hurt.'

I also told Dean about the infamous IRA Security Teams.

'They're evil bastards, Marty. What have you been told about them?' he asked.

'I learned that when an IRA member has been picked up and interviewed by the RUC, a special IRA Security Team will sometimes follow them from the moment the man is released from custody. The man doesn't know he's being followed, but for two or three days he is watched by members of the team. They take note of everyone he talks to, everywhere he goes, everything he does.

'A couple of days later he is told to report for questioning. The man goes to a safe house. Inside is total darkness, no lights whatsoever. The man is taken to a room and told to sit down while men in balaclavas question him, asking him a hundred questions about his time inside, the police questioning, the details and, more importantly, his answers.

'The man is made to feel like a leper, a traitor. They question him harder than the CID ever did. If they think he's talked or betrayed the cause, then he's fucking had it. And if they think he's been turned and become an informant, they will beat the shit out of him, torture him and whatever. And before they've finished with him, they will have discovered every tiny piece of information that he gave about members and the IRA operations. If he admits to being turned, then he's fucked – just a bullet in the back of the head.'

I told Dean that I understood there were two IRA Security Teams, one operating in Belfast, the other in 'Derry. I also told him that the names of the Team members were kept so secret that even IRA men who had been in the organisation for years had no idea as to their identities.

'I understand that their main job is to root out those IRA members who are turned during their interrogation and persuaded to become police informers. They have now become a law unto themselves with the power of life and death.'

*   *   *

From the day I took the oath of allegiance and became a fully-fledged member of the IRA, sometime in the autumn of 1989, I found myself working more frequently for Davy Adams and the IRA's Belfast Intelligence Unit. He asked me to call at his house once or twice a week, where he would give me details of potential targets he wanted me to reconnoitre.

One of my first tasks was to check out the movements of a Major in the Ulster Defence Regiment (since re-named the Royal Irish Rangers), who lived on the Cregagh Estate in the heart of Protestant Belfast. Davy Adams had been told that this man rode to work each day on his powerful motorbike.

'I want you to go and take a look at this address,'

Davy said to me as we chatted in the back garden of his house. 'See if there is any way one of our active service units could put a Semtex booby trap in one of the motorcycle's panniers.'

When he gave me details of the location we would move back inside the house because he did not want anyone to see him poring over a map. We walked into the kitchen where he took out a large map of Belfast and laid it on a work-top. He signalled for me to come over and pointed to a street in the Cregagh area. Throughout, he never spoke a word. He pointed to the exact street with a pen so that I would not make a mistake. Then, using his forefinger, he outlined the number of the house he wanted me to check out.

On those occasions I, too, never spoke a word. When I wasn't sure of the exact number, I would write it on a scrap of paper and, if correct, he would give me the 'thumb's up' sign.

Only when I was leaving and we moved outside his home would he say anything to me, perhaps suggesting that I should check out the target at night time, or whatever was best for the particular operation. On this first occasion, Davy told me to survey the Major's home at night, check out the panniers on the bike and to make sure we were targeting the right bike by checking the registration number.

The following morning, I phoned Dean and gave him details of the task I had been set, giving the address and all the facts I knew of the UDR Major and the IRA's intention to place a bomb in the pannier of his motorbike.

I would no longer use Dean's name during phone conversations because he believed the time had come for us to both operate under aliases. From now on I would always refer to him as 'Felix', and he would always refer to me during phone calls by my new code name 'Carol'. He told me always to use his new name 'Felix' so that I would not make a mistake if emergencies arose. At first, it seemed odd using the new names but after a few days I became used to it.

'Well done,' Felix said, 'leave it to us.'

I told him that I intended to check out the Major's house that night and report back to Davy Adams the following day.

I drove in my car, which was still fitted with the tracker device, to the Cregagh address and, though lights were on in the house, I could see no sign of the motorbike. It was possible that his bike could have been kept in a shed at the back of the house which was just visible from the road, but it would have been too risky to check that night without arousing suspicion. I considered it highly likely that the Major might hear me as I made my way to the shed to check its contents.

I reported back to Davy Adams and he told me to continue surveillance of the house. He also gave me £30 in cash as petrol allowance. During the next few days, I checked the Cregagh house on a number of occasions but never saw the motorbike. Then, one afternoon I saw a man riding a powerful motorbike along the street where the Major lived. I took the registration number and gave all the details to Davy. He told me later that I had indeed targeted the right man.

A few days after that, Davy said he would arrange a meeting for me with another IRA member, one of their gunmen, who would be taking over the operation. We met under cover of darkness at the Bull Ring shops on the Ballymurphy Estate.

The gunman, clean-shaven with fair hair, was nearly six feet tall, with a strong muscular body and in his mid-20s. He took me to a nearby house where we met a third

IRA man, a skinny, scruffy-looking fellow who hardly said a word throughout the 20-minute meeting.

'Have you looked at this job, Marty?' the fair-haired man asked.

'Aye,' I replied, 'I've been keeping the place under surveillance for more than a week.'

'What's your thoughts about it?'

I told him that I had checked out the house on many occasions but had only seen the man once, as he was riding his bike along the street.

'Would it be easy for us to get away if we arranged a car?'

I told him straight, 'No chance, there's too many RUC in the area.'

In fact, I knew it would have been easy for an IRA squad to shoot the man in the street, and make their escape, but I had to play for time. I knew there was a possibility that if I gave the go-ahead, those two hit men might go out that night to shoot the Major. I knew I had to warn Felix if the man's life was to be saved.

After several minutes, I gathered that the gunman had decided not to risk an attack on the Major near his home, but to hijack a car and wait for him to pull up at some convenient traffic lights. One man would drive the car while the other would hide under a blanket in the back seat, an AK-47 at the ready. When the driver decided that the moment was right, he would tell the gunman, who would sit up and spray the Major with a full magazine.

Within 30 minutes of leaving the house, I phoned Felix and told him of the IRA's plan to assassinate the Major. I also told him I had no idea when the IRA gunmen planned to strike.

Later, I was informed that the targeted man was indeed a UDR Major who worked in the Tyrone area.

As a result of the information I passed to the SB, the man's life had been saved. That made me feel good and inspired me to continue working for the IRA so that I could continue to pass intelligence material to the Special Branch. I also realised that I felt a buzz of adrenalin, an excitement, now that I had succeeded in infiltrating the IRA's intelligence unit and dealt with their top men, at the same time as working with the Special Branch.

*   *   *

It may seem incredible, but at that time the thought that I might have been taking extraordinary risks hardly ever crossed my mind. To me, it had become a job that I had to carry out. So I did it.

Davy Adams would not be the only person who briefed me. My pal, Harry Fitzsimmons, would also occasionally ask me to carry out intelligence work, checking on someone the IRA planned to target.

One day, Davy told me they were interested in a UDR man who worked in the Antrim UDR base, drove a silver Nissan Sunny hatchback and lived in Springfarm, an Antrim housing estate a short drive from the base. They planned to put a booby-trap bomb – known in the IRA as 'a charge' – under his car. At one stage, I was asked to check out the man, but before being given the go-ahead I was moved to another job. Fortunately, I had discovered sufficient details about the man for the Special Branch to be able to identify him. Some time later, Felix told me that the RUC had managed to identify the officer concerned and immediately moved him to a new address.

On another occasion, an IRA man was driving his wife along Tennent Street off the Protestant Shankill

Road when he saw a silver Mark IV Ford Escort pull out of the RUC station, drive into the Shankill and park outside the TSB. The IRA's Commanding Officer told him to make checks during the following few days but the man never reappeared. They decided to make another check at the same time as the original sighting, about 2.30 on a Friday afternoon.

Around 2.30pm the following Friday, the same man appeared in his Escort, drove to the TSB and parked for about ten minutes before returning to Tennent Street RUC base. The IRA man noted that when the RUC man returned to his car, he neglected to check under his vehicle to see whether a booby trap had been planted. One of the golden rules that every RUC man was encouraged to carry out was to check under his vehicle for bombs, each and every time he got into a vehicle.

I was detailed to drive the IRA man, who had been tasked to plant the charge, to the bank so that he could make one last check of the location. The plan was to carry out the bombing the following Friday. I notified the SB and they warned the RUC man of the danger. The next Friday, the IRA active service unit was driven to the bank, armed with a 1.5lb Semtex magnet bomb, enough to severely damage the car, killing the occupants and probably injuring any passers-by. But to their annoyance, the Ford Escort never appeared.

I would sometimes pass on information that I happened to hear whenever I was with other IRA men from other active service units, perhaps in a bar, a club, or maybe travelling together in a vehicle. At first, IRA members were reticent to talk in front of me because they weren't sure of my background and whether I could be trusted. But the more they saw me hanging around with men they could trust, and the fact that Davy Adams himself wanted me as part of his intelligence unit, helped tremendously to give me the credibility I needed to infiltrate the very heart of the IRA network.

The IRA had worked the 'cell system' for years so that members only knew for certain that those in their cell were trusted IRA men. In this way, of course, if one member of a cell was arrested he could only reveal details of his own cell and no other. That kept to a minimum the possibility of agents infiltrating the network and gaining information across the whole hierarchy of the organisation.

However, having been brought into the organisation as part of the intelligence wing, I came into contact with numerous IRA men from many different cells. And because of my role, they automatically came to trust me in a very short time. By accident, I had fallen into a most privileged position of trust which provided me with an extraordinary range of contacts, all involved in carrying out the IRA's dirty work. As a result, they would often speak in my presence of planned targets, murders, bombings and future operations before final decisions had been made. More importantly, it provided the Special Branch with a remarkable early-warning system.

Sometimes, I would take the opportunity, with one or two other IRA members, to practise shooting with various types of weapons; AK-47s, 9mm hand-guns and Smith & Wesson .38 Specials. After dark, we would place scouts at street corners and fire the weapons at targets on a blank wall on an estate where we knew we were safe from RUC and Army patrols. I realised that practising with live ammunition with known IRA members would further help to guarantee my reputation as a staunch IRA man. Within a few months of officially joining the organisation, my credibility as a trusted member had been secured.

Such close relationships with so many different IRA

cells would pay dividends throughout the years I was working inside the IRA. On one occasion, a chance remark saved the lives of two RUC men who were on foot patrol in Upper Antrim Road, near Glengormly, North Belfast. I was in a house waiting to see someone and I overheard two IRA men discussing the operation. They had been watching the spot for some time and believed it would be an ideal location for a bomb attached to a command wire, blowing up the RUC men with little or no danger of being caught. They also had a secure escape route.

I phoned Felix and warned him of the planned attack, although I had no idea at that time when the attack was due to take place. The RUC stopped patrolling the area for a few weeks but then restarted foot patrols. One evening, I heard on the radio that a bomb had gone off at the location I had targeted.

On another occasion, Harry Fitzsimmons and other IRA men were planning to execute a 26-year-old Protestant, Lee Samuel Livingstone, who lived over the peace line not far from my mother's home. They believed he was responsible, among others, for a rocket and gun attack on the Sinn Fein Centre in the Republican Ardoyne.

The plan was for an IRA active service unit to go to his house one night, break in and shoot him in his bed. I informed the SB and the man was alerted and advised to move house. However, the IRA have long memories and two years later another IRA unit decided to ambush Livingstone as he walked to work. By luck and incompetence on the part of the Ballymurphy IRA, Livingstone escaped and, to make matters worse, the two gunmen were seen and identified by passers-by. They were arrested, charged and sentenced to long jail terms.

But my daily routine wasn't totally dominated by my

double life. My first son, Martin, was born on Sunday, 4 February 1990, in Belfast's Royal Victoria Hospital. Angie was wonderfully happy and young Martin helped to cement our relationship.

But the fact that Angie was now spending most of the time at home with young Martin meant that she met those IRA members who would call at my house for a meeting or just a chat. At first, of course, she believed the young men dropping by for a cup of coffee were just friends, but Angie was nobody's fool. A few weeks after Martin's birth Angie realised that I had become a member of the IRA for she had recognised some of the visitors as members of the organisation.

When I had first met Angela, she had been very supportive towards the IRA and told me on a few occasions that she had considered becoming a member. After she became pregnant, however, her views changed and she did not like the thought of her boyfriend risking his freedom and maybe his life by joining the organisation. At no time, however, did Angie ever have the slightest idea that I was also working with the Special Branch.

One evening, when I called to see Davy Adams, he signalled me to follow him into the garden.

'Marty,' he said, 'I want you to come and meet someone, a good friend of mine.'

'Who's that?' I asked.

'Gillen,' he replied.

I had not the slightest idea who Gillen was, but I was happy to go along, curious as to his identity and, more importantly, why Davy Adams would want me to meet him.

I drove Davy to Lenadoon Estate in Suffolk, and parked the car in a little car park reserved for the residents of the nearby houses. We walked through a couple of streets, down a back lane and Davy stopped by a gate. He looked around him before putting his hand inside the gate, flicking open the latch and walking into the back yard of a terraced house.

A young woman with a baby opened the door and motioned for us to come into the kitchen. Then a man in his 30s, whom I recognised as Brian Gillen, one of the IRA's top commanders, walked into the room. The two men immediately began speaking in Gaelic and, although I did not speak a word of the language, I could tell they were both fluent.

After a few seconds chat, Gillen introduced himself to me and we shook hands. 'I'm Brian,' he said. 'Pleased to meet you.'

'How are you doing?' I asked, not sure how I should address him.

Davy said, 'This is Marty, the man I've been telling you about. He's a good lad. I wanted you to meet him because I was thinking of him for the new job that's coming up.'

This was news to me. No mention had been made to me of any new role or new job.

Gillen looked at me and said, 'Hey, Marty, I hope you're not working for the fucking Branch.'

Somehow, I reacted so quickly I surprised myself. 'For fuck sake, are you mad?' I exclaimed.

The two burst out laughing and I joined in the joke, hoping that I didn't laugh too nervously. The immediate danger had been averted, but I'm sure I must have flushed red.

Ten minutes later, Davy and I left the house and returned to our car using the same route. I dropped Davy at his house and immediately went to see Jimmy and Steve, two IRA members with whom I had become friendly over the previous few months.

'Do you know who I've just met, Jimmy?' I said to my mate.

'Don't tell me, the Prime Minister,' he said and roared with laughter at his joke.

'Brian Gillen,' I said, wondering what their reaction would be.

'Fuck, you mean Carrot Head,' he said. 'What the hell were you doing with him?'

'Why do you call him Carrot Head?' I asked stupidly.

'Because of his bright red hair, of course'.

I had come to visit my two mates to find out more about Brian Gillen. I knew a little about him because Felix had mentioned his name on a number of occasions and shown me photographs. But I had no idea just how important he was in the IRA hierarchy.

In the hope of gaining more information, I asked, 'Why did Davy Adams want me to drive to the other side of Belfast just to meet him?'

'Do you not know what Gillen does?' Stevie asked.

'No,' I said, 'Should I?'

'Gillen is to be the new head of the Belfast Brigade, one of the most important people in the whole organisation,' said Jimmy.

'Shit, I didn't realise that. I thought Spud was still the boss.'

'No,' he replied, 'Spud's been given the boot. He's no longer the top man, but he's still operating.'

'What the fuck happened?' I asked.

I knew, of course, that both Stevie, an experienced IRA gunman, and Jimmy, known throughout IRA circles as a ruthless bomber, would know exactly what had happened to Spud and the reasons why.

Stevie said, 'He got the boot for misusing IRA funds.'

Later, I asked Davy Adams the same question about Spud. He told me, 'It's true; Spud did get demoted. I heard within the IRA that Spud had stolen IRA money.'

'Really?' I asked.

'No,' Davy replied, 'he never stole any money. Basically, Spud's a good lad and a very dedicated volunteer. He was simply using the IRA's funds too liberally. Activists were asking him for £200 for an operation and he would give them £250 instead. He was just being too generous with the funds and his bosses thought he was behaving in a reckless way. That's the reason he was demoted. If he had stolen the money, he would have been for the high jump.'

The following day I spoke to Felix and told him about my meeting with Brian Gillen and the news of his promotion. He seemed excited by the news and, seemingly, surprised and delighted that I was meeting top IRA men like Adams and Gillen and bringing Special Branch such valuable information. Changes at the top of the IRA were of extreme importance to the Special Branch and the other government secret services like MI5. He explained to me that Gillen had been jailed for ten years back in the 1970s, having been convicted of being a member of a bombing team and possessing explosives and a gun.

I continued to work with Davy Adams and after a few weeks he encouraged me to meet him at least once a day, not necessarily to discuss new operations but simply to chat to him. He also enjoyed telling me something of the history of the IRA and the gallant deeds former heroes carried out both before and after World War II. He would also talk to me about his wife and kids, but what impressed me most was the amount of attention he paid to his appearance, always immaculate in well-pressed trousers, a smart shirt and, often, a fancy waistcoat. His beard was always neatly trimmed, his hair perfectly combed. Usually, before leaving the house, he would stand in front of the mirror and preen himself, checking his hair and his beard, his clothes and his shoes.

'How do I look, Marty?' he would say as he looked at himself in the mirror. Before I could reply he would continue, 'Good; isn't this the business; don't I look nice tonight, Marty?' as he showed me a new shirt or new pair of trousers. Some IRA members called him 'Swallow-the-Piano' because his white teeth looked so perfectly even and brushed – he would smile frequently, revealing his teeth, snow-white in contrast to his full black beard, so that one could easily understand how he had earned his nickname.

In many ways, I respected Davy Adams. He was a true IRA man, absolutely dedicated to the cause. And I always found him scrupulously honest. Although he would always have several hundred pounds of IRA money at his home at any one time, he would be meticulous in dividing his own money from IRA funds. In fact, he made me smile whenever he told me how he was saving his dole money so that he could buy a new shirt the following week. Sometimes he would ask me to loan him £20 for a few days and I would happily do so. And, as soon as he had any money, he repaid me.

Sunday, however, was sacrosanct for Davy Adams. He reserve every Sunday for his friends and his mates, and not necessarily IRA members. On a number of occasions, he invited me, but the fact that I didn't drink and would quickly become bored sitting around pubs and clubs while others drank meant that I didn't often go along.

Something else that I liked and respected about Davy Adams was his attitude to the IRA punishment gangs. Several times, I heard him denounce punishment beatings and he would frequently insult and ridicule members of the punishment gangs whom he believed brought the IRA into disrepute and dishonour. He would sometimes sit in a pub with his mates and watch a punishment gang sitting across the room, chatting, laughing and drinking, openly boasting that they were the true law enforcers of the organisation, the men who protected the IRA's strict disciplinary code. Davy Adams would treat them with contempt, because he believed that they should have been involved in doing valuable IRA work, like targeting soldiers or police, risking their lives and their freedom, rather than chasing, beating and sometimes maiming kids and others with their baseball bats and iron bars.

He never forget those IRA members who had been caught and jailed, fighting for the cause, because he had served a long jail sentence himself. He would ask people for books to send to the inmates and provide food parcels. He would also write secret letters to personal friends inside jail, which would be smuggled inside by sympathisers and relations of the imprisoned men.

Immaculate, good-looking and proud, Davy Adams often found himself receiving attention from various women but I never saw him take advantage of any of them, as though he didn't welcome their attention. He seemed totally dedicated to his wife and kids and even, on occasions, when he had a pint too many, he would always leave the pub and go straight home. As I watched, sober as usual, I always saw a number of women endeavouring to attract his attention, openly flirting, virtually offering themselves to him. He didn't want to know.

To many Republican women, senior members of the IRA have always seemed especially attractive, not only because of the dangerous lives they lead but because of the romantic image the organisation has created over the decades. Many are still fêted as heroes and some women seem to find this very seductive. Though Davy Adams wanted none of their attention, there were many other senior IRA men who revelled in the limelight and took advantage of their positions to conduct many illicit affairs.

It appeared to matter little to many of these women that they were already married, so strong seemed the attraction of the IRA image. Many affairs took place because the women found the men irresistible, but for the men it would usually be for different reasons. Most IRA members enjoyed the attention and took advantage of the situation, but for others it would only be a means to an end. The men often used their relationship to gain access to the lover's house or flat, so they would have yet another secret hideout for storing their guns, ammunition and bomb-making equipment. Sometimes the women would be persuaded to look the other way while men turned their homes into bomb-making factories.

Occasionally, Davy Adams would accompany me on IRA targeting operations, surveying possible locations. We even walked up and down the Protestant Shankill Road, which took considerable nerve. Every Loyalist would have recognised him as easily as they would have recognised his uncle, Gerry Adams. To walk along the Shankill revealed his courage.

Once, Davy and I went to survey a flat in the Shankill Parade which had been identified as a late-night drinking den of members of the hard-line UVF. We had parked the car a few hundred yards away, parted company and approached the flats from different sides. We both knew that if we were caught in that area we would be kidnapped, interrogated and, more than likely, beaten to death, our bodies discovered the following day down some alley with a bullet through the head.

That night, we walked along the road and looked up, checking the exact address. As there was no one on the streets we stood watching as ten or more UVF members, some obviously drunk, enjoyed their late-night binge. I constantly looked around, checking to see if anyone was approaching, but Davy didn't seem to care a damn about his own safety.

He told me that he wanted me to go to a house in Kerrykeel Gardens, in the Suffolk area of Belfast, to meet some IRA members. I had no idea why he wanted me to go, nor did Davy offer any reason. He liked to work in that way with me because he knew me to be naturally curious and was confident that whatever he suggested I would wish to investigate. This would be no exception.

A freckly-faced young man in his late teens, with a noticeable baby face and dark ginger hair, opened the door and motioned me to go into a downstairs room. Once inside, he told me to sit on the single chair which was facing the wall and wait. I did as I was told but became worried when I heard no voices, because I wondered if my identity had somehow been revealed or, perhaps, that someone had seen me making phone calls from public call boxes, arousing suspicion. Five minutes later, I heard some people enter the room and my heart began to beat faster, but at no time did I even think of turning round.

'OK, Marty,' a voice said, 'did Davy tell you why you're here?'

'No,' I replied. 'He just told me to come to this address.'

'I'll tell you what it is Marty,' the voice continued. 'We want to know some things about you.'

That question put the fear of God in me. I became convinced that my true identity had been rumbled. I wondered what would happen next.

'Is it true you have your own car?' he asked.

'Yes,' I said, fearful that someone may have found the tracking device.

'Have you ever been in trouble with the police?' the voice asked.

'A few times, yes,' I replied, 'but nothing serious.'

Another voice spoke up, 'Are you well known to the peelers in your area?'

'No, not really,' I said.

The first voice asked, 'Marty, tell us, why did you join the IRA?'

I had been briefed some months earlier by the Special Branch as to exactly what I should say if IRA members ever asked me why I wanted to join the organisation. They hadn't told me anything specific to say, never giving me the exact words to remember, but they said that I should tell them that I believed in the IRA, that I wanted to serve the cause.

'I joined because I believe in what the IRA is doing,' I said, 'and so that I can help protect the people in the area where I grew up.'

They asked me how well I knew Davy Adams and I told them that I had known him for a couple of months. They asked me what I thought of him and I told them I found him to be honest and dedicated to the cause.

'Do you know that he's also well known to the peelers?' the voice asked.

'I don't know,' I lied.

They asked me how I had first met Davy Adams and I told them that it had been through Harry Fitzsimmons, a lad whom I had known all my life.

Another voice piped up, 'Fuck, I know Harry well; he's a good lad. But he's also well known to the peelers.'

After a few more questions the men left the room. I still did not move but sat facing the wall. I could feel my heart thumping, wondering what would happen next, fearing the worst. The minutes dragged by like hours.

Ten minutes later they returned. 'OK, Marty,' said the voice, 'you can turn round now.'

When I turned round I saw the two men, one of whom I recognised from the Special Branch files. The first voice belonged to Spud. The other man was in his 30s, about 5' 7" tall, medium-built with a high forehead.

Spud said, 'Now I can tell you why you're here. I'm sorry you had to face the wall while we questioned you, but it's for everyone's safety.'

'It's OK,' I replied, 'don't worry about it.'

'Marty,' he went on, 'we're setting up a new IRA unit, a new cell and we have been told a lot about you. We think you would fit in well for what we have planned. Basically, we need people who can get in and out of areas where UDR soldiers and peelers live, where they feel safe from IRA attacks.'

'OK,' I replied, 'I've been stopped by the army and the peelers many times, made to show my licence and insurance and things and then told to be on my way.'

'Do you want to come in with us, then?' he asked.

'Yes, I would,' I replied eagerly, 'that would be great.'

'There is one important point, Marty,' Spud said, sounding grave and somewhat ominous.

'What's that?' I asked, wondering what the hell he was going to say.

'You will have to keep away from Davy Adams.'

'Why's that?' I asked, knowing that Felix wouldn't welcome that news.

'Through no fault of his own, Davy is too well-known to the Branch,' he said. 'He may draw attention to you without realising it and we can't risk that. We don't want the Branch to get to know about this squad because we are going to be really successful.'

'Fair enough,' I said, but I knew that, somehow, I would continue to see Davy Adams from time to time.

Spud told me, 'I'll tell you what I want you to do, Marty. I want to put together a new cell and recruit young men, new recruits to the organisation, who are totally unknown to the RUC. I intend to use these recruits to carry out dangerous operations where the enemy feels safe: in their own homes.'

I was told to report the following night to another address, a flat in the same area of Belfast. In all, seven of us were in the room that night and our leader told us that we were all part of the new cell, along with three others we would meet at a later date.

As he talked, I checked out every one of the team, trying to remember their looks, their faces, height, weight, anything that could identify them from photographs. I was sure that I had never seen a single one of them before on any Special Branch file, except for the leader. I knew this would spell trouble for the Branch because it meant that the members of this new cell were all recent recruits. I anticipated that if this cell was being created from raw recruits, unknown to the police or Special Branch, there was the distinct probability that other cells were also being created around this time.

When I left the flat that night, I had a good idea of each man and knew that, if shown a photo, I would be able to recognise most, if not all of them.

I was surprised that at that initial meeting our first major operation was discussed. The leader told us that two RUC patrol men had been targeted in the Rathcoole area north of Belfast, a fiercely loyalist area.

He said, 'This area is full of UVF and UFF loyalist paramilitaries and if we can kill two RUC men in that area it will be a real fucking embarrassment to the Loyalists and also a very good result for us.'

Within an hour of leaving the meeting, I phoned the Branch and spoke to Felix, who called me back at the phone box. I explained in detail what had happened that night. He sounded concerned at the news and told me it would be necessary for me to meet him, as a matter of urgency, the next morning. I also told him of the planned attack in Rathcoole and he said he would take care of that.

The following morning, I met Felix and Mo at one of our meeting places. They were waiting for me in their parked car. As they listened to me relating everything that had happened the previous night, I could see they were both worried men. Felix told me that the previous night he had spoken to senior officers within the Branch. He asked if I would drive off and return an hour later to meet one of their most senior officers.

Felix, Mo and the senior officer were sitting in the blacked-out van when I returned. Felix asked me to explain to the officer, who surprisingly wore a hand-gun in a shoulder holster, everything that had happened the previous night. He also produced three more photographic files which I had never seen before, full of pictures of IRA suspects from other areas of Belfast. Once again, I went diligently through each page of photos, but recognised none of those whom I had met the previous night.

Before I left, Felix asked me to keep them closely informed of any meetings that I was asked to attend and, more importantly, if I heard of any operations being planned.

Over the following months, the cell meet, on average, once a week. We would be encouraged to find sympathetic Republicans prepared to offer their homes to conceal weapons, Semtex, ammunition and bomb-making materials. We were actively discouraged from keeping any IRA material or weapons in our own homes, for fear of being raided.

I decided to discuss the matter with my Special Branch controllers and suggested to them that I should keep whatever was necessary in my home because I knew the Branch could then ensure that the flat would never be searched. They agreed and told me that they would organise for a block to be put on my address, which meant that no police or army patrols would ever be permitted to enter or search my home.

At a cell meeting one night, I volunteered to keep some arms and explosives in the roof space of my flat and was advised to go and see a member of the IRA who was the area Quartermaster. I was told to go to an address off the Falls Road where I would meet a 40-year-old man with shoulder-length fair hair.

The man they described opened the door to me. 'I've been sent down to you to get some stuff,' I said.

He asked who had sent me and I gave him the name of our IRA boss.

He never asked any other question, but told me to wait until he returned. 15 minutes later the man came back and handed me 5lb of Semtex, three detonators wrapped in toilet paper and two battery packs fitted with tilt switches and timers, enough to make three under-car booby traps. He also gave me a 9mm Browning automatic and a small sock containing about seventeen 9mm rounds.

I drove straight home and immediately took the gear inside, because I knew Angie had taken baby Martin to her mother's for the day. I went into the hallway where I knew there was a small opening in the ceiling, no more than a foot square, above the cupboard. I put the gear in there, convinced that Angie would never search the roof space.

A few weeks later, my pal, Harry Fitzsimmons, asked

me if he could use my flat for a few hours one day because he needed to build an under-car booby trap. I did not bother to tell the Branch because there was no danger of anyone suddenly raiding the flat. He brought the equipment, including a magnet, in a plastic supermarket bag.

Harry put the fear of God in me that day. I knew nothing whatsoever about explosives or how they should be handled. To me, explosives spelt danger.

We went to the bathroom and Harry laid out everything on the linoleum floor. He began to cut the Semtex with a pen knife and gave it to me to hold. It felt like squidgy chewing gum, yellowish in colour with mottled orange and brown specks. It was also very, very difficult to get off any surface, including skin. We wore pink kitchen gloves. By accident, Harry cut a hole in the forefinger of one of his gloves and he was so worried that his finger-print could end up on the materials that he wound some black tape around the finger before continuing with his work. He then began to hit the Semtex with a piece of wood, striking it really hard.

'What the fuck are you doing?' I shouted. 'You'll blow us up if you go on like that.'

He just laughed at my reaction and went on beating the Semtex into the shape he wanted. I became convinced that the whole lot would explode, and backed out of the room and went and stood in the hallway expecting an explosion, fearing the worst, wondering what on earth I would tell Angie if our flat had been blown apart by an IRA bomb exploding accidentally.

About 90 minutes later, a long time after I had become bored watching him, Harry announced, 'That's it, come and have a look.'

He was proud of his work, very proud. He explained to me exactly what he had done, but I didn't pay that much attention for I had no wish ever to become an explosives officer for the IRA.

Despite my forebodings about the bomb, I agreed to keep it in my flat for a few days, in the same space I had hidden the weapons.

I immediately informed my handlers about the bomb and they told me they were keen to see it.

Because of the possibility of Angela seeing the bomb, I arranged a meeting after midnight. I waited until she had gone to bed and then told her I had to go out and see someone. I quickly took all the gear out of the roof space and put it into a carrier bag before driving off to meet Felix and his mate.

On this occasion, the Branch were taking no chances. I drove behind Felix and Mo in their car and another Branch car immediately drew up behind me as protection, escorting me to Castlereagh Police Station. I carried the bag in and they immediately took out the contents, spreading everything on the table. A photographer and a bomb expert came into the room, photographed the booby trap from every conceivable angle and then took it away for examination. They were gone the best part of two hours.

When they returned to the room, the bomb expert explained to me that the Semtex had been injected with a chemical of some type, which would ensure that the bomb would never explode. They produced the Polaroid snaps to check that the bomb had been re-assembled in precisely the same manner, so that not even the bomb-maker himself would think anyone had tampered with his masterpiece.

When I arrived home, however, sometime after 3.00am, I was about to put the booby-trap bomb back into the roof space when I noticed a small piece of black wire was missing. I searched everywhere, but to no avail. And after twice searching my car I phoned the Branch.

'This is Carol,' I said to the telephonist. 'Is there any chance of contacting Felix very, very urgently. Please tell him to phone me at home.'

I sat by the phone not daring to move until Felix phoned back. The last thing I wanted was to wake Angie. It was almost dawn when the call came through.

'What the fuck's up with you?' Felix said jokingly, 'Do you never sleep?'

'No, this is real serious shit,' I said. 'I've lost part of the bomb.'

'Jesus,' he said, sounding concerned, 'are you sure?'

'I'm positive.'

'Have you checked your bag, your car?'

'Yes, yes,' I said, 'I've been here for the past hour searching high and low. I can't find it.'

'Stay by the phone and I'll call you back. I'll get someone to search the office.'

Fifteen minutes later Felix phoned back. 'Found it,' he said. 'Now for fuck's sake, go to bed and we'll meet tomorrow. Will you be able to connect it?'

'Yes, it'll be easy,' I said, 'It just connects to the battery.'

The following morning, I met Felix as arranged and took the little piece of black wire back home. As I was kneeling on the hall floor connecting the piece of wire, I heard footsteps on the stairs. I froze, hoping the person was going to one of the other three flats on the floor above. The footsteps stopped outside the door and I knew instinctively Angie had unexpectedly returned. In desperation, I stuffed the bomb back into the plastic bag before she opened the door.

I am sure that Angie could see by the look on my face that I had been caught red-handed, though I tried to act as nonchalantly as possible.

'What are you doing on the floor?' she said, rather bemused.

'I'm just putting some stuff in this bag,' I said, collecting it up.

'What is it?' she asked.

'It's just some stuff for the car,' I lied, trying to sound matter-of-fact.

She asked no further questions and went through into the sitting room with Martin and the shopping. From that day on, however, Angie knew that I was hiding something from her.

A few days later, I decided to tell Angie the truth because I realised that this secret life I was leading was beginning to break down the trust between us.

One evening, after tea, I said, 'Angie, listen. I have something to tell you.'

'What's that?'

'The other day when you came into the house', I said, 'and you found me in the hall with this stuff I was putting in a bag.'

'Yes, I remember,' she said. 'Well, what about it?'

It seemed as though she knew what I was about to tell her and she looked me straight in the eye.

'It was stuff that I was making for the IRA,' I said.

The news didn't seem to shock her at all. 'What were you doing with it?' she asked.

'Because, Angie,' I said, taking a deep breath, ' I am now a member of the IRA.'

Her face changed. She looked worried, anxious, and I wondered what she was about to say. After a few seconds she told me, 'Well, I hope you know what you're doing, Marty ... I hope you know what you're getting yourself involved in.'

I had thought that Angie would be furious at my confession and was surprised that she showed so much maturity about the whole affair. I realised in that instant, however, that Angie had hit the nail on the head when she said she hoped that I knew what I was becoming involved in.

Angie's remark made me think seriously about everything I was doing for the first time since I had officially joined the IRA. And the more I thought about it, the more I realised that I seemed to be on a slippery slope, from the day I agreed to work for the Branch to the day I swore an oath of allegiance to the cause. I realised how deep I had become involved with both organisations, and matters seemed to be accelerating. The IRA was keen for me to become a member of an active service unit involved in killings and bombings. I was now storing bombs and guns in my own house, risking trips at night to show them to the Branch and knowing that, at any moment, that I could be seen and identified by one of the many IRA men who knew me. From the daily conversations I had overheard, I knew that the IRA were always suspicious of their own men, and I knew what the consequences would be. The thought sent a shudder through me.

CHAPTER EIGHT

THOUGH SPUD, MY NEW IRA BOSS, HAD WARNED ME to keep away from the IRA's intelligence wing, Davy Adams still stayed in contact, asking me to carry out intelligence work on his behalf. My Branch handlers were keen for me to continue my burgeoning relationship with Davy, because they were confident that the relationship would lead them to more IRA members, widening their network of known suspects.

I kept quiet about the work I did for Davy, never even mentioning his name to other IRA members, because I had no wish to be the centre of controversy between two such powerful men within the organisation. I realised that I would be the loser, and the Special Branch could possibly lose valuable contacts.

There was so much happening in both Davy's intelligence area and Spud's active service unit that Felix wanted me to meet them four or five times a week. I knew that at some future date the Branch would probably arrest both Davy Adams and my pal Fitzi, if they could be sure a serious charge would stick. In the meantime, however, I didn't want them to arrest either man because of the close relationships I had developed with them.

I would tell Felix, 'It's bad enough giving information about these two whenever I have something to tell. But it would be virtually impossible for me to provide the Branch with this intelligence if I believed that as a direct result of my tip-off either of these men would be arrested, charged and probably end up doing 20 years.'

I would appeal to Felix and his mate Mo to understand my viewpoint, and I believe he did take note because no move was made against either men from any piece of intelligence supplied by me. I also realised, of course, that the Branch was receiving high-quality intelligence from my close involvement with both men, which would immediately dry up if they were arrested.

From the beginning of our relationship I had faith in the Branch and I trusted those men I dealt with on a day-to-day basis, particularly Felix. I realised that my handlers had superior officers who would order the arrest of both Davy and Harry if they believed it would be beneficial to the wider intelligence scene. Throughout the years I worked with the Branch, my handlers constantly give me advice, and their advice always turned out to be honest and beneficial to me. I knew that I was putting my very life in their hands on a daily basis, and I believe that they never betrayed that trust. Felix became someone special to me because of the understanding and trust we built up during the years I was working as a British agent. If I was ever in doubt I would seek his advice and always take it. He never let me down. But I was also vaguely aware that, if the senior officers believed it necessary, they would sacrifice me, probably without a second thought!

There were occasions, however, when I did not

report certain IRA activities to the Branch, particularly if they involved Davy or Harry. If, for example, either of them were organising arms, ammunition or bombs to be moved from one hiding place to another, I would not bother to tell the Branch. But I always made sure the Branch knew if either Davy or Fitzi were involved in activity that might result in the death or injury of anyone.

*   *   *

One evening, in early September 1990, I was driving home with Angela in the car when I was amazed to see Harry Fitzsimmons walking along near my home dressed in a smart suit, collar and tie and with his hair smartly combed. I ususally saw Harry wearing jeans, a sweat shirt, trainers and a baseball cap. With him, also dressed smartly in a blazer, blouse and skirt was Caroline Mooreland, a woman whom I knew to be a stalwart IRA sympathiser.

I stopped and, laughing, asked Harry, 'Where are you going dressed like that? Are you going to some wedding or something?'

'Alright, kid?' he asked, not answering the question. Caroline said nothing.

'Where are you going?' I asked again.

'Just going down the town,' he replied.

I asked them if they wanted me to drive them into town and Harry said, 'Great,' and got in the back with Caroline. During the ten-minute drive neither spoke a word, which surprised me. However, I thought they were probably being ultra cautious because they did not want to speak openly in front of Angie.

I dropped them opposite the Royal Courts of Justice in the centre of Belfast. As I drove away, I checked in my rear-view mirror and saw them run across the road and disappear into the Buttery Bar, a well-known pub frequented by lawyers, court officials and police officers.

I sensed that Harry and Caroline were bent on causing trouble that night, dressed as they were, and I wondered if they could possibly be planting a bomb. I immediately returned home, dropped off Angie at her mother's house and said I would return shortly to pick her and the baby up. Then I raced home, pressed the radio button and drove for a meeting with one of my handlers. I told them about Harry and Caroline and they told me they would immediately arrange for the pub to be checked for any suspicious packages. Before I went home, they also asked me to keep a close eye on the couple.

By accident, I ran into Harry the next morning and he told me that he had stayed the night at Caroline's place. He winked and asked me to cover for him if his wife asked where he had spent the night.

Exactly seven days after I had dropped Harry and Caroline at the Buttery Bar, a home-made hand grenade was thrown at the back of the Law Courts shortly after midnight and a search of the area began. As a result of the information I had given the Branch, however, army bomb disposal experts immediately searched the Buttery Bar and quickly discovered a large 15lb Semtex bomb in a woman's handbag hidden under a seat. Because of the intelligence they had received, the experts were able to defuse the bomb with time to spare.

Later, I heard from other IRA sources that the plan had been for the bomb to explode one hour after the grenade had been thrown, expecting that the area would have been flooded by Army and RUC personnel. No one would know, however, why the bomb failed to go off.

Four years later, Caroline Mooreland, 34, the mother of three young children, who was separated from her husband, would be murdered by the IRA as a police informer. She had been kidnapped, held, interrogated and tortured for three days before being shot, her body dumped near the border at Rosslea, County Fermanagh. According to the IRA, Caroline Mooreland had been interviewed by the RUC and had been persuaded to become an informer. She would be only the second woman to be murdered by the IRA as an informer over a ten-year period.

Father Brian McCluskey, from Rosslea, who was called from his church to give Caroline the last rites of the Catholic church, described her face as 'mutilated beyond recognition and her head completely disfigured'.

But many of her friends and neighbours in the Catholic Republican area of Belfast did not believe that she had ever worked for the RUC. Caroline Mooreland was a quiet woman, who had not only raised three children and worked with the IRA but had also found time to organise the West Belfast Muscular Dystrophy Association for a number of years, raising thousands of pounds for the charity after her brother died from the illness.

The Catholic community was outraged by the torture and murder of Caroline Mooreland. Father Luke McWilliams told mourners at St Paul's Church that the community had been 'revolted by the barbarous savagery and shocked by the vile manner of her dying.'

He added, 'Like all of you, I'm sure, I was haunted by the cruelty and inhumanity meted out by her murderers.'

Reading of the appalling torture and murder of Caroline some three years after leaving Belfast, I realised how ruthless the IRA could be with either guilty or innocent suspects.

*   *   *

I never flattered myself with the idea that Davy Adams found my companionship to be anything other than a means to an end. I am sure that the principle reason Davy and I spent so much time together was the simple fact that I owned a car and was happy to drive him around. Davy had never learned to drive and, to my knowledge, never owned a car. I, on the other hand, was only too happy to drive him wherever he wanted to go, checking possible targets, meeting other IRA members and attending meetings. The Branch were also very happy for me to drive Davy around the city because they could track our vehicle and I would be able to inform them whom he had met and what the conversations had been about.

It was during one of our car rides across the city that I heard about a possible IRA operation being planned on the Larne–Stranraer ferry across the Irish Sea which the IRA heard was being used every other week to transport 15 British Army three-ton trucks bringing supplies from Scotland to the troops stationed in the Province.

An IRA intelligence unit had managed to plant one of their young volunteers, whose first name was also Martin, on the ferry. He worked as a ship's hand and he reported back that the dozen army vehicles were loaded at Stranraer every other Saturday, arriving at Larne the same afternoon. He also reported that the last two army trucks leaving the ferry on arrival in Northern Ireland were usually full of soldiers.

Davy Adams decided that I should become involved with this operation because I would be happy to drive to Larne and report back to him. I met Martin outside a café in the centre of Larne and he told me the details of the fortnightly crossing of the army supply vehicles. He also told me that the RUC, responsible for checking security and keeping an eye out for known IRA and

Loyalist terrorists, would drive a van to the port and leave it unattended while they checked the ferries arriving at Larne. He thought that the RUC van would be a perfect target for a booby-trap bomb.

'How often do you see the van?' I asked him.

'Every time a ferry arrives, the RUC arrives in the van while they check the passengers and cars coming off the ferry.'

'Are you sure no one is left in the van as a guard?' I asked him.

'No, definitely not,' he said, 'I couldn't believe it myself, but every time I come into port I see the van, left on its own and unattended.'

I had been told to check that the intelligence he had supplied was accurate, so the following Saturday I drove back to Larne and made my way to the ferry port. I checked the army trucks being loaded that day and counted 15 vehicles.

Having reported back to Davy Adams, I was sent to discuss the operation with a highly experienced IRA explosives officer named Tony. This man had a formidable reputation and he would be responsible for many of the huge IRA bombs that devastated the centre of Belfast during the late 1980s.

Tony, a quiet, dark-haired man in his mid-30s, asked me questions as we discussed the operation.

'What is the objective?', he asked. 'What does Davy want to do?'

I told him that the idea was to plant a bomb at the side of the road and take out the last two trucks, which were understood to be full of soldiers returning from Scotland.

He asked me for details of the road that the army trucks drove along as they left port.

'It's single-lane traffic.'

'Are cars parked on the road at that point?'

'No,' I replied, 'but there are a few lay-bys for vehicles along the route.'

'That's good,' he said. 'This should be a real easy one. What I propose is to stage the bombing at holiday time. We can put a caravan packed with explosives on the back of a car, as though a family is visiting Northern Ireland for a holiday.'

Tony became so keen to carry out the operation that he asked me to drive him to the area so that he could select the exact spot to park the caravan and where he could lay a command wire to trigger the bomb. I drove into Larne pointing out two of the lay-bys.

'This is very, very good, ideal,' he enthused. ' Drive on, turn round and drive slowly past the first lay-by. I'm certain that's the spot to park the caravan.'

When we turned round and drove away from Larne, Tony became even more enthusiastic. 'This is brilliant, fucking fabulous,' he said. ' If we can't stiff at least a dozen Brits in this operation we're real wankers.'

After passing the spot, he asked me to take the first left turn off the main road and drive as near to the lay-by as possible, so that he could estimate the length of the command wire and the best vantage point from which to trigger the bomb. He also wanted to ensure that the bomber would be capable of making a quick getaway.

As we drove back to Belfast, Tony enthused about the operation. 'I'm going to go and see Davy Adams about this one. This is a cracking op. I think I should get involved in this.'

Later, as though speaking to himself, Tony said, 'To carry out that job, a 1,000lb of mix would blow one of those lorries off the fucking road. But this is a chance of a lifetime, so I think we'll up the mix to 1,500lb. That should really blast the fuck out of both vehicles. If both those trucks are full of soldiers, hardly any will get out alive. Something like this only comes once and you have to get it right.'

The following day, I contacted the Branch and met Felix and Mo at a pre-arranged spot. I told them everything I had learned during my trips to Larne and the conversation with Tony.

As soon as I mentioned Tony's name, both Felix and Mo became extremely interested. 'If Tony's involved it means they are deadly serious,' Felix said. 'He is one of their top bomb makers. He is also an evil bastard; we will have to sort this one out, and quickly.'

As Felix sat thinking of what I had told him, he commented, 'My God, I could tell you some stories about that man. Over the years, he has been the bomb-maker in some of their most spectacular bombings.'

Before I left my handlers, I told them that I would not be able to supply them with any further intelligence about Larne because I had only been helping out Davy Adams and I doubted if I would be given any further information about the bombing.

I added, 'I don't often ask you this Felix, but on this occasion will you make sure the information is treated very carefully, as there are only very few people who know about this operation and they could easily put two and two together and realise I tipped you off.'

'Yes, you're right,' he said, 'OK.'

I had realised that this would be a perfect operation for the Special Branch to monitor and arrest the IRA bombers as they were parking the caravan in the lay-by or laying the command wire. And as I had told them that Tony himself might be actively involved, there would be a golden opportunity to arrest one of the IRA's most experienced bomb-makers. As I would have nothing further to do with this operation, however, the finger of suspicion could well be pointed at me.

I told all this to Felix and Mo.

'Yes, you're right,' Felix said, 'we won't wait until the bombers strike; we will find out which units of the British Army are using Larne and warn them to stop using that route for a while as the IRA are planning a spectacular. In that way, no one in the IRA will suspect the information has come from you.'

I respected Felix for saying that because it showed me that protecting me had become more important than arresting one of the IRA's top bomb-makers.

A few weeks later, I was chatting to Tony about another project. He told me, 'Hey, Marty, did you hear about the Larne job?'

'No, why?' I asked.

'It seems the bastards were only using the Larne ferry for a short while, because they don't go there any more. We had the gear already, the mix prepared and packed in the caravan. As usual, before an operation we took a last look one Saturday afternoon and there were no army trucks to be seen. I don't think they've used the port since.'

'That's surprising,' I said, 'from what the lad told me.'

'I was devastated when I heard there were no more trucks,' he said. 'I thought that job was too good to be true.'

The more time I spent with the IRA, the less I was seeing of Angie and Martin. Angie would be out of bed early in the morning taking care of Martin, and I would awake most mornings at around eight o'clock. I never bothered with breakfast or even a cup of tea, but would leave the flat for a meeting with either the IRA or the Branch. For a young man who was permanently on the dole, I must have been one of the busiest lads in the entire Province!

It seemed that I hardly had any time for myself, let alone Angie and Martin, and that concerned me. Our relationship was still strong and I loved being with her. When we were together we still laughed and joked and our love life was still great.

Most of the time, including weekends, I hardly ever return home during the hours of daylight. And I never ate at home, not even on Saturdays and Sundays. I would usually grab a bite to eat in the cafés around Belfast or simply eat a couple of sandwiches on the hoof. I would try to return home each evening at about 6.00pm to relax with Angie, watching TV or lying around with her on the settee. But I was serving two masters and both were becoming increasingly demanding. If they wanted to see me, no matter if it was day or night, I could not say no, but would have to leave whatever I was doing and report in.

Time and again Angie would ask whether there was any chance of me doing less running around. She complained that I hardly ever played with Martin, or fed or cuddled him. As I would feel guilty about not seeing either Angie or Martin I would salve my conscience by giving Angie loads of money. I would hand her perhaps £100 or £200 a time to go out and buy clothes for Martin and herself or toys.

I didn't realise it at the time, but that would be a big mistake, for Angie wondered how a young man on the dole had access to so much money. Her mother would also ask Angie where I was getting all the money, for she would often accompany Angie on her shopping sprees and would see the amount of money I had given Angie to spend. They had always been close and their relationship strengthened after Martin's arrival.

When I felt guilty about neglecting Angie and Martin, I would spend more time with them for a while until the pressure mounted once again and I would be flying around Belfast, attending meetings all over the place, checking out possible IRA operations, running Davy Adams around the city and making sure I had time enough to brief my handlers.

On one occasion, I took Angie down south across the border to the Republic and stopped in a little café for a meal and we went for a walk together. On the way back, we stopped at a toy shop just north of the border and I bought a child's swing and see-saw set which came in a large pack. We had no garden, but Angie fell in love with it and, as she had applied for a council house, she hoped the swing might bring her luck.

On another occasion, I returned home to find Angie in tears. She told me that her elder brother, Thomas, had been horrifically beaten by an IRA punishment squad for simply joy-riding. They had left him semi-conscious in a deep hole so badly crippled that he could not climb out to get assistance. He was fortunate to survive.

The beating of Tommy angered and frustrated me. I was angry that some pathetic IRA men could beat a young Catholic lad for simply driving around in stolen cars, and was frustrated that I could do nothing to avenge him. Angie behaved brilliantly, handling the situation with great maturity. She knew that I was involved with the IRA, and yet she never asked me if I could find his attackers or do anything to have them punished in return. All this despite the fact that she had always been close to her brother, who had been her protector and friend when they were growing up together. Their mother, who had separated, brought them up alone and determined that they should remain a close-knit family.

I never forget what those bastards in the punishment squad had done to Tommy. I kept my silence, however, determined to wait until an opportunity arose for me to tackle them and, if possible, take revenge on the cowards.

I decided that it would be impossible for me, given my position inside the IRA, to organise for the bastards to be given a bloody good beating. But I was determined to get even with the evil thugs.

A year later, I was driving through the Ballymurphy Estate when I saw one of the bastards who had beaten Tommy walking into a house. During the 12 months since his beating, Tommy was never far from my mind. And yet I was also angry at the senior Republicans, men whom I respected, who could apparently permit such awful beatings. The time had arrived for me to get my own back.

With revenge in my heart, I phoned the Special Branch and told them that they should search the man's address within hours because I had seen him carrying a hold-all into the house. Because of my position as an agent, I had no need to give any reason why a search should be implemented immediately but the intimation was that he was carrying weapons.

Within an hour I saw a large number of RUC personnel and the Army descend on the street, surround the man's house and begin a room by room search of the premises while the man was held in the house. Six or seven hours later, after tearing up the floor boards, pulling down the ceilings and smashing the walls in their determination to find arms or explosives, the search was called off. Nothing had been discovered.

It did not surprise me one jot for the man was carrying nothing when I saw him. I knew it was wrong for me to abuse my position, but I simply could not resist the temptation of giving this bastard a taste of his own medicine. He may not have received a beating, but his house had been trashed.

The next time I met Felix and Mo I broached the matter.

'Hard luck, Marty,' Felix said, 'there was nothing in that house. You're usually a hundred per cent with your intelligence.'

'I know,' I replied, and I could not stop laughing.

'What are you up to, Marty, you little cunt,' said Felix. 'When you laugh like that, I know you're up to something. Come on, what is it?'

'Felix, mate,' I replied, ' if you had found something in that house it would have been a fucking miracle,' and I burst out laughing again.

'Come on,' he said.

'Do you remember I told you about the bastards who beat Angie's brother?'

'Aye,' he said, 'about a year ago?'

'Yes, that's it. Well that person's house you searched the other day was one of the bastards who beat him.'

They both roared with laughter. 'God, Marty,' he said, 'I have to hand it to you; you never forget a thing.'

'Listen, Marty,' Felix said, 'do you still want to get even with them?'

'Of course I fuckin' do. It still upsets Angie and I'm not going to rest until I get those bastards put behind bars.'

'Marty,' Felix said, 'give me their names will you and I'll see what can be done.'

Happily I gave their names and addresses and wondered what would happen. Sometime later, an IRA friend of mine, named Jimmy, who also despised the punishment squads, called me over as we were having a drink in a Republican club. More than a year before I had explained to Jimmy that I knew the names of four of the men who were involved in some way in Tommy's beating.

'Did you hear what happened to your mates?' Jimmy asked.

'Who are you talking about?' I asked.

'Some of that punishment squad,' he replied.

'Why, what happened?' I asked.

'Three of them were stopped by the DMSUs the other night as they were driving through the estate. They got into a bit of an argument with the RUC officers. They were arrested and given a bit of a hiding at the same time.'

As I drank my glass of Coke I couldn't hide a smile, for I realised that the hiding they received bore the hallmark of one of Felix's little 'behind the scenes' operations. He had kept his word.

*   *   *

It appeared to me that the IRA were stepping up their campaign of violence, because I became even busier throughout 1990. They appeared to stop targeting major populated areas or destroying shops in Belfast and other major towns in Northern Ireland, preferring to concentrate on taking out RUC men and soldiers with booby-trap car bombs.

The IRA's intelligence unit had one of their men working full-time as a taxi driver and he would frequently pick up soldiers from Palace Barracks, Holywood, to take them out to clubs and pubs in Belfast City Centre. No one would have known that these lads were soldiers, for they always wore civvies and were permitted to wear their hair quite long so that they would not be conspicuous with an army-style short-back-and-sides.

The driver got to know some of the soldiers quite well and would sometimes take them to Belfast City Airport when they were going on home leave. At other times, he drove soldiers to Larne to catch the ferry.

The taxi driver reported back that most Friday evenings he would drop four or five paratroopers at one particular spot near Belfast City Centre and they would then walk 50 yards down a narrow lane to one of their favourite pubs. Down one side of the lane was a building site. I was detailed to reconnoitre the site to see if an attack could be made against the paras. It was decided that the only possible method would be for an IRA man to climb the scaffolding overlooking the narrow lane and drop a large, spring-loaded sweet jar packed with Semtex, which would explode on impact. The bomb officer predicted that the resulting blast would kill or maim most of the soldiers.

Having checked out the operation it seemed to me that it would be quite easy for an IRA unit to carry out the attack. I passed all the information to the Branch and, as a result, British Army commanders declared a number of Belfast city pubs and clubs out of bounds for a while.

I had no idea at that time that a taxi driver had been responsible for targeting the soldiers. It would be nearly a year later when I discovered the identity of the IRA man responsible, and immediately informed my controllers. The taxi driver was arrested.

In August, 1990, Harry Fitzsimmons asked me to travel with him to Gilford, a pretty village in County Down, to check out an RUC Constable who parked his red Fiat Regata outside his home each night. The car was parked behind a row of terraced houses off Stanmore Road on the outskirts of the village.

After Fitzi and I checked out the location, it seemed a straightforward operation. Fitzi would have no problem attaching a booby trap bomb under the car one night. Another man, John McFadden, would also be involved in the operation.

I notified Felix of the plan and he asked me to pick him up and take him to the Gilford house. After checking the house, he told me to go ahead but to keep him updated at every stage.

On Wednesday, 29 August, I drove the booby-trapped bomb – 1.5lb of Semtex – having been informed by Felix that the road I would use between Belfast and Gilford would be free of check points at that hour. I was still desperately worried that I might be stopped by an RUC or army patrol or, even worse, that the bomb might explode prematurely. Having left the bomb in a pre-arranged spot, I knew that Harry and his mate John would take over, fix the booby trap, and drive away.

I knew that the Branch had moved the man and his family out of the house earlier that day, and had stationed their own armed men inside, in case of trouble.

Early the following morning, I turned on the radio to hear the news on Downtown Radio which reported that a bomb had been discovered under an RUC's man's car in the village of Gilford.

Later that morning, I went round to see Harry, to commiserate with him for the failed operation. He was drinking a cup of tea.

'I'm fucking depressed,' he said. 'All that work and the fucker goes and finds the charge. I could have sworn that we were told that he never checked his car.'

After a few minutes, I left Harry and went for a pre-arranged meeting with Felix. He was happy at how well the operation had gone. I was happy that the Special Branch had kept their word and had not arrested Harry. It also meant, of course, that no suspicion would fall on me.

About two months later, Harry, John and I were given another job to carry out by IRA intelligence, placing a booby-trap bomb under a Black Mark 3 Ford Fiesta

1.6S, which was parked in the loading bay at Carryduff Shopping Centre, in the south of Belfast. The car was owned by a member of the Security forces.

I told Felix about the planned operation, and, after checking with senior officers, he told me to let the operation go ahead.

The plan was for John and Harry to place the bomb under the car while I would stand at the entrance to the loading bay with a 9mm Browning, keeping watch for any RUC or army patrols. As John was lying under the side of the car the alarm suddenly went off. Shocked, John automatically jerked his head, cracking his skull on the underside of the vehicle. The three of us walked away from the bay, climbed into the car and drove off.

The following day, Felix told me they had deliberately set off the alarm as they watched the operation from a vantage point not far from the vehicle. They had also videoed the entire operation. The next day I read about the incident in the Belfast Telegraph, which reported that the device, containing 1.5lb of Semtex had been been defused by army bomb experts. Sadly, however, the article went on to report that in another IRA operation, a 42-year-old, part-time member of the UDR, Albert Cooper, had been killed by a booby-trap bomb in Cookstown. When I read of such cowardly killings it made me realise that I was indeed carrying out vital work. When I thought of the people whose lives we were saving, I felt happy that I was working with the Special Branch.

But Harry Fitzsimmons' days as an IRA bomber would soon come to an end.

On the morning of Monday, 3 December 1990, Harry and his IRA mate, John McFadden, were arrested by the RUC in a rear attic bedroom of a house in Brookvale Street, north Belfast. The two men were discovered kneeling on the floor. Next to them was a white plastic bag containing gloves and a torch. In a bedroom opposite, police found a quantity of Semtex explosive, a timer power unit and magnets, all of which were neatly laid out.

In the roof-space, police also found another plastic bag containing a nearly-completed under-car explosive device, a 9mm Browning, ammunition, detonators and adhesive tape.

The day before, I had arranged to meet Harry and had given him the 9mm Browning, an under-car booby trap and other bomb-making equipment, which he had asked me to supply for a planned operation. He must have been followed by an RUC surveillance team from the moment I handed over the gear. I had no idea that the RUC were targeting Harry, for I believed that no decision had yet been made to arrest him.

I only discovered that Harry had been arrested when I called at his house later that day. I was sitting chatting to his wife Charlene when an RUC Land Rover pulled up and an Inspector knocked at the door.

He walked into the house and told Charlene, 'Your husband has been arrested.'

She asked why, but the Inspector would not say. He asked who else lived in the house and demanded my name and address.

I was furious. The Special Branch, my mates, had told me that Harry Fitzsimmons would not be arrested and yet he had been. At a meeting with Felix the following day, I said, 'I'm not happy with Harry being picked up.'

Felix replied, 'Listen, Marty. That had nothing to do with us or with you.'

'Bollocks,' I said. 'I just told you only two days ago that I was giving him that stuff and, surprise, surprise, he gets arrested.'

Felix said, 'Marty, there are other people targeting IRA suspects as well as you. The information that got Harry Fitzsimmons came from someone else at the other side of Belfast.'

'I don't believe a word you're telling me,' I said. 'Of course you knew what the fuck was going on. If you're going to start telling me lies, I'm going to stop working for you, because I won't have any trust in you.'

'Listen, Marty ...' he began, but I wouldn't let him finish the sentence.

'If I'm prepared to put my life on the line for you people, the least you can do is tell me the truth. I live among these people, I'm a member of the IRA only because *you* want me to be, not because *I* want to be. I haven't got a gun under my pillow every night like you fellas.'

Felix and Mo could see that I was deeply angry at what had happened. But I also wanted them to see things in perspective, to see things from my point of view.

'It doesn't matter to me what the fuck Harry Fitzi does with his life,' I shouted, 'but I don't want to be held responsible for him getting arrested.'

After I had vented my fury, Felix tried to calm me down. 'Marty, there's an old saying which I agree with one hundred per cent: never bite the hand that feeds you. I would not do anything to expose you or harm you in anyway. I've known you for three years, you little cunt, and I've got to like you. I can promise you that we had nothing whatsoever to do with his arrest.'

That day I left the meeting feeling unhappy and depressed and not sure whether Felix and Mo were, on this occasion, telling me the truth. I wondered if the decision to arrest Fitzi had been taken by a superior officer and was therefore out of Felix's control. I had no idea whether Felix was telling me the truth but I gave him the benefit of the doubt. I understood that there would be other agents working for the SB who would also come across vital information. I decided to forget the matter but to make sure that I took even greater care what intelligence I passed on in future.

*   *   *

In December 1990, Davy Adams introduced me to a close friend of his whom he had known for many years, a man named Paul, slightly built and clean shaven with dark brown hair, who would usually wear an open-necked shirt with a T-shirt beneath, and jeans and trainers. Whenever Davy and I met this man, I would be surprised how openly Davy talked in front of him, discussing IRA business that I would only have discussed with Davy in private, when no one else was around.

On one of these occasions, I was introduced to Paul's girlfriend, a slim, short, blond-haired woman in her 40s who had obviously taken good care of herself. Davy explained that the woman was a celebrated actress who had appeared in many plays in Ireland as well as a number of television films in the UK. Remarkably, she was also the mother of seven children.

At one of my regular meetings with Felix and Mo, I mentioned that I had met a woman with Davy Adams, for whom he showed a certain respect, as though she was a woman of some importance. Neither Felix nor Mo took much notice of what I was telling them, nodding and taking the occasional note.

'What did you say was this woman's name?' one of them asked.

'I didn't,' I replied.

'Well, did you find out her name?' Mo said.

'Yes.'

'Can you remember it?' Felix asked.

'Of course I can,' I replied, 'do you think I've no brain in my head?'

'What was it?' he asked again.

'Rosena Brown,' I said.

I had barely finished telling them her surname when they yelled 'Rosena Brown!' in unison, and turned to look at me in astonishment.

'Yes,' I repeated, 'Rosena Brown.'

'She is perhaps one of the most important IRA operators we have ever had to track,' Felix said. 'She's dynamite. She has been questioned time and again by our people, put under tremendous pressure, but has never said a word.'

He went on, 'Marty, I can't impress on you how important she could be. She's a dangerous woman. We have been trying to get someone close to her for years but we've never succeeded. Get as close to her as you possibly can and keep us informed.'

CHAPTER NINE

SOME DAYS AFTER MY CONVERSATION WITH FELIX AND MO, I was given an opportunity to establish some sort of relationship with Rosena Brown when Davy Adams asked me to accompany her to Andersonstown. She was going to visit an IRA activist.

I took her to the address and waited outside in the car for ten minutes. I had no idea whom she was seeing, but I knew that the Branch would be tracking my car and would probably discover the name of the person living at the address.

On her return, Rosena said, 'Marty, would you do me a favour?'

'Yes,' I replied, happy to maintain the relationship with one of the IRA's most important operators, 'what is it?'

'Would you take me to the city centre, because I have to meet someone there?'

'Yes, of course,' I said, 'but I don't want to take the car because of all the parking restrictions and RUC check points. It would be better if we went in a black taxi.'

'That's fine, thanks.'

Rosena Brown always dressed smartly, usually in new jeans and a fresh, clean shirt or smart sweater. Her hair always appeared well groomed, her make-up was applied immaculately with only a hint of lipstick, and her nails were manicured. She also smoked, although she wasn't a chain-smoker, and she would carry small, smart hand-bags.

Seconds after the taxi dropped us at the rank in Castle Street, Rosena and I were nearly knocked over by another taxi which was speeding to join the rank. Rosena had to jump, literally jump, out of the way of the taxi, otherwise she would have been hit.

Rosena put her hand to her heart, realising that she had narrowly escaped being run down, 'Jesus!' she said. 'What an idiot. He would have hit me if I hadn't jumped out of the way.'

I shouted at the driver, 'You fuckin' dickhead! Watch where you're going.'

He replied, 'Shut the fuck up,' as he parked his taxi in the rank.

I turned and walked up to him as Rosena said, 'Don't worry, Marty, come on, let him be.'

But the driver had annoyed me, for he was swearing at us when he had been entirely at fault. I walked up to the driver's window.

'What are you slobbering about, big mouth?' I asked him as I stood with my face only a few inches away from him.

He must have realised that I was furious, as he tried to apologise saying that he hadn't seen us crossing the road.

Rosena came and pulled at my sleeve, urging me to leave the taxi driver alone. But I wanted to have the last word. Seeing that he was wearing glasses, I said, 'You should get yourself a pair of fucking binoculars instead of those glasses, then you might see people. Are you fuckin' blind or something?'

I was on the verge of thumping him in the face but the driver looked away and said nothing, so I walked away with Rosena.

'You must take care,' Rosena advised me as we walked down the street, 'you've got a terrible temper.'

During the following few weeks and months, I sometimes saw Rosena every other day. Now and then I sent to her home, a terraced council house in Cliftonville. The house was tidy and the three younger children whom I saw from time to time always appeared well behaved. I would often see the children cleaning and tidying the house which surprised me. I could tell that they respected their mother, never giving her cheek and always appearing to be obedient and polite.

There were those in the IRA, however, who were becoming concerned about Rosena's safety. They were worried that she could be easily targeted and executed by the loyalist paramilitaries, because the area where she lived was surrounded by staunch Protestants.

On one occasion, I heard Brian Gillen, who was then head of the IRA Belfast Brigade, speaking of his concern for Rosena. 'I think we should try and get her moved,' he said, 'she's far too exposed where she lives. She's a sitting duck in that house.'

Senior IRA men knew that it would be a brilliant coup for the Loyalists if they managed to kill her. It would also be highly embarrassing for the IRA, for Rosena was known as one of the organisation's most important and successful intelligence officers.

Extensive media interest centred on a court case in March 1990, when Rosena Brown had been named as the IRA intelligence officer who had persuaded a principal officer in the infamous H Blocks of the Maze Prison to give her information, including the home addresses, of fellow prison officers.

Belfast Crown Court was told that Christopher John Hanna, aged 45, had passed the information to Rosena Brown, knowing it would be used to murder fellow officers. Rosena obtained the address of one of Hanna's colleagues, Brian Armour, 48, Vice-Chairman of the Northern Ireland Prison Officers' Association, and passed the information to an IRA active service unit. They checked out the officer's address and placed a booby-trap bomb under his car in October, 1988. The following morning, as Brian Armour drove to work, the bomb exploded, killing him instantly. The following day, a bomb was placed under the car of Thomas Murtagh, the Governor of a young offenders' centre near Belfast, but it failed to detonate.

In the court case, Mr Ronald Appleton, QC, for the prosecution, said Hanna had collected information about fellow prison officers and passed them to a woman he knew as 'Anne'. Hanna told a fellow prison officer that he had been meeting the woman, described as a 'Mata Hari-type spy'. After Rosena had picked him up in a hotel bar one night, they would kiss and cuddle in a lay-by, or meet and chat in a cemetery where his parents were buried. He told his fellow officer that he believed Anne to be a 'Provo'.

Hanna claimed that he was acting under duress, after being intimidated by threats against his daughter and grandson. He was jailed for life.

The court was told that Rosena was questioned several times by Special Branch officers but was never charged. It was also stated in court that the Special Branch went as far as trying to recruit Rosena as a double agent but with no success. During questioning,

Rosena would sit saying nothing, refusing to answer questions thrown at her. The IRA's anti-interrogation lectures would have prepared her for all types of interrogation, and she had obviously learned their lessons well.

Early in 1991, I was asked by one of the IRA's intelligence officers to go and see Rosena at Whiterock Further Education Centre, situated in my old school, St Thomas's.

I was always impressed by how polite Rosena was to everyone, and sometimes I wondered if there was a touch of snobbery about her politeness, engendered, perhaps, by her years as a successful actress.

'Nice to see you, Marty,' she would say, in a friendly, genuine voice. 'How are you?'

It wasn't the usual way people addressed each other in West Belfast. Her politeness made me more respectful and polite as well and, whenever we were together, I made a conscious effort to behave well. 'What can I do for you?' I asked.

'Will you be able to take this to Davy?' she asked, taking from her mouth what seemed like a small, screwed up piece of paper, not much larger than an aspirin tablet, wrapped in cling film.

'Aye,' I said, taking the note from her.

As I drove back to Davy's house, I thought hard about whether I should open the note and read it. The fact that Rosena had kept the note in her mouth made me think it was of some considerable importance, something that the Special Branch would dearly like to scrutinise. But I realised that Davy would probably have been able to tell if I had tampered with the cling film, and that risk was was not worth taking.

I decided to be cautious and immediately took the note to Davy and, to my surprise, he opened and read the contents of the note in front of me. In that instant, I realised the considerable trust that Davy Adams now placed in me. Though pretending to take no interest, I watched intently and saw that the message had been written on two cigarette papers glued together.

After a few moments reflection, Davy said, 'Marty, I want you to do me a favour. Go to the nursery in the Turf Lodge district and give this to a man whom I think you know – Matt Lundy. It's urgent.'

As he handed back the cigarette paper, I noticed that he had not re-sealed the cling film. In the past, I had seen other top secret IRA notes delivered in this way but usually, when the contents were highly confidential, the cling film would be slightly burned with a match or lighted cigarette, totally sealing the note. But not this time.

Five minutes down the road I pulled into the kerb and gingerly opened the note. It contained a list of no less than a dozen names, addresses and car registration numbers of RUC officers. Some of the addresses had also been given post codes. At the top of the note were the three letters 'RUC'. This, indeed, was dynamite intelligence and I realised that all those officers were now at serious risk.

Several options raced through my mind. I thought of stopping and phoning Castlereagh, but realised that would be suicidal, for if some IRA man spotted me in a phone box in that Republican area, suspicions would be aroused. I thought of copying down the list of names and addresses but knew I didn't have time to stop, buy a pen and paper and sit for perhaps ten minutes diligently writing down the list. I also knew that I had to get to Lundy's school quickly, because if Davy Adams phoned and asked whether I had arrived safely, arriving late would have aroused serious suspicions. It was only a seven-minute drive and I had already stopped for two minutes to read the note.

I had no option but to drive on. I could see that Matt Lundy was surprised to see me for he obviously had no idea I was a member of the organisation. I handed him the note. At first he seemed reluctant to take it but when I explained to him that Davy Adams had sent me he happily accepted it.

Immediately, I drove to a safe phone box outside the Republican area and called the Branch, telling them I needed to see someone as a matter of urgency in the usual meeting place.

'I had to see you,' I told Felix and Mo as I climbed into their car. 'You'll never believe what's just happened. I met Rosena Brown and she gave me a bit of paper to take to Davy. He opened it, and after reading it told me to go and take the note immediately to Matt Lundy.'

'Did you manage to read the note?' Mo asked.

'Yes,' I replied, 'it contained the names of about twelve RUC men with the addresses, and the car registration numbers. Some names also had post codes. I think this means that Rosena has access to someone who has a computer with details of RUC personnel.'

I could see from their reaction that both Felix and Mo were extremely concerned with the news. And they even seemed a little annoyed that I hadn't taken a copy of the note, because it was obvious that the IRA now intended to target those officers, who were now at serious risk.

'Give us a break,' I said. 'If I'd had the time I would have copied the note, but that would have been far too risky in the middle of Turf Lodge.'

They nodded in agreement for they knew I was right.

A few days later, they came to the conclusion that Rosena may have formed a relationship with an RUC officer who was supplying her with information, the same way as she had persuaded Hanna, the prison officer, to provide her with names and addresses. They also asked me if I thought there was any possibility of me retrieving or even just seeing the note again.

'Go and fuck yourself,' I replied, angry that they should even ask me to risk my neck to that extent. But I forgave Felix believing that he had probably been put under pressure to have a sight of the note by one of his superior officers.

*   *   *

Throughout the early months of 1991, my IRA cell was becoming more active. One evening, a young woman knocked at the door of my flat and gave me a piece of paper with an address written on it. Speaking in a whisper, she said, 'Marty, you have to go here at eight o'clock.'

This was normal practice for calling members to meetings of IRA cells. I left immediately to drive to the meeting at Gortna Mona in Turf Lodge, and after ten minutes everyone had arrived.

Spud pulled the phone socket out of the wall. 'Why did you do that?' Peter asked.

'Because the Branch can listen in to our conversation if you leave the socket in,' he explained.

He said that the cell needed dumps in which to store gear –explosives, guns and ammunition – and he wanted everyone to find two or three places in which to store the weapons that the cell was beginning to acquire.

After 30 minutes or so, the meeting ended and Spud told everyone to leave the house separately, one or two at a time, some using the front door, others the back.

As I was about to leave, Spud stopped me. 'Marty, can you stay behind for a minute?'

'Aye,' I said, wondering why I had been singled out.

'Have you got your car?'

'Aye,' I said. 'What do you want?'

He explained that IRA intelligence had given him the name and address of an RUC Inspector who lived off the Antrim Road in Lisburn. The Inspector was understood to travel most days along back roads from Lisburn to Belfast in a blue Vauxhall Belmont, which he never garaged at night but left in his driveway.

Spud gave me £20 petrol money and I drove to Lisburn that night to check out the Inspector's house. Fifty yards from the end of the street, I saw the Vauxhall parked in the driveway. The following day, I returned to the Inspector's house. The car had gone, but as I surveyed the house I saw two lovely little girls, not yet teenagers, both with blond hair, playing in the driveway.

I looked at the two girls with warmth and happiness in my heart for I was confident that, now I had become involved in this IRA operation, there would be no way that I would let their father die, nor would there be any risk to either of those two innocent children. As I drove back home, I pondered how IRA or Loyalist bombers could go through with their evil work having come face to face with their victims' children.

I returned a third time to the house, this time at night, and saw his car parked in the drive. It seemed obvious that he had a regular police job with regular hours, which would make him a sitting target for any bomber. I reported back to Spud that the Inspector checked under his car each morning, in the hope that Spud would tell me to forget the operation. But he didn't.

He suggested that we would need a car thief to show us how to open the passenger door of the car, silently, so that a booby trap could be placed under the driver's seat. By tampering with the passenger door, Spud hoped the Inspector would not notice when getting into his car.

I became concerned that Spud intended to carry out the bombing in the immediate future and notified the Special Branch to treat the planned operation as a matter or urgency.

They took immediate action, moving the Inspector and his family to a new house. When the IRA bomber returned to survey the house, there was a 'For Sale' notice outside. The house was empty.

A week or so later, I was contacted again and told that Spud, my new boss, needed to see me urgently. It seemed he was taking up more and more of my time.

'We have a problem,' Spud told me as soon as I reached the agreed meeting place.

'Do you need driving somewhere? ' I asked, because Spud would often ask me to carry messages or people from place to place around Belfast.

'No,' he replied, 'nothing like that. This is a major problem.'

I wondered what on earth Spud was worrying about, acting mysteriously and yet wanting me to become involved. I smelt danger.

He told me that a couple of nights earlier, two members of our Active Service Unit had burgled an RUC officer's house outside Ballymena and had stolen his rifle, hiding it in a hedgerow on the edge of a field near his home. The plan had been to take the rifle, hide it nearby, and then return a couple of days later and shoot the peeler when he arrived home at night, using his own rifle. But the two-man IRA unit team had lost their bottle and were frightened to return. They believed that the peeler had notified his senior officers of the theft and that the SAS were lying in wait for the thieves to return.

'We need you to go and get the rifle,' Spud said in a matter-of-fact voice.

'You fuckin' what?' I exclaimed. 'You want me to risk my neck because some other cunts have lost their bottle. You must be joking.'

'We need that rifle,' Spud explained trying to interest me in carrying out the plan, 'We need it desperately for other operations we have planned.'

'I want nothing to do with it,' I told him.

'Well, if I show you on the map where it is will you go and take a look? Just drive past to see if you can see any activity and report back.'

'But you know,' I went on, 'that if the SAS are involved I won't see fuck all from driving past. Those guys can lie buried in the ground for days without moving. When I show up, they'll just let fly.'

'Just take a look,' Spud pleaded, 'just take a look.'

My mind was racing. I knew that if Spud needed the rifle for other planned operations – in other words, for executions – then maybe I should intervene and try to get hold of the weapon.

'OK,' I said, 'I'll take a look, but I'm not promising.'

'You're a good lad, Marty,' he said, 'I knew we could rely on you.'

Twenty minutes later, I phoned Felix and explained my dilemma.

'I'll check it out. We'll meet at the usual place in an hour. OK?'

'OK,' I replied.

An hour later, I was face to face with Felix and Mo, telling them once again exactly what had happened.

'OK, let's go,' said Felix.

'Where are we going?' I asked.

'We're going for a ride to Bellymena to pick up the rifle.'

'But what about the fucking SAS?' I asked, anxiety in my voice.

'I've made enquiries,' Felix replied. 'I don't think they're there yet, but they may be. We'll have to tread carefully.'

'Fuck me, Felix,' I protested, 'Are you mad or something?'

When we arrived at the location Spud had indicated, it was still daylight. Having driven along the hedgerow five or six times, we stopped. Felix decided that Mo and I should go and search for the rifle while he stayed in the blacked-out van with his radio, in case of trouble.

'Shit, Mo,' I said as we clambered out of the van, 'do you think this is stupid?'

'Aye,' he said with a grin, 'but Felix knows what he's doing. He's nobody's fool.'

'I fuckin' hope not,' I said as we crossed the road and began searching the hedgerow. I kept looking around me, fearful that at any moment an SAS man in camouflage would pop up, as if from nowhere, and either shoot me or smash my head in.

We searched for more than ten minutes without success, and I began to wonder whether Spud had deliberately sent me on a wild goose chase, possibly to check me out, perhaps even having detailed someone to follow me, suspecting something.

'Marty, come here.'

It was Mo, further down, working along the hedgerow on the other side.

I stopped looking and ran towards him. He was holding the rifle which was partly covered with a bedsheet.

'Let's go,' he said and we walked down the field towards Felix and the van. I was still looking around anxiously, fearful that the SAS may have been waiting to catch us red-handed. But nothing stirred. I felt massively relieved when we finally clambered into the van to see Felix beaming, a huge smile across his face.

'There you are, Marty,' he said, 'I told you it would be a piece of cake.'

'Fuck off,' I said, but I was happy to be in the safety of the van and driving back to Belfast.

'And what do I tell Spud?' I enquired. 'What shall I say?'

'Tell him that you went to have a look,' Felix said. 'Tell him that you drove along the road, backwards and forwards a few times, and then got out and had a look, but you found nothing. Tell him you searched for five minutes or more but with no success. Not wanting to call attention to yourself, you pushed off.'

'Will he believe me?' I asked.

'Fuck knows,' Felix said with a smile, 'but I expect he will. Remember, Marty, he couldn't find anyone else to go. Don't worry, you'll be OK.'

I was worried when I called to see Spud, but I had rehearsed my story a dozen times or more in my head before going to see him.

'Did you go?' he asked me. 'Did you really go, Marty?'

'Aye,' I said, 'if you want, I'll tell you what it was like.'

'No, no,' he said, 'there's no need for that. But you couldn't find anything?'

'Nothing,' I said. 'But to search the whole long hedgerow would have taken a dozen men an hour or more. I wasn't going to be seen searching the undergrowth, in case I was spotted and people asked questions.'

'Don't worry,' Spud said, 'you did well. Shame about the rifle though.'

'The dozy cunts should have brought it back with them,' I said.

'Perhaps,' he said. 'Now we'll have to get another one from somewhere.'

Agreeing to that mission seemed to enhance my reputation within our cell and Spud became more deferential towards me, marking me out for praise, and seeking my advice when he hadn't done so in the past. It also meant that I was learning about other IRA activities which I wouldn't have known about otherwise.

It was about this time that Angie told me that she was pregnant again. I sensed, however, that she did not seem as happy as she had been when she was expecting little Martin. Understandably, she was worried because she believed that I had become deeply committed to the IRA and believed I was spending 90 per cent of my waking hours talking, planning and doing God-knows-what with other members of the organisation.

'You know I don't like what you're doing, Marty,' she would say, an anxious look on her face.

I would try to calm her, tell her that everything was fine; that we would all be OK.

'But now I'm pregnant again,' she would say, 'and I don't know whether you're going to be with us this week or next week. I keep reading in the paper and hearing on the news that IRA people are being arrested, others killed, and I keep thinking that could be you.'

Perhaps I hadn't realised the extent to which she worried, for she would continue, 'It's awful being here on my own, knowing you are getting mixed up in trouble and not knowing what I would do if anything happened to you.'

These conversations, which would arise from time to time, always put me in a quandary – I wanted to tell Angie the truth, but wasn't able even to hint that I was, in fact, an agent working with the Special Branch and therefore would never be arrested and imprisoned. I felt desperately sorry for her. I had tried to put her fears out of my mind, but when she spoke openly to me, I realised the hell she was going through alone, at home each night, waiting for me to return. There was simply no way for me to tell her that I was working for the Branch, for the British Government, and not the IRA.

I would lie awake at night, unable to sleep for hours, thinking of a way I could allay Angie's fears without telling her that I was working for the Government. But the one fact that I kept telling myself was that Angie was worrying unduly; the chance of my being arrested and jailed was nil, and one day we would all live together as a happy family. But not yet. First, I reasoned, I had to finish the job I had started, helping to save people's lives. I believed that my life was safe and my future secure, but there were others depending on the job I was doing.

Often, Felix would tell me, 'Remember, Marty, what you are doing. You're not simply saving a man's life, but the life of someone's father, someone's husband or someone's son. They will never know what you did for them. But you will know. When all this is over, you will realise the lives you saved by your courage. And you must never forget that. For me, it's easy, telling you what to do from the safety of this place, but you are out there, risking your neck every day.'

In March 1991, I determined to spend more time with Angie, to help her through the last weeks of her pregnancy, as well as to give her the emotional support which she needed.

I had been detailed by Spud to check out a house in Richhill Crescent, near the RUC headquarters in Knock, East Belfast, where an RUC Constable lived alone. He was in his 50s, without a car and would walk to the bus stop each day on his way to work. The IRA decided that they could not shoot him in cold blood, because a safe getaway could not be guaranteed in an area where so many RUC officers lived.

They finally decided that the only way to kill the officer was to place a booby-trap bomb in the wheely bin in his back garden. They knew that, once a week, he would push the bin into the street for collection. I warned the Branch of the planned attack and they told me to watch developments and to keep them notified.

The police officer was advised to move immediately but when I went to check the house I saw a number of people moving about inside, as though a party was in full swing. It seemed strange for this was the first time I had ever seen anyone, except for the policeman, in the house. I became convinced that the Branch had laid a trap for the IRA bomb squad, and I feared that someone would be killed if an attack was mounted.

So I decided to lie to both the IRA and the Special Branch. I told Spud that the RUC man kept his wheely bin locked in a shed in his garden, and told the Branch that the attack was still being planned. Spud decided to call off the planned attack, but the Branch repeatedly asked me for progress reports on the attack. I constantly fed them the same intelligence – the operation was still on.

I continued to watch the house, wondering what was really being planned, either by the Branch or the RUC. Sometimes I discovered lights on all over the place, at other times hardly anyone seemed to be about, but generally there appeared to be a number of people living there. One night, I took the unusual step of taking Angie with me because she seemed to be on the point of giving birth. Our son Martin was staying the night with Angie's mother.

We parked the car, picked up a bite to eat at the

Kentucky Fried Chicken nearby, and walked the mile-and-a-half to the street where the RUC man lived. Then we walked back again. Angie had said she wanted to take a long, slow walk in the fresh air and it seemed an ideal opportunity for me spy on the house and for Angie to stretch her legs. At no time did I tell Angie anything about the planned attack, nor that there was an RUC man living there.

Later, I dropped Angie at her grandmother's house in Ballymurphy for the night. The following morning – 16 March – I received a call saying that Angie had been taken to hospital in the early hours of the morning. I went straight to the hospital and hours later, baby Pódraig was born, a healthy, bouncy baby boy with dark hair like his mother.

A few weeks after Angie and Pódraig came home from hospital, a Housing Executive official came to tell her that her application for a council place had been successful. They had arranged for her and the children to move into her grandmother's house in Glenalena Park on the Ballymurphy Estate, where her mother had spent her childhood years. This was good news and I gave up my flat and moved ino our new place, rent free. Angie's grandmother would be moved to a smaller house off the Falls Road.

Before leaving our flat, I made sure that every piece of IRA equipment had been moved to a new safe house in the area.

I was still involved with both my own IRA cell and working as often as possible with Davy Adams, gathering information and targets that I would pass on to the Branch.

*　　　　*　　　　*

In the Spring of 1991, Davy Adams phoned me as I was having a glass of Coke in a Republican bar.

'Marty,' he said, 'can you come down and have a drink with a couple of friends. I'm in the club on the Falls Road.'

Davy and his pal Paul were having a drink and chatting to Rosena Brown, who was working a shift as a barmaid.

'I'm going to Scotland tonight,' Davy told me, 'and Paul wants to bring Rosena along, too.'

'How are you getting there?' I asked.

'We've got a lift laid on.'

I wondered why Davy would be so keen to visit Scotland. Convinced it had to be serious IRA business, I volunteered to drive him.

'Would you really drive us?' he asked.

'Yes, sure I will,' I replied. 'I'll have to go and get some money from home. I'll see you back here in 20 minutes.'

I went to a cash machine and withdrew £200. I also took the opportunity of phoning Castlereagh and left a message with 'B' Division, asking them to tell Felix that I was going to Scotland.

'Put your foot down,' Davy said as soon as we were all in the car, 'the ferry sails in 45 minutes.'

Davy sat beside me in the front, while Rosena and Paul sat in the back.

I enjoyed that drive, racing at speeds in excess of 100 mph along the back roads leading to Larne. Davy loved the fast driving, yelping and whooping as we tore along the narrow, twisting roads. In the back, Rosena and Paul were screaming blue murder, shouting for me to slow down, convinced we would all be killed in a pile up. But Davy was determined to make that ferry.

'Calm yourselves,' Davy told them, 'Marty is a bloody good little driver. He'll get us there.'

We made it, with five minutes to spare.

It was the first time that I had ever left my native Ireland. And I did not enjoy the journey one bit. The crossing was rough that night, and Davy and I were seasick on the way over to Stranraer. But as soon as we reached port and I stood on dry land again, I felt better. We were met by two lads from Glasgow and we followed them in our car. We finally reached our destination at about 2.30am, a small terraced house on a run-down housing estate. Rosena and Paul took the only bedroom, while Davy and I had to sleep on the floor in the front room. I was so tired, though, I fell asleep within minutes.

Early the following morning, Davy phoned Brian Gillen back in Belfast who seemed agitated that Davy, Rosena and I had travelled together to Scotland. He feared that the Special Branch might be watching the ferries.

That afternoon, we all walked to a flat on the estate and met two Scots, both in their 30s. They were introduced to me as two strong Republican supporters. The two men explained that they had been able to trace some hand-guns which they were acquiring from Glasgow criminals. At that time I was well aware that the IRA in Belfast were desperately short of hand-guns, though we had plenty of AK-47s. To carry out most of the operations the IRA planned at that time, hand-guns were essential, because they could be easily concealed and moved from place to place.

Having completed the business, we all went to Parkhead the next day to see the crunch match of the Scottish soccer season, Celtic versus Rangers, viewed for generations as Catholics versus Protestants. Rosena was in her element, shouting and screaming whenever Celtic gained possession of the ball or came close to scoring.

Throughout the match, we heard some supporters shouting IRA slogans at the Rangers supporters on the terrace opposite and they, in turn, would hurl Loyalist abuse at the 'Micks'.

Later that night, I went out alone for a McDonald's, and took the opportunity to phone Castlereagh, leaving a message for Felix, telling him what had happened in Glasgow. I was very happy to return to Belfast the following day, as I had missed Angie and the kids. Before that weekend, I had never been away from Angie and it made me realise how involved I had become with her. It made me think how good our relationship was and how much she meant to me.

Angie's mother was the first person I saw as I came into the house and she gave me a cold look, as though I had a nerve walking into the house as though I hadn't been missing for four days.

Angie walked in from the kitchen. 'Where have you been?' she asked, not wanting to give me a roasting in front of her mother. On the way back I had discussed with Davy what I should tell Angie. I had done nothing wrong, but I didn't want Angie to think that I would simply push off and leave her for a long weekend without telling her first. Davy advised me to tell her that he and I had been arrested and held by the RUC.

She believed the story I told her, but I could tell she was far from happy with what had happened.

I felt bad about having to lie to Angie, and even worse that I had left her for so long without telling her. I was determined to make it up to her. I had genuinely missed her and I felt I wanted to spoil her, to show her how much I cared for her and the kids. I hadn't been spending much money on Angie and my bank balance was healthy. After my recent pay rise, I was earning more than £3,000 a month from the Special Branch and decided to make our three-bedroom home really comfortable.

Felix had decided the time had come to change my car, and I had been given £3,300 to go and buy something suitable. With Angie, I went to Wilson's Car Auctions and we bought a two-year-old Mark IV Ford Escort 1.4 LX, which had been a Bank of Ireland company car.

I decided I wanted to park the car in the front garden rather than leave it in the road where, I figured, it could have been the target of joy-riders. I walked to a nearby building site and asked a JCB driver if he wanted to earn a few quid for doing a little job for me. He agreed to drive over to our house, knock down the front wall and scrape out the crazy paving, levelling the area. The job took him a little over an hour and he was happy with the £30 I gave him. The next day, a load of concrete was delivered and I laid and levelled the concrete. I arranged for a pair of wooden gates to be erected, hoping that would deter would-be car thieves. At the same time, I put up the swing that Angie and I had bought on our trip down south.

But I wanted to show Angie that I really cared, and was only too happy to spend my money on making our new home really beautiful. I paid a joiner to clad the bathroom with pine and paid a decorator to wallpaper the entire house. We bought new carpets for the whole house, purchased a three-piece suite from her mother, bought a new bed, wardrobe and side tables for our bedroom and two single beds for the other rooms. For the kitchen, we bought a new washing machine, fridge/ freezer and cooker. I spent over £4,000, but it was worth every penny for Angie was thrilled with her new home.

I knew I was taking a risk spending such money, arousing suspicion with Davy Adams and other IRA men calling round to see me from time to time. But I accepted that risk because I wanted to spoil Angie, to show her I cared and that I could be kind and generous. After all, she had to endure an odd life with me, not knowing where I worked, what I did or when she would ever see me. I tried to lead as normal a life as possible, but it was becoming increasingly difficult with the demands the IRA was making on my time and the need to keep my handlers notified of everything that was going on.

I did, however, become increasingly concerned about Angie's mother, because she began asking questions about the cost of our new car and all the work carried out on the house. She would tell Angie that she was surprised that a young unemployed man like me, with no job, could have found such an amount of money, not only to spend so much on our new home but also to have had enough funds to buy a smart two-year-old car which she knew had cost over £3,000.

Without thinking, I made another mistake a couple of weeks later. I bought Angie a £300 double pram for the kids, and gave her a further £200 for clothes for her and the children.

Her mother saw the bundle of notes in Angie's handbag one day and, with some concern in her voice, said, 'I don't know how your Marty does it. He's just spent a fortune on the house and now he gives you all this money. Where does he get it all from?'

'I don't know,' Angie replied. 'I never know where his money comes from. He's always out working.'

More worrying, however, would be the fact that Davy Adams, who often called round to visit me, began cracking jokes when he visited our newly furnished home. I began to suspect that I had been foolish, even stupid, to spend so much money in one go. When he came to visit us, I watched to see if our new home, with all the redecorations, aroused any suspicions. Davy did make some jokes about our new furniture, at one point pretending to be concerned when he spilt some milk on the kitchen floor. He never asked any questions directly nor suggested how I was able to afford such luxuries, yet I felt increasingly awkward whenever he came round.

'Have you been robbing banks?' he joked on one occasion and that made me feel paranoid. I had always respected Davy's intelligence. If anyone was going to put two and two together, I knew it would be Davy. And I knew what the consequences would be.

From time to time, other IRA members would call at the house and they all seemed highly impressed with our new home. Some made comments suggesting that I must be into drugs or had a secret supply of money. None suggested, however, that I might be working for the Branch, but I would always wonder if the thought crossed their minds.

Whenever they asked awkward questions, I would suggest that Angie and I had been saving for some years and had now decided to splash out.

But I wondered whether, behind my back, they were beginning to speculate as to the real source of all my money.

CHAPTER TEN

THROUGHOUT THE TWO YEARS that I worked with the intelligence wing of the IRA, I would learn many of the organisation's intimate secrets, as well as discovering the detailed command structure responsible for finance, planning, intelligence, ordnance and the operations at street level where the bombings and shootings took place.

During the late 1980s and the 1990s, Sinn Fein, the political wing of the Republican cause, worked hard to distance itself from the Provisional IRA, the military wing which was prepared to shoot and bomb their way to their ultimate goal of a United Ireland.

And no one worked harder at this than Gerry Adams, the President of Sinn Fein since 1983, a man who believed that Sinn Fein should become more involved in and committed to a wide range of political activity at community level. In the early 1980s, Sinn Fein decided that they should enter the political arena, putting up candidates in democratic elections, hoping to prove that they had a mandate from the Northern Ireland electorate. By 1983, Sinn Fein received 13 per cent of the vote throughout the north, and in the 1983 British parliamentary election, Gerry Adams was elected as Member of Parliament for West Belfast which he continued to represent until 1992.

Adams set out to secure the support of the West Belfast voters by pushing for housing campaigns, which in time culminated in the wholesale demolition of old houses and flats and the building of new homes. At the same time as initiating social, economic and cultural issues, Adams sought to open discussion and public debate about the achievement of peace through talks and a democratic settlement.

In 1986, Adams claimed that a military stalemate existed between the IRA and the British Army, which he maintained could only be resolved by a political settlement. So he launched a peace strategy, engaging in talks with church and reconciliation groups in Northern Ireland.

Throughout his years as a Member of Parliament, Gerry Adams tried to distance the political party from the bombs and the bullets of the IRA, which during those nine years continued to claim the lives of innocent people. He would claim that he had no links with the organisation.

But Adams was denying his past. In the early 1970s, the young Adams' organisational skills were recognised by the then leadership of the Provisional IRA, and he was promoted to Quartermaster of the Ballymurphy Battalion, the man ultimately responsible for storing and issuing weapons, ammunition and bomb-making materials to active service units.

He would later be appointed Officer Commanding the Provisional IRA in Ballymurphy, the man primarily responsible for the IRA offensive in that area. In a ten month period, when Adams held the position of Officer

Commanding the 2nd Battalion, a total of 52 people were murdered, including soldiers, police and civilians. As a result of those 'successes', Adams was promoted, becoming Commander of the IRA's foremost operational command, the Provisional IRA Belfast Brigade, with three Battalions under his authority.

I witnessed at first hand the constant interplay between Sinn Fein and the IRA during the years when Gerry Adams claimed there was no link between the two organisations. Despite his denials, Adams himself was not only President of Sinn Fein but was also a member of the seven-man Provisional IRA Army Council, the authority responsible for strategy and planning of both Sinn Fein policies and tactics, and all military operations.

Martin McGuinness would also later hold dual roles – as Chief Negotiator for Sinn Fein, as well as being one of the most influential members of the IRA Army Council. In 1974, he was found guilty of membership of the Provisional IRA before a Dublin court, and was given a six-month jail sentence. In court, he said he was the commanding officer of the 'Derry Brigade of the IRA for two years. McGuinness later returned to jail, again for being an IRA member.

During my years inside the IRA, a number of senior Provo intelligence officers confirmed to me that, during the late 1980s and early 1990s, McGuinness had been Head of the IRA Northern Command, one of the most senior positions throughout the entire IRA organisation.

More disgracefully and, I would suggest, more sickening, was the fact that McGuinness was widely known in the 'Derry area of Northern Ireland to have been responsible for the loss of several people's lives, as well as being the authority behind many savage punishment beatings.

Over recent years, it has been extraordinary to hear the Sinn Fein leadership declaring to British and American politicians, as well as the media, that they had no knowledge of the decisions taken by the IRA Army Council, while both Adams and McGuinness were Council members.

The IRA Army Council also decides when a ceasefire will commence and finish, when bombing campaigns will be conducted, and whether those campaigns should be aimed at targets in the Province or on the mainland. Adams and McGuinness would have been among those directly responsible for taking the decision to declare a ceasefire, as well as deciding when the ceasefire would end and the bombing recommence.

And that working relationship between the IRA and Sinn Fein reached from the top to the very bottom of both organisations. To many working for either the IRA or Sinn Fein, the two organisations often seemed indistinguishable, because many people worked for both the military and political wings. To those inside both organisations, there is no doubt whatsoever that the military and political wings work closely together. And yet Sinn Fein continues to deny the relationship.

One example of how closely the two are linked was revealed during the British parliamentary or local Northern Ireland elections. During the years, I become involved in helping the Sinn Fein cause, along with many other young men and women, many of whom were members of the IRA.

From their headquarters in Connolly House, Belfast, Sinn Fein organisers would try, with the assistance of the IRA, to do everything in their power to rig the elections. The plan would be to distribute false identification papers to IRA men and women and other Republican sympathisers, and send them around to a number of polling stations so that they could cast votes in perhaps six to ten different places.

The problem was be identification. One way Sinn Fein circumvented this was by asking the IRA to steal a large quantity of brand-new medical cards, which the IRA workers would then fill out with various false names and addresses, filling in dates and places of birth which would not arouse suspicion with the officers at the various polling stations.

On election day, fleets of taxis would be hired, which would then drive around the city dropping people off near various polling stations. They then walked the short distance to the polling station, produce their medical cards as evidence of identification, date of birth and address and would be permitted to vote.

The taxis would then take their 'voters' off to another station and would continue this process for most of the day.

It was, of course, difficult to estimate how many illegal votes were cast in this way but there would certainly have been around a thousand or more, often enough to swing a local election. Even if the Sinn Fein candidate didn't win, the large Sinn Fein turnout gave Gerry Adams and the organisation a certain mandate, claiming increasing support for the Republican cause.

I would spend election days with Sinn Fein and IRA sympathisers, driving from polling station to polling station. Most of the young men and women volunteers considered the whole business great fun, particularly as their efforts would result in one of their own Sinn Fein candidates being voted into power to the chagrin and surprise of other law abiding candidates.

There were more sinister operations going on, however, which continue to have serious repercussions in Northern Ireland, and which could not only endanger many lives, but also provide the IRA with valuable information.

The IRA intelligence wing, with the approval of the IRA Army Council, decided on a major long-term campaign to infiltrate many organisations throughout the Province, including the Department of Health and Social Security, the major high street banks and building societies, British Telecom, the vehicle licensing centre in Coleraine, the Post Office, leading insurance companies, universities and travel agents.

I was led to understand that, by 1991, the Republican sympathisers, including many Sinn Fein activists who had been recruited and, in some cases, trained to infiltrate the various organisations, had successfully penetrated these institutions and businesses and were now in place. They would remain as 'sleepers', waiting to be activated whenever their IRA masters needed their help in providing information.

Some sympathisers were encouraged to become computer experts so that they could find positions in organisations where access to computer files would provide the IRA with most of the information required to target members of the RUC, the security forces, prison staff and anyone the IRA decided they wanted to nail. It seems that the great majority of these men and women are still employed in the organisations, and are capable of handing over information which would put their targets at risk from attack. One phone call or late-night visit would be sufficient for the information to be 'requested' and provided, and more often than not, within 24 hours the vital information would have been passed to the IRA's intelligence wing.

One IRA man, a schoolteacher, has a part-time job and is employed and paid a monthly wage by the intelligence wing of the IRA Belfast Brigade, spending his spare time feeding information into a computer; details of thousands of men and women whom the IRA believe that it might want to target at some future date.

Every known detail is contained on computer floppy disks, which list an extensive range of Northern Irish citizens, including senior officers of the RUC and the Royal Irish Rangers, judges and lawyers, prison officers, Loyalist paramilitaries, building contractors and politicians of Unionist parties. The information includes their positions, ranks and precise occupations, their place of work and, more importantly, their private addresses and telephone numbers. The make, model and age of their cars, including the registration number and tax dates, are also often included on the disk.

But as well as gathering as much information as possible on potential targets, the IRA decided in the 1980s to change its entire command structure from the battalion-strength strategy, employing perhaps 40 people, to the far more secure and clandestine plan of working in separate cells of only eight people. This caused the security forces far greater problems, because infiltrating agents into so many cells proved almost impossible.

When cell commanders sometimes became suspicious that one of their members might be a British agent, arrangements would first be made to track down the spy and question him, and then the cell would be disbanded, its members fading away into the community until contacted some weeks or months later to carry out other IRA tasks.

The man whom they believed to be betraying the cause, however, would face a hell on earth. Several times, IRA investigators targeted the wrong man and no matter how much he pleaded his innocence, his interrogators would beat a confession out of him.

Whenever someone 'confessed', regardless of whether he was innocent or guilty, the sentence would always be the same – one or two bullets in the back of the head. Some suspects would face up to seven weeks of horrific interrogation and torture before being executed.

*   *   *

Throughout my years inside the IRA, there was always a desperate shortage of good-quality, modern hand-guns. The IRA had ample supplies of AK-47s, hundreds of which had been supplied virtually free of charge by the PLO (Palestine Liberation Organisation) and Colonel Gaddafi of Libya.

A few of these were kept in 'dumps', in the roof spaces of safe houses dotted around Belfast and 'Derry. The vast majority of AK-47s, however, had been buried in protective wrapping in dumps around Northern Ireland, particularly in South Armagh, the border county where the IRA had established a virtual no-go area for British troops and the RUC.

Whenever individual IRA cells needed more weapons and supplies of Semtex, arrangements would be made for the necessary equipment to be collected from IRA dumps in the Republic. A convoy would be formed – some cars would be bought or borrowed for the trip south, others would be hijacked. Usually, three cell members would call at houses where they knew there were reliable cars, the families would be held at gun-point and the cars would be taken. The families would not be released until the cars were returned later that day.

One such convoy of five cars was convened in Dundalk in the autumn of 1990. Two of the cars were loaded with AK-47s and Semtex, which were being moved to safe arms dumps in and around Belfast. Two of the remaining cars led the convoy as 'scouts', and the fifth car brought up the rear, acting as 'tail-end Charlie'.

The five cars, driving about a hundred yards apart, made their way through the back roads to a border crossing where they knew there was no RUC crossing or army checkpoint. The convoy then made its way to Belfast via Newry to Hillsborough, joining the M1 at Lisburn for the drive to Andersonstown in West Belfast.

Before leaving Belfast, the cell commander would brief the drivers, telling them that under no circumstances were they to risk being caught with the arms in their possession. 'We can always get more arms and Semtex,' he told them, 'but we can't afford to lose valuable members.'

The drivers were also told that they should never use their indicators, whether turning off the road or overtaking. These were only to be used if it looked as though the Army or RUC were about to act or, of course, if they came across a road block. If the drivers carrying the equipment saw a light flashing on one of their leading scout cars, they were instructed to take the first available turning. If they were on the motorway, however, with no slip-road nearby, the drivers were to abandon their cars and walk back a few yards to be picked up by the tail-end vehicle. The run in autumn 1990, only one of many, went without a hitch.

The excellent AK-47, though, was no good for the great majority of operations undertaken by active service units – they were bulky, difficult to conceal and useless at close quarters. Except for sniper work, hand-guns were preferred in nearly all circumstances. As a result, IRA activists became remarkably attached to their hand-guns, loath to loan them out to other cells.

The IRA organised sympathisers in Glasgow, Manchester and London to contact known villains and buy the guns on the black market. After the fall of the Soviet Union, hand-guns were also bought from gangsters in Moscow, mostly weapons stolen from the former Soviet bloc forces. There would, however, never be sufficient for the IRA's purposes.

There was always a severe shortage of detonators, too. The IRA had access to as much Semtex bomb-making material as they could use. The problem was acquiring reliable detonators. On a number of occasions during my years with the IRA, a few active service bombing operations were postponed, and others cancelled, because there were no available detonators.

IRA bomb-makers were encouraged to construct home-made detonators, but these often proved embarrassingly unreliable. Several times, IRA members risked carrying out a bombing only to find that the detonator was ineffective and the operation a waste of time.

As a result, orders were issued to the effect that detonators should be assembled by bomb-makers in batches of ten, so that three or four of them could be tested – exploded, in effect – hopefully ensuring that the home-made detonator would perform correctly when the bomb was laid. If two or three tests proved negative, then the whole batch would be scrapped and the bomb-maker would start again from scratch. The problem caused anger and frustration among the highest echelons of the IRA.

Making big bombs, designed to cause massive damage to town centres, such as those which exploded in the City of London and Canary Wharf, was a perennial problem for the IRA bomb-makers. This was due to the time needed to grind the fertiliser and pack the explosive material into lorries, vans or cars. Usually, this would be carried out under cover of darkness, which added to the problems.

After much consideration, it was decided to follow the example of the Viet Cong and construct an underground bomb-making factory. It took months of painstaking intelligence work to find a suitable site, as the IRA leadership decided that it had to be based in the countryside but not too far from Belfast. It also had to be located in an area where the local population would not become suspicious. At the beginning of the 1990s, with no sign of a ceasefire, the IRA believed it would continue its major bombing campaigns in Belfast and elsewhere, and that it would need a location where its bomb-makers could work in secret.

Usually, the IRA bomb-makers worked under pressure. Accompanied by gunmen, they would take over a house for the night, forcing the occupants into a single room where they would remain with an armed guard. The bomb-makers would then work throughout the next eight to ten hours, hurrying to complete the bomb before daylight. It would then be transferred, often in a wheely-bin, to a waiting car or van. A house with a rear kitchen was often chosen, so that the RUC would not be alerted by lights being on throughout the night.

Eventually, a near-perfect site was found on a deserted farm between Glenarm and Carnlough near the coast, twenty-five miles from Belfast. The farm had an old barn big enough to hold a lorry and one or two cars, which could be parked out of sight of the general public and army reconnaisance helicopters.

The plan was to construct a shaft beneath the barn which would lead down to a well-built, well-equipped small factory, where a group of IRA members could make various sizes and types of bombs without the worry of a knock at the door. Most IRA bombs had been assembled in sympathisers' homes or lock-up garages where problems inevitably occurred.

The new factory was to be equipped with industrial coffee-grinding machinery to handle the fertiliser, and work benches with lathes, vices, power drills and other essential tools. These could all be powered by on-site generators, concealed below ground to dampen the noise. The team of workers would have the comfort of heating and lighting, and would enter and leave the site after dark.

Money was never a problem for the IRA. From enquiries I made of various high-ranking IRA personnel, it appeared that between US$10 million and US$12 million a year was pouring into the coffers of the organisation during the late '80s and early '90s.

Most of this money was laundered through European banks and invested by professional investment managers, some of whom had no idea that the funds they were caring for were associated with the IRA. I was aware of one senior IRA official who lived and worked as an accountant in Belfast and another, whose name I could never trace, lived in Dublin. These funds had been built up over many years, mainly from North American sources sympathetic to the cause of a united Ireland, and it seemed that the money never entered the Republic of Ireland or the Province, but would be invested mainly in Europe.

There was also income from protection rackets, bank robberies, post office raids, black taxis, DSS scams, video and CD pirating, fruit machines, Republican clubs and pubs and local collections among sympathisers. This money would be collected and handled locally to buy guns or ammunition, getaway cars or trucks, as well as to pay full-time IRA staff who were too busy to hold down regular jobs. It would also be used to take care of the families of IRA men serving jail sentences, as well as to finance recently released IRA men who had served long prison sentences and had little or no chance of securing a proper job.

The IRA needed to keep its tills ringing to cover its considerable overheads. All IRA cell members received £10 a week, and the cell commanders received between £30–£50 per week. The great majority of the IRA's income, however, went on intelligence gathering, and organising and carrying out active service missions. Occasionally, money was needed to buy second-hand cars, pay for transport, food and lodgings outside Belfast. Sympathisers who agreed to hide arms and ammunition in their homes and garages would also be paid, not only to ensure that they kept their mouths shut, but also because of the considerable risks they faced.

The construction of small arms dumps in Belfast and 'Derry would go on for about a year. The RUC and the Army were always on the lookout for arms dumps, so it was necessary for IRA teams to move the weapons continually to and from different locations, and to build more secure and secret hiding places. If the Special Branch ever suspected that a house had become an IRA arms dump, the place would be ripped apart, every floorboard would be pulled up, the walls would be left with gaping holes and all the kitchen, bathroom and bedroom cupboards would be taken apart. The house would, literally, be trashed, and made virtually uninhabitable until major repairs had been carried out.

Most flats and houses were quite small, ordinary council-owned homes without much space. As a result, an average arms dump, possibly secreted behind a false bathroom wall, might contain three AK-47 rifles, two hand-guns and 5lb of Semtex. Sometimes, the IRA had great difficulty of persuading people to allow their homes to be used as a dump, as the occupants would be fully aware of the threat of long jail sentences if the weapons were ever discovered in their homes. Consequently, many of those who agreed to hide weapons were widows or young, unmarried mothers who desperately needed the money.

Most of the IRA men who handled income from whatever source seemed to be meticulous in their accounting. There were also examples of punishment beatings handed out to those few who misused IRA funds for their own ends. Those men would not only be beaten but would also earn the scorn and contempt of their IRA mates, friends and often their families.

Throughout the years I worked with the IRA, I was left in no doubt that the cardinal sin, above all else, was the betrayal of the cause.

And yet many people, including escalating numbers of former IRA personnel, did betray the cause by volunteering to work for the RUC, the British Government and, occasionally, the Security Services. Some of those would be police informers, others intelligence agents like me.

During the 25 years since the Troubles began in earnest, hundreds of people have happily worked for the Government in a desperate bid to end the violence and the killings, the bombings and the shootings, which have made life so miserable for the entire Northern Ireland population.

And a few hundred people, who risked their lives working for the Government or the RUC, have been pulled out of the Province because their undercover work had been detected by the IRA. It is always necessary in such situations to pull out the person immediately, and often their families as well, and re-settle them in different locations throughout the mainland. They are then given houses or apartments, new identities and sometimes a job. Often, as the IRA keeps up its attempts to find and target these families, they have to be moved three or four times in an effort to keep them one step ahead of the gunmen. I understand that these rescue missions, which are still carried out, have so far cost the British taxpayer between £75–£100 million.

CHAPTER ELEVEN

My increasing concern over suspicious IRA members began to make me feel nervous, but I would tell myself that I had to look forward and get on with the task in hand, maintaining my apparent enthusiasm for working with the IRA, as well as trying to do all I could to frustrate their murderous intentions.

Though I sometimes had sleepless nights worrying that my cover would be blown, I did try to ensure that many of the IRA operations I thwarted were ones in which I had only been one of many people involved in their planning.

My handlers would impress on me, time and again, to be vigilant, to keep a low-profile, and never to take risks which might expose me as an agent working for the Special Branch. And the more intelligence I supplied, the more they would seek to protect and advise me. In my naïveté, I sometimes thought they were being excessively cautious.

'Remember, Marty,' Felix would stress, 'It's not only us who need your help, it's all those other poor bastards who might be on the receiving end. Promise me that you'll take care. Remember, never take risks; too many people rely on you ... although they will never know.'

Many of the operations I helped to ruin had been brought to my attention because of my position as a member of the IRA Intelligence wing, a position far removed from the actual Active Service Unit that would carry out the task. On a number of occasions, I was one of 20 or 30 people in the chain of command with knowledge of a particular operation and, as a result, escaped suspicion.

I would also deliberately loan out my Special Branch car, with the secret tracker bleep attached, to anyone who wanted to borrow it. As a result, these personnel would be automatically tracked by the Special Branch and some of their nefarious activities ruined by some unknown intervention which no one could pin-point. I did not know about those operations, but it was obvious to those involved in the IRA's internal security network, the men constantly watching for agents and informants, that I had nothing whatsoever to do with many of the jobs that were ruined before they ever reached fruition.

My first real concern for my position occurred after I was drafted into Spud's IRA cell. From that moment, I became intimately involved in direct action, gaining first-hand knowledge of potential targets and operational details at the point of execution.

There were only eight of us in the cell with that privileged knowledge, and whenever I provided the intelligence that scuppered an operation, I knew that suspicion of having betrayed the cell's plans would initially point to one of the eight, including me.

From the moment I joined Spud's cell, I realised that my life was at risk; yet I knew that I could not permit an innocent man or woman to be targeted and murdered without trying everything in my power to stop it. And whenever I did prevent a bombing or a shooting, I knew that I was one step closer to having my cover blown.

*   *   *

On Saturday, 15 September 1990, an RUC detective, Louis Robinson, aged 42, who had been with the force for 20 years, was kidnapped on the border at Killen, Co Armagh, as he returned from a fishing trip in the Republic. Dressed in jeans and a Guinness T-shirt, Detective-Constable Robinson, who had been on sick-leave for three years, was travelling with some friends, serving prison officers, when a gang of eight armed IRA men ambushed their vehicle at a bogus checkpoint.

D/C Robinson's abduction had been planned by the IRA's Belfast Brigade after they received information that the officer was planning the fishing trip to County Kerry. The IRA intelligence wing passed the information to an active service unit in Armagh, an area where the IRA retained a deadly freedom of movement in the Irish border hills. Some years before, the British Army had been forced to abandon movements of troops by road for it had become too risky. Since that time, the Army had relied on helicopters to ferry them around the border area because of the high risk of ambush. Even then, the IRA continued to harry the army, staging lightning attacks on the army helicopters, firing at them with automatic weapons as they landed and took off from exposed places.

Within hours of her husband's kidnap, Ann Robinson appealed to the IRA to spare her husband's life, claiming he had been ill and off duty for three years, suffering from depression. The Catholic Bishop Cahal Daly, describing the abduction as 'repugnant' and 'an outrage to all humanitarian feelings' called for the IRA to release the officer unharmed.

In fact, D/C Robinson's abduction, and the appeals for his release, caused problems for the IRA leadership in South Armagh. Robinson had been seized because the Belfast leadership believed he could point the finger at RUC officers known to be particularly hard on IRA men arrested and taken to Castlereagh for questioning. They hoped to uncover identities, addresses and movements.

D/C Robinson, a powerfully built man, was put through hours of interrogation and torture. It had always been the IRA's intention to find out what they could and then shoot their prisoner. His fate had been sealed from the moment he was taken, but appeals from the Roman Catholic clergy caused concern. Factions inside the IRA High Command believed that they should heed appeals by Roman Catholic clergy, for fear of alienating Catholics who had nothing whatsoever to do with the IRA but who were, nevertheless, sympathetic to the IRA cause. For the IRA, however, there could be no turning back. The appeals from Church leaders had come too late to save Robinson's life, because by then he had seen the faces of a number of his interrogators. He had to die.

One of the names Robinson was forced to reveal would be a serving member of the CID in Belfast, who had a reputation for intimidating and terrorising suspected IRA men brought in for questioning. His name was immediately placed at the top of the IRA hit list.

My Belfast cell was given the task of checking that the information Robinson had given was correct. We had been informed that the officer lived in Garnerville Road, near Belfast City Airport, drove two cars and never revealed, not even to friends or neighbours, that he worked for the RUC. Most of the time he drove around in a battered 1979 Toyota, but he also kept a new Renault which he garaged some distance away from his home. We were told that he played golf with other police officers at Helen's Bay, near Bangor. One plan under consideration was to target the man's car while he was playing golf, placing a charge under the vehicle which would explode when he drove away.

I was detailed to survey the officer's home, check out the information and report back. As soon as I saw the man's house and the old Toyota standing in the drive, I realised that the information the IRA had acquired from Robinson was accurate. I knew the IRA intended to place a bomb under his car within the next couple of days, if not the following night. As soon as I had checked his home, I immediately phoned Castlereagh because I realised this was a matter of urgency.

'Carol speaking,' I told the Castlereagh operator. 'It's urgent.'

Thirty minutes later, I met Felix and Mo in Knocknagoney Park, a few hundred yards from the man's home.

'Can you take us to the house?' Felix asked.

'Jump in,' I said.

As I slowed down and drove past the front of the man's house, Felix said, 'My God, Mo, do you realise who lives there? We know that man, Marty, he works at Castlereagh. We had better do something, and fast.'

Felix decided that the only way we could save the man's life and keep my identity safe would be to pretend that I had accidentally driven into a police checkpoint. Felix told Mo and me to wait in the car park while he returned to Belfast and picked up an RUC form demanding that I produce my driver's documents at a police station within five days.

When Felix returned, I drove them back to Belfast and immediately went to see my cell commander, Spud, reporting everything I had seen.

'Good,' he said, 'that's OK.'

'But I had a problem,' I added, 'I got stopped at a checkpoint.'

'You fucking what?' he exploded. 'For fuck's sake, Marty, tell me you're joking?'

'It was not too far from his house,' I said. 'Are you surprised? For fuck's sake, there is an RUC training camp just up the road from his house.'

He began to lose his temper, shouting at me. 'What the fuck is this, Marty?' he said. 'Every time you get involved in a job it's a fucking disaster. How the fuck did you get stopped at a sodding checkpoint?'

'What the fuck did you expect me to do?' I said. 'What did you want me to do, do a handbrake turn and speed away? I had to just fucking stop, like all the other traffic.'

I could tell he wasn't very happy, but I had to continue with my story. 'The RUC man gave me this form, and told me to produce my licence and insurance at New Barnsley police station.'

He looked at the evidence I produced, realising I was telling the truth. His temper subsided but he seemed far from happy.

As I drove back home that night, I worried that someone within the IRA organisation might begin to suspect that there was a connection between me and all the operations that had gone wrong whenever I had become involved. As I approached my home, parked the car and walked inside, I also realised how vulnerable I was if the IRA ever wanted to pick me up.

Only a couple of weeks later I would become involved in another IRA operation where, once again,

I would have to risk exposure to save the lives of two RUC men.

IRA intelligence had learned that two RUC officers, stationed at Antrim, would stop at a take-away Chinese restaurant every Saturday night. They drove an ordinary, unmarked blue Ford Sierra without bullet-proof glass or reinforced steel doors, as there was little IRA activity in that area.

My cell commander told me to check the following Saturday night to make sure that the two RUC men still called at the Chinese restaurant on their way home. I knew that if I was involved in another operational disaster my integrity would be called into question, my identity put at risk. So I phoned Felix and told him I needed to discuss a new situation with him.

The following night, we met as arranged and I told him of the IRA plan to kill the two Antrim officers, emphasising that there was a real possibility of the attack being organised for the coming Saturday, two days away. I also told him that I felt Spud and certain other cell members may have begun to suspect me and that if he wanted to protect my identity, he should take preventative measures.

'What have you in mind?' he asked.

'I believe you should tell the two officers from Antrim that the IRA have targeted their Saturday night visits to the Chinese restaurant, and tell them to stay away from the place from now on.'

'Do you know what they plan to do?' Felix asked.

'Yes,' I said. 'The preferred plan is to shoot them,' I told him, 'or, because the Sierra isn't armoured, they were thinking of throwing a Semtex coffee-jar bomb at the car instead. That would certainly kill them both.'

'Too right,' Felix said. 'Go on.'

'But I will have to tell Spud that when I checked out

the restaurant there were no police at the restaurant and no Ford Sierra. Because of their growing suspicions, they won't believe me and will send someone else to check. If the police never turn up there again, my story will be seen to be true, no matter how often they check. I'm not saying they won't suspect me, but it should help me.'

'I agree,' said Felix, 'good idea.'

Once again I returned to my IRA boss and told him the bad news – no blue Ford Sierra had turned up at the restaurant. At first he seemed somewhat annoyed, but told me he would be sending someone else to check the following week. That pleased me because it would prove I was telling the truth and, hopefully, would arouse no suspicion. I would hear no more of that particular operation and hoped it would help to rebuild my credibility within my cell.

* * *

On the odd occasion, black humour would surface during an IRA operation, but not very often.

Once, though, I had been asked to target an RUC man who frequently visited his brother's house in Ballysillan, North Belfast.

After I had reported the operation to Castlereagh, the Special Branch went to see the man who lived at the house to warn him of a possible IRA threat. They were somewhat surprised when they discovered that the man who lived at the address was a vicar. They asked him who the car belonged to, and the Vicar told them that his brother was an RUC officer.

The Special Branch officers said they would warn the vicar's brother now they knew his identity.

'No, no,' said the Vicar. 'Leave it to me. I will give a

press conference telling the IRA not to target me because I am a man of God. I will go on television and make an appeal through the newspapers revealing who I am. Don't worry. God will ensure we are safe.'

The Special Branch officers told the vicar in no uncertain terms that he must do absolutely nothing of the sort; he must tell no one of their visit to his house because someone else would get hurt, if not killed, if he uttered a word about their visit.

'My God, I wouldn't want that on my conscience,' he protested. 'But I believe God will protect all of us.'

The officers made the vicar sit down and listen very carefully to what they had to say.

'Listen, and take note,' one explained. 'One of our agents has risked his life saving your brother's life. You must do nothing and say nothing to anyone, otherwise this young man will be shot dead by the IRA.'

At that, the vicar looked surprised and began to shake.

'Do you understand?' they asked. 'Are you sure you understand?'

'May God forgive me,' he said. 'Now I understand everything. I will say nothing and do nothing. I will say a prayer for him, instead. Will that be all right?'

'That would be fine,' one said, 'I'm sure the young man would appreciate that.'

Having been told of the vicar's reaction by the Branch officers, I watched every TV news bulletin during the following few days, fearful that the vicar would blurt everything out, despite the fact that he had been warned to keep quiet. Thank God he never did. Later, we had a laugh at the vicar's naïveté. But such humour was scarce.

Some IRA plans seemed downright foolhardy to me. One such example was the attempted assassination of an RUC Divisional Commander who lived in a large bungalow in Hillsborough, south of Lisburn.

I was told to pick up Paul Lynch, a young though highly-dangerous IRA gunman with a baby face and a reputation for being both a crack shot and a ruthless killer. I was to drive him to Hillsborough to check out the vicinity around the Commander's home.

I dropped him at the end of the road, which had a number of expensive, detached homes and returned 15 minutes later to pick him up.

On the way back to Belfast, Lynch told me, 'That job's a gift, Marty, an absolute gift from God. Just now I was in the man's back garden and no one could see me from the house. I've worked out exactly how I will deal with him. I plan to lie in wait for him in his garden, and when he comes to the patio doors leading from the sitting room to the garden, I'll just knock him off, give him the whole magazine from an AK-47. Easy as ABC.'

I couldn't believe that it would be that easy for an IRA gunman to kill a Divisional Commander. I was convinced that they would have better security than Lynch was suggesting. To me it sounded like a mad idea.

As we drove back, he continued to chat about his operation. 'Marty,' he remarked, 'that bastard's already as good as dead.'

The following day I informed Felix. His attitude was as positive as always. 'I'll tell the Commander to ensure his safety.'

Within 24 hours, the Commander and his family were moved to a safe house and eventually relocated to another. I realised that once again I had taken a risk, making yet another set of IRA men suspicious of me. But I also realised that another man's life had been saved.

I was beginning to believe that I would never survive the career I had accidentally become involved in, working as an agent between the two hardest organisations imaginable. Sometimes Felix and I would discuss my situation.

I never forgot the words Felix said to me during one of our chats, words which sounded like a warning that I should heed. 'Marty,' he said, 'I'm going to tell you something.'

We were sitting in the back of the van chatting about the IRA and their punishment squads.

He went on, 'Listen carefully to what I have to say. If the IRA ever make the connection between you and us, you know exactly what will happen if you ever admit you ever had dealings with us.'

'I know,' I said, not wanting to think too hard about the horrible consequences.

'If those people ever get you,' he continued, 'they will try every trick in the book to get you to admit that you're an agent, working for the Branch. If you're not giving them the replies they want to hear, they will turn very nasty and they will torture you with atrocities that you and I could never imagine. They're sick bastards, Marty.' He paused. 'You have to be very, very good and totally determined to cope with their interrogation. If you deny ever working for us and keep telling them the same story, I will guarantee that you will eventually walk out of there. It may not be the next day or the next week, but one day you will walk out.'

'But, I will also promise you, that if you admit for one second that you ever worked for us, you will never see daylight again.'

I respected Felix for telling me that. I felt he was the most honest man I had ever met. As I walked away from that chat, I knew that the only reason I was continuing such a risky job, day in, day out, was because I trusted the man who, in effect, was my boss, but who had become almost family and certainly my closest friend.

I also realised at the same time that Felix's bosses wouldn't care a damn about me, whether I lived or whether I died. While Agent Carol was proving useful to them, providing intelligence to help the RUC and the politicians in their battle against the IRA, saving the odd policeman's life, then I was useful to them. I also realised that once the IRA had rumbled me, I would be of no further use and I feared they might wash their hands of me, leaving me to my fate. Events later confirmed my worst fears.

I also began to wonder if it ever came to the crunch, whether Felix would put my life first, and refuse to obey orders that his RUC bosses gave him, orders that could perhaps lead to my arrest by the Provisionals, a searching interrogation, torture and almost certain death. I trusted Felix implicitly and hoped he would never have to make such a decision.

*   *   *

One day, Spud told me to go and watch an RUC man who, every day, rode his moped to work at Queen Street Police Station in the centre of Belfast. He would park the scooter outside a Heel Bar, 20 yards from the police station and walk, still wearing his crash helmet, into the RUC base.

The IRA planned to use two gunmen to shoot him on a busy street corner, a few hundred yards from the RUC base, as he arrived for work. I notified the Special Branch and the man was ordered to stop riding the moped. Whether on purpose, or by accident, it was fortunate that the officer never removed his crash hat until he had walked into the building, so the IRA had no idea what he looked like.

I waited for some reaction from Spud or my other cell members, but none came. This worried me, because if there was no reaction to an operation in which I had been involved, and which had subsequently collapsed, and no one made any comment to me, I feared I might have been placed under suspicion. In IRA language that meant they thought I could be a traitor, working for the hated Special Branch. I re-doubled my attention to detail, determined not to put a foot wrong. I had always taken care to make sure I was never followed, by foot, motorbike or car, but now I took greater precautions than ever.

Now, whenever meetings were planned with Felix and Mo, I would make a deliberate detour, check out whether I was being followed and, only then, would I make my way to the rendezvous. Another evasive tactic would be to use the housing estates to lose anyone trying to tail me. I would drive slowly into an estate, and when I rounded a corner I would accelerate hard and race out of the estate via another exit and on to the main road. I checked continually, but never saw anyone following me. I began to relax again.

I knew that the Special Branch sometimes followed me to check that I wasn't being tailed by the IRA. They would produce photographs of me taken all over Belfast and throw the pictures down on the desk for me to examine. Throughout the years I worked for them, I could never remember anyone ever taking my picture while I was racing around the city. Some of the photographs were even taken in Republican strongholds, where anyone seen taking photographs would have been questioned, if not instantly taken away and beaten up, before being closely interrogated. And some of the photographs were close-ups, as though taken only a few feet away!

It made me realise that if the Branch could secretly tail me with such ease without me ever realising it, then so could the IRA.

The man the IRA planted on the Larne–Stranraer ferry discovered another wonderful target – an RUC minibus which was parked each day near the ferry. The unmarked bus was used to transport RUC officers from the nearby police station to the harbour whenever a ferry docked. It was their job to monitor cars and foot passengers, looking out for possible IRA suspects.

Their man had checked the minibus and I was sent with another cell member to survey the possibility of an attack and report back to Spud at the next meeting. We saw at least six RUC men clamber in and out of the minibus whenever a ferry docked. It was decided that a Semtex booby-trap bomb should be planted with a mercury tilt-switch under the vehicle. I realised that such a powerful bomb would completely destroy the entire minibus, killing everyone inside and probably seriously injuring bystanders within a 20 yard radius.

As soon as I returned home, I dropped off the other IRA man and pressed the secret switch on my radio. An hour later, I explained to Felix that the IRA man on the ferry had discovered another ideal target and I had checked it out that night.

Felix discussed my plan to prevent the bombing and keep my involvement secret. We decided that the minibus should not suddenly disappear, because that would arouse suspicion. So it was decided that the Larne RUC would be advised to make sure the minibus would never be left unattended in future. Felix believed that not even the wildest IRA active service unit would try to plant a bomb with an officer sitting in the driver's seat.

As a result, the operation was called off with no suspicion that I had been responsible for another débâcle. The plan was not forgotten, however, for in September 1993, Rosena Brown and two new recruits, Paul 'Bun' McCullough, 30, and Stephen Canning, 21, were each jailed for 20 years, having been found guilty of conspiracy to murder, conspiracy to cause an explosion and having a Semtex bomb with intent. Their car had been stopped as they headed towards the Larne Harbour to carry out an attack on an RUC minibus.

Another reckless raid planned by our cell was to hurl two coffee-jar bombs, packed with Semtex, into an office of the Protestant Ulster Defence Association on the Shankill Road in the heart of Loyalist Belfast. The IRA had received intelligence that the offices were allegedly used for meetings by Loyalist paramilitary squads.

Spud told us that two IRA bombers would be dropped off by car about 20 yards from the building, and the driver would remain in the getaway car with the engine running. The two men, the coffee jars concealed under their jackets, would hurl the jars into the first-floor offices and make their escape.

I was not directly involved in the operation in any way but I heard of its planning. I immediately called Felix, believing the attack would take place within the next 48 hours, and told him everything I knew during a three-minute call from a phone box. I had hardly left the phone box when I heard the DMSUs racing towards the area, where they threw up road blocks and checkpoints, stopping and examining every vehicle coming from republican parts of the city towards the Shankill.

Once again the operation was postponed but would not be forgotten.

Eighteen months later, in October 1993, nine innocent people and an IRA bomber, Thomas Begley, were killed when Begley walked into the fish shop below the UDA offices and put down a bomb. It exploded immediately, wrecking the building and killing those queuing for their fish.

*   *   *

One IRA operation which I helped thwart gave me great satisfaction. A middle-aged RUC patrol officer, who worked in the New Barnsley police station near my home, had been targeted. Most days he would take his wife to work in Belfast City Centre, and the IRA planned to shoot him as he drove off after dropping his wife. To the IRA he was an easy target. To me he was simply 'Bumper', a small, rather fat policeman with a large moustache, who was easy-going and friendly to everyone he met, both on and off duty.

I heard of this so-called 'easy target' and told the Branch. To me, targeting policemen like Bumper was totally unfair and unwarranted. I asked Felix to make sure he was OK. I had also discovered that the IRA weren't sure of his exact address. Ironically, when I told Felix of the planned murder he was also outraged, as Bumper was also a colleague and friend of his.

There were numerous other operations, some of which I would be involved with, others that I simply heard about through IRA intelligence or my cell. Only once, throughout my four-year career as an Intelligence Agent with the RUC, did I ever fail to save someone's life after I had become inextricably involved. And I never forgot that night.

CHAPTER TWELVE

I WAS SITTING AT HOME, LISTENING INTENTLY TO THE RADIO with Angie and my two boys on the evening of Wednesday, 19 June 1991, when I first heard the news.

The male newsreader said, 'Reports are coming in of a man having been shot dead in the Holywood Road area of East Belfast. It is thought he could be a member of the security forces.'

In that instant, I knew that I had been caught in the trap I had always feared since I began working for both the Special Branch and the IRA. I had known about the plot to kill a soldier in that part of East Belfast from the very beginning and circumstances had forced me to play a role in his murder.

As I listened to the news I felt sick and left the room unable to hear any more, asking myself how I could have done anything else to save the poor man's life. I blamed myself for his murder, and yet, I believe, there was nothing I could have done to save him. But I would never forget. The horror of his death would never leave me, nor the nightmares that followed.

I knew the dead man had to be the person I'd heard was to be a possible IRA target four weeks earlier. The first I heard of the intended victim was one day in May when an IRA man I knew as Jimmy asked me, as a favour, to drive him over to East Belfast.

During the drive, Jimmy explained, 'I'm watching for a soldier who gets a bus on the Holywood Road. I think he must live in one of the streets nearby.'

Jimmy told me, 'The IRA want me to go and shoot him as he's standing at the bus stop, and I've told them to fuck off because that would be a stupid idea, bloody suicidal. So I want to go and take a look to try and find where he lives so that we can shoot him in his home.'

After checking the bus stop we drove into Nevis Avenue off Holywood Road, looking for the target. We then drove into Irwin Drive and I kept looking at Jimmy to see if I could tell if he had any real idea where the soldier lived. But I had to do this surreptitiously, so that Jimmy didn't think I was keeping an eye on him.

I had to bear in mind that some elements in the IRA might now be suspecting that I was indeed a British agent, and this could have been a way of testing my commitment to the cause. I came to the conclusion that Jimmy had no real idea where the soldier lived and had been on a scouting exercise, either hoping that something would turn up, or perhaps noting my reactions. After passing the bus stop again we left the area and drove back to West Belfast.

After dropping Jimmy, I found an inconspicuous phone box and called Felix. I told him exactly what had happened.

'I think I had better take a look,' he said.

'Fine,' I said, 'when do you want to go?'

'Meet me in 45 minutes at the usual place.'

Felix and a new side-kick, a tall, athletic man in his 40s called Ray, picked me up.

'Marty,' Felix said, as he usually did on these occasions, 'tell us exactly what happened.'

I told them everything that had happened since picking up Jimmy a couple of hours earlier. We drove to Holywood Road and retraced the exact route I had taken with Jimmy. The two men took notes of the bus stop and the names of the surrounding streets.

Felix said, 'We must check this out. Because you're not directly involved with this case it is possible it could happen at any time, even tonight.'

'Felix,' I said, 'I doubt it because my man had no idea where this soldier lived. I could tell by the way he was looking around him all the time, asking me to go up and down three streets as if searching for a clue.'

'I hear what you're saying,' Felix said, 'but we have to make sure. We must do everything to safeguard this man's life. We must keep checking.'

Forty minutes later, Felix decided that we would have to call off the search and return to Castlereagh. They intended to contact the UDR to check if any of their personnel lived in any of those streets off the Holywood Road. They also intended to check their street registers of the area to discover the names and occupations of all the residents.

I heard nothing more about the mystery soldier from either my IRA contacts or Felix and forgot about the affair. At that time, I was probably making five or six separate journeys throughout Belfast and beyond every other day, ferrying IRA men around. I listened to their conversations and I passed on anything worthwhile to Felix. Many of the journeys, and much of the information I learned, was inconsequential, but such frequent meetings with senior IRA personnel meant that I was becoming accepted as a staunch IRA member and, hopefully, earning their trust.

In particular, I would listen to every tiny hint of a forthcoming IRA operation, whether it was planned bombings, shootings or robberies, and call Felix. I would also tell him if I heard of any planned operations that had been halted or postponed.

On the morning of 19 June, I was contacted by one of the IRA couriers and told to attend a cell meeting that afternoon. As usual I went along. But there were only three people present, instead of the usual eight or nine.

Spud said, 'This is not a meeting Marty, we've got a job for you. You're to drive Stephen and Paul on an operation. My heart sank and I feared the worst. I knew Paul Lynch to be one of the IRA's top assassins, a ruthless bastard who had a reputation for the most daring attacks and a ferocious hatred of anyone who opposed the cause. Even his mates believed he was a man without feeling.

The other man I knew as Stephen, who was also a recognised IRA gunman.

'The car's outside,' Spud said. 'It's hot; it's just been hijacked, so dump it immediately afterwards.'

'Let's go,' said Paul and we walked to the car.

Spud had decided that Paul should make his own way to the target, as all RUC patrols would be highly suspicious of three young men driving around Belfast together. Spud realised that it would be stupid to jeopardise the operation and risk losing three IRA men after failing to take such a simple precaution. He wanted nothing to go wrong.

'Do you know East Belfast, Marty?' Stephen asked as we drove away.

'Aye,' I replied.

'That's where we're heading,' he said. 'A house in Nevis Avenue off Holywood Road.

I knew then that I was driving to the home of a

soldier whom they intended to shoot in cold blood. I wondered what I should do; I wondered if there was anything that I could now do to save the man's life. As we drove along, I prayed that Felix had been able to trace the man and have him moved from the house, but he had told me nothing of the soldier since we had first checked out the area a month before.

I debated whether I should try any trick, like stalling the car or crashing it into a vehicle, as if by accident. But Stephen sitting by my side was armed with a hand-gun and I knew that if he suspected I was not playing straight, he would shoot me and walk away without a second thought.

I was already convinced that Spud was suspicious of me. It seemed most unusual to call me to a meeting and then surprise me by announcing that I was to accompany two of the IRA's most notorious killers on a high-risk operation the instant I arrived. I also had no idea whether Spud would have passed on his suspicions to either Paul or Stephen.

'Stop here,' said Stephen, who was sitting in the passenger seat, as we turned into Nevis Avenue. 'I'll be back soon.'

A few minutes later, Paul arrived in a hijacked car and parked nearby. As Stephen got out of my car and walked away I prayed to God that the soldier had been spirited away, as most men had been when I had discovered that the IRA were targeting them. I knew that the Special Branch, and all the security services, did everything possible to save targeted men.

I wound down the car window so that I would hear if any shots were fired. I prayed that I would hear nothing. I waited what seemed an age, but it was probably less than 60 seconds. Then I heard the shots – one, two, three, four, five – I counted them, and knew in my heart that some poor bastard had been murdered in cold blood.

My hands were shaking and I broke into a cold sweat as I rammed the car into first gear and drove towards my two IRA murderers. They appeared from the house and jumped into the car as I slowed for them. They seemed to be in black moods, and I remained silent, not wanting to know whether they had found their target, or had just fired off five shots in anger at having found the house empty.

'Fuckin' drive,' said Paul as he climbed in the back, 'fuckin' drive.'

No one said another word and I drove, not fast or furiously.

Two hundred yards down the road, Paul said, 'Stop the car.'

I braked and stopped.

'Dump it,' said Paul. 'Dump it here, then fuck off.'

Both men got out of the car and walked away. I turned off the engine and left the vehicle, walking away in the opposite direction, hoping that the two men were in black moods because they had found no one at home. But I was wrong.

Forty-eight hours later, the newspapers reported that a member of the 3rd Parachute Regiment had been murdered while at his fiancée's home off the Holywood Road, Belfast. Private Tony Harrison, 21, from London, was on leave, finalising wedding plans at the home of his fiancée Tracey Gouck in Nevis Avenue, one of the roads we had checked.

Tracey had described that at about 6.30pm the previous evening, she had answered a knock at the door. One man put a gun to her head and forced her into the living room. The second gunman then fired five shots at her fiancé, hitting him in the head and body. Tracey's widowed mother, Agnes Gouck, and a ten-year-old girl were also in the house when the killers struck.

At a meeting of my IRA cell a couple of days later, the man who had murdered Harrison described to me and others what had happened. He seemed satisfied with his evening's work.

Paul said, 'The cell wanted to carry out this 'op' in the morning with two or three of us actively involved, but I decided it would be better to carry out the job alone, dressed as a postman. I was sitting on a wall at the bottom of Nevis Avenue reading a newspaper, waiting for the soldier's girlfriend to leave the house. I had the Magnum, cocked and ready, in the postman's bag. I saw the girl leave her house and walk straight past me on the opposite side of the road. She turned the corner as if to walk to Holywood Road and looked straight at me; it was eyeball to eyeball.'

He went on to explain how he had walked to the house, knocked on the front door, but no young man had answered so he left and returned that evening with an accomplice.

'It was a piece of piss,' he said. 'The bastard didn't even move. As soon as he appeared in the hall, I let him have it firing into the body and the head, just to make sure.'

Later, I discovered that the man who posed as a postman had carried out a similar killing two months earlier, once again shooting a man at point-blank range. Businessman Wallace McVeigh was at work in the family's fruit and vegetable depot at Balmoral when the killers struck.

On that occasion, the two IRA men had walked into the depot and asked for McVeigh. When he came to see the two men, one said, 'Are you Wallace McVeigh?'

'Yes, can I help you?' he asked.

Without saying another word, the men pulled out

their hand-guns and shot him six times at point-blank range. They then turned and walked out of the depot and into the main road where a getaway car was waiting. Later, claiming responsibility for the killing, the IRA said the man had been killed because he was supplying the Security Forces with fruit and vegetables. McVeigh would not be the only person to die for such a tenuous reason – many businessmen would be murdered in cold blood for similar 'activities'.

Throughout the summer of 1991, I began to suspect that my IRA cell mates were becoming suspicious. It was the way they would occasionally fall silent when I entered the room. Some would also look at me in a way they had never done before. And that worried me. I became even more concerned days later when, for the first time, they lied to me about an operation in which I had been initially involved.

In July 1991, another IRA cell with whom I had occasionally worked asked me to become involved in an operation they were planning. Their EO, a young man called Tommy, someone well known to the Special Branch, asked me to drive him to Dunmurry off the M1, south of Belfast.

On the way there, Tommy told me, 'Marty, I've decided to plant a Semtex bomb in a shop in Kingsway, Dunmurry, below what I have been told is an empty flat. I plan to put the bomb in the shop and then set off a burglar alarm by breaking a window. I will run a command wire through the back of the shop, across the garden and over a railway line where the bomb will be triggered. When the peelers come running towards the shop, we'll let it rip.'

Together, we checked out the shop by driving past the building a few times before heading back to his house at Twinbrook, a mile or so from Dunmurry. Before we parted, Tommy had asked me to find someone who would set off the burglar alarm by breaking the window. I asked a friend of mine called Paul, who had nothing to do with the IRA, if he would carry out the job. He was happy to do so because he knew it was for the IRA.

Two days later, I drove down to Twinbrook and told Tommy I had someone who would set off the alarm. To my surprise, Tommy said, 'Marty, the job's been called off. The Operation's Officer in Belfast has told me to leave it awhile; we might take a look at it some time later.'

This news worried me. I was well aware that the IRA's Operations Officer – always called 'Double O' – one of the most important officers in the entire Belfast Brigade, and had overall control of every IRA cell and their active service units. He had the power to give the go-ahead or to stop any IRA operation and, furthermore, I knew he had to give no reason why a particular operation should be halted. He would know of every IRA operation being prepared and planned and would always be notified when an operation was to go ahead. He was the man at the nerve centre of the entire IRA network. He needed to know details of every operation to prevent any possible conflicts, with perhaps two cells planning similar operations at the same time or near the same place. He would make the decision as to which operations would go ahead and which were to be delayed or called off.

At that time, the Double O was Paddy Fern, a quiet, intelligent man in his late 30s, a man of medium build with greying dark hair and a thin moustache. IRA men from different cells and squads would call at Paddy Fern's house on the Falls Road day and night and his home would be kept under almost constant Special Branch surveillance. They knew his home was the nerve centre of IRA activity in Belfast and, as I would learn later,

Special Branch would use their latest, most sophisticated listening devices to try and eavesdrop on conversations inside the house.

Because Tommy had told me his Dunmurry operation had been called off, I did not bother to inform the Branch. Three days later, on the morning news of July 8, I was shocked to hear that an 80-year-old woman had escaped with minor injuries when an IRA booby-trap bomb demolished her flat above a shop in Kingsway, Dunmurry, as she slept in the early hours of the morning.

Two police officers, whom I knew to be the intended targets of the attack, had been slightly injured. The radio report said they had been lured to the area after a burglar alarm in an adjacent shop had been activated.

From that moment, I knew in my heart that the IRA suspected I was an agent working for the Special Branch, because I could conceive of no other logical reason why I would have been told the operation had been called off.

I debated whether to go and see Felix to ask his advice. But I knew there would be no future in that course of action. I tried to convince myself during the next few days that I had become paranoid about the whole business, that the IRA may have called off the Dunmurry bombing and then decided to put it back on again. I had no other first-hand evidence to suggest that they suspected me. I decided to continue, reminding myself to pay attention to every minute detail, watch peoples' reaction to my presence and to see if I was still included in surveying and planning forthcoming operations.

To my surprise, two days later, my IRA cell boss Spud asked me to store two AK-47s in one of my dumps. Some months earlier, the IRA had given a woman £350 to convert her bathroom, so that AK-47s and explosives could be stored behind wooden cladding. At that time I had four dumps, dotted around different houses in the Ballymurphy area in which I kept the two AK-47s, 200 rounds of ammunition, a Magnum, a Smith & Wesson .38 Special, two Semtex coffee-jar bombs, detonators and a 5lb block of Semtex.

I phoned the young woman who was storing the two AK-47s and arranged for her to bring them to me, along with the ammunition and the Magnum. She brought them in a holdall having taken a taxi, handing over the weapons and ammunition to me at a restaurant car park in Andersonstown. I took them to another of my secret dumps in a house belonging to another woman. I would give the woman £20 or £30 every few weeks, hinting that the money was coming from IRA funds. In reality, I paid her from my own pocket. I also ensured, through my Special Branch handlers, that the womens' homes would never be raided.

After phoning Felix, I arranged to meet him at a spot not far from where I had stored the weapons. With one Branch car in front of my vehicle and another behind, I drove to Castlereagh in the early hours of the following morning. As we left the area, I noticed more than half a dozen RUC and army Land Rovers patrolling the area. They were taking no chances.

I parked my car outside the back entrance to Castlereagh and, keeping the weapons in a holdall, lay on the back seat of Felix's car while he drove inside. My car had to be parked outside in case any RUC men noted the number of my vehicle. Felix always stressed that the Branch would never permit RUC personnel to know anything of their business or their contacts unless they needed to be informed for a specific operation. Even then, they would only be given the most minimal information.

The weapons were taken away by a Branch expert

and 'doctored'. A tracking device was attached, so that whenever the weapons were moved, their exact whereabouts could be monitored. Felix, Ray and I played cards, and at 2.00am Felix, who never seemed to stop eating, went down to the canteen and brought back three huge fried breakfasts. Once again, Felix lived up to his reputation of being a massive and speedy eater; I had only eaten one sausage by the time Felix had cleared his plate!

I was told of a famous occasion when another officer had been so foolhardy as to try and steal one of Felix's sausages, simply as a joke. To Felix, taking his food was not a laughing matter, and he stabbed the man's hand with his fork, forcing him to drop the sausage. Legend had it within the Branch that no one else ever tried the same trick again.

Before we returned home some 90 minutes later, Felix radioed through to check that no Land-Rover or foot patrols were in the Ballymurphy area when I returned home. As sometimes occurred when I was involved in such late night activities I didn't want to waken Angie or the boys so I would sleep on the sofa downstairs.

Some days later, Spud asked me to attend a cell meeting. He spoke to everyone separately, calling each of us into the room, one after the other, and gave us our instructions, while the rest of us waited in the sitting room. While we were waiting, I am certain I saw some of my cell colleagues giving me suspicious looks, but no one said anything to my face.

When I went into the kitchen, I closed the door. Spud was sitting at the table.

'Sit down, Marty,' he said, 'I've got something to tell you.'

I feared the worst, but Spud simply began to give me the details of the latest operation he was planning.

'We have information from one of our good sources that there is a bar in Bangor, called Charlie Heggarty's, which is frequented by Paras every weekend. Your job is to go and buy a car. Here's £300 to get a vehicle we can use to park outside the pub all day, so that we've got a parking space for the getaway car. Make sure it's taxed. It doesn't matter a fuck about an MOT. Just get something clean that won't attract attention. It'll never be used again so £300 should be enough.'

I nodded.

He went on, 'I've given the lads the jobs they must carry out. Some are to check the pub this weekend, others are arranging to hijack a car for the operation, and others are to plan the best route for our escape. If this job goes according to plan, Marty, you'll make your name. I believe it will be one of the most successful jobs the IRA has ever pulled off. If we kill as many soldiers as I'm expecting it will be a great coup for the organisation and for all of us who have taken part. It will also be a hell of a setback for the fucking Brits.'

Before I left the room, Spud added, 'Marty, I'm expecting at least 20 dead Paras from this one job and maybe more. The information came from one of our best sources, a taxi driver who has dropped off loads of soldiers at this bar over many weekends. The bar's been checked out once already and every man in the place had an English accent. You could tell by looking at them that they were all fucking British squaddies.'

I could see from the look on Spud's face that this operation had gripped his imagination. He hoped to make his reputation within the organisation with this one and was excited by the prospect.

The fact that Spud had trusted me with the details of such a major operation gave me fresh confidence that perhaps all was well, that my fear of having been suspected of working for the Branch had been misplaced and that I had, stupidly, over-reacted and allowed myself to become paranoid about the whole business.

And yet my mind was working overtime. Before ringing Felix to tell him of the plan, I sat in the car, thinking through the whole scenario. If this operation went wrong or failed spectacularly, I realised that suspicion would be bound to fall on me. I wondered if I would be able to withstand a full IRA interrogation, and the mere thought of the sort of torture of which those men are capable made my mouth go dry. I knew that some agents and police informers had been held for several weeks before finally being killed, their face and bodies almost unrecognisable due to the terrible beatings they had been given. After five minutes of privately debating the pros and cons, I knew that I had no option but to phone Felix and tell him.

I got out of the car, slammed the door and went and called him.

'I need to talk to you,' I said, sounding serious.

Felix, however, hadn't noticed my tone of voice and began happily cracking a couple of jokes, as he sometimes did.

'We must have a meeting, Felix,' I began, my voice sounding anxious. 'This one's urgent.'

'Alright, alright' he said, '30 minutes, usual place.' And he was gone.

All the way to the meeting, I kept telling myself that I was about to commit the greatest mistake of my life. Something inside told me I was putting my head in an IRA noose.

When I told Felix of the plan, however, his mood changed abruptly. He looked perturbed. I knew Felix had handled many agents since the Troubles began in the early 1970s, but the audacity and the numbers of soldiers due to be killed in this operation surprised even him.

'When's this going to happen, Marty?'

'I don't know, but everyone is checking it out this weekend.'

'So, you're sure it won't take place this weekend?'

'I'm as sure as can be,' I said, 'because they're not checking it out till this Saturday.'

'Go ahead with everything but make sure you keep us informed of any changes. Alright?'

'OK', I replied.

A couple of days later Spud called another meeting, but this time he addressed everyone together.

He asked one man, named Philip, if he had organised a getaway car; he asked me if I had the two AK-47s safe and ready, and asked others about the escape route they had mapped out. Everyone answered in the affirmative. There seemed to be no reason why we could not now check out the bar over the next weekend.

Spud told the eight people present, 'I'm convinced the recce will show we have an easy and straightforward operation, so I want to run through the plan once again. I want you to drive the getaway car, Marty.' I nodded.

He told Paul and Philip, 'I want you two to carry the AKs.'

'How many rounds have we got, Marty?'

'Well, I've got 189.'

'I want you to tape two magazines to each AK, so you each have 60 rounds, a total of 120. The two spare full magazines will be kept in the getaway car with Marty. Those magazines will only be used in an emergency when we are driving away.

'I want you, Patricia, to make sure you are in Bangor with all the gear. Marty will pick you up outside the railway station in the hijacked car at the time I will give you later.'

'I want you, Skin, to pick up the old banger parked outside and drive back to Belfast.'

Looking directly at me, Spud said, 'And as soon as Skin drives away, you, Marty, must immediately take the place to ensure a fast getaway. By the time Marty is parked outside with all the gear in the boot, everyone taking part will have been having a drink in the bar for 20 minutes. While you're all drinking, I want you to spend the time eyeing everyone who is a potential target. We want to get every fucking bastard we can.'

'And another point,' he said. 'Make sure when you've finished your drinks you put the glasses back on the bar so they can be washed. We don't want any finger prints left for forensic.'

Everyone in the room remained hushed as Spud continued outlining the details of the plan. 'When you three, Phil, Paul and Kieran, have identified your targets and when you are all confident the time is right, I want you all to make your way towards the door. Marty will be parked outside and the guns will be in a holdall in the boot, which will be unlocked. Just walk out, open the boot, take out the rifles and the hand-gun. You will find the AKs' magazines already taped together, so you will only have to push home the magazines. I want you, Kieran, to take the hand-gun and stand by the door and don't let anyone in or out.

'Phil and Paul, remember, hold the rifles by your leg until you reach the door. Then as soon as you go inside, open up, shooting at everyone you targeted earlier. Make sure that you have the rifles on semi-automatic. You know these rifles can fire 100 rounds a minute on automatic, so you must keep them on semi-auto so you can be accurate with the shots.

'If you have any of those stupid women wanting to act as heroines by throwing themselves in front of the soldiers, take no fucking notice. Just shoot them. I'm not going to let any Brit's whore fuck up an opportunity like this.'

Once more, Spud turned to Kieran. 'Remember, all of you, that you will have loads of time. The peelers won't be there for at least ten minutes. When Phil and Paul have done the business, Kieran, you must place the bomb by the exit to stop the emergency services, the peelers and the ambulance men getting into the bar to attend to the dying and the injured.'

Spud looked at Kieran, who said, 'Got it.'

Spud continued, 'As soon as you get out of the place, walk to the car, get in the back and put the rifles in the golf bag you will find on the back seat. There are also two magazines in the car just in case of trouble. Marty knows the escape route and he will drive away as normally as possible. No speeding unless absolutely necessary.'

It was intended that I should drive along the sea front road for about two miles and drop off the three lads near the entrance to a golf course. Then I would park the car in a nearby old people's home only yards from the main Bangor–Belfast road. It was hoped the peelers, if they found the car, would believe that we had parked a second getaway car there and were heading back to Belfast.

In fact, Spud planned that I would join the three lads at the golf club, hiding under a hedge for two hours or so until the last train to Belfast had left Bangor. Then we would walk along the railway track as quietly as possible, as there were houses either side of the line. At the same time, we would listen to the high-frequency radio receiver for any police activity. If we heard any, then we would hide in the undergrowth until the danger passed.

IRA intelligence thought it would take us a couple of hours to walk the six or seven miles to Holywood, where we would sleep in the hedges until morning before making our way to the car park of the Ulster Folk Museum. We would take it in turns to stand guard.

Parked there would be the old £300 banger and we would put the golf bag, containing the gear, into the boot. At 9.00am we had arranged for a minibus, hired for the day by an IRA sympathiser, to arrive, packed with children visiting the museum. All the children would be wearing white T-shirts bearing a logo and in the bus were similar T-shirts for the four of us to wear. After mingling with the children for an hour or so, we would all return to Belfast, raising no suspicion if we were stopped at any checkpoint.

After leaving the museum, Spud had arranged for a breakdown truck to pick up the banger and return it to Belfast.

Before we left the meeting that evening, Spud told Pete, Phil and me to go that weekend for one final recce of the bar. He wanted the operation to take place the following Saturday.

I immediately phoned Felix and told him that the final recce would take place in Bangor that Saturday night and the operation had been given the go-ahead for the following weekend.

When Paul, Phil and I arrived at Heggarty's Bar that Saturday night we saw an army helicopter hovering over the town. I was amazed to see RUC foot patrols all over the place and concentrated in and around the bar we were checking out. I looked at Phil and Paul, checking their reaction to the scene, for it seemed we had accidentally stumbled upon a major security alert. I, of course, understood all too well what had happened, that some stupid RUC Chief Superintendent, or whoever, had ordered the Army and police to swamp the area around the bar.

As we parked the car and walked into the bar to have a drink, I looked around me, furious that the RUC had risked exposing me when there was no need whatsoever for such a heavy-handed police and army presence.

The pub was full of people, perhaps more than a hundred, and I wondered how many SB undercover officers there were in the bar that night. Many customers were obviously off-duty soldiers. We could tell by their accents that they were from the mainland. As we drove to Bangor that evening we had all been chatty in the car, discussing the operation. Once inside the bar, however, Phil and Paul seemed to shun me, talking quietly between themselves and saying hardly a word to me. I became very worried.

We stayed for about 45 minutes, and as we emerged from the smoky bar we could see the Army chopper still hovering over the area. Hardly a word was passed between us on the return journey and I dropped them at Andersonstown.

The following morning, I pressed my secret button on the radio and met Felix an hour later. The moment I clambered into the back of the blacked-out SB van, Felix could see that I was far from happy.

'What's up?' he asked.

'I'll tell you what's fucking up,' I exploded in anger. 'I told you nothing was happening this weekend, and when we turn up in Bangor there is a fucking army helicopter nearly sitting on the roof of my car and the whole fucking town swarming with peelers.'

'Calm down,' he urged. 'Cool it, will you, Marty?'

'No I won't fucking cool it!' I yelled at him. 'You know I am under the deepest fucking suspicion and you have probably sealed my fate. How the fuck could you do something like that to me, Felix?' I paused for a moment, my head hanging in frustration and dejection at what had happened. But I hadn't finished yet. 'I kept you notified of every step of that operation, Felix,' I continued, 'and you have to put your bloody great foot in the middle of it and expose me to the fucking IRA. I don't know how you could do that to me, Felix, I really don't.'

Before I left him, he knew that I was both furious and upset. He also knew that, for the first time, I felt he had failed me and I now doubted if there was real trust between us. Kicking the van as I clambered out, I told him, 'I'll phone you if I can. But remember, this might be the last time you ever see me alive. And if it is, then it will be on your fucking conscience.'

Later, after I had calmed down a little, I wondered if I had been too heavy-handed with Felix, because I knew that he was always under incredible pressure from his bosses. I presumed that overriding Felix's authority, the faceless officers at the top had probably ordered the army and RUC presence. I wondered if Felix had argued my case, insisting that by carrying out their orders they were in grave danger of sacrificing one of their agents. I hoped he had, and I wondered if I would ever know.

Extraordinarily, however, the following day I heard that the planned attack on the paras visiting Heggarty's Bar would go ahead, as I was notified of a meeting due to take place the following Thursday, two days before the attack. Felix also asked for a meeting and apologised for what had happened, explaining that he had been ordered to watch Bangor by his superior officers. He told me that he had argued our case but had been overruled.

'All I can do is apologise, Marty,' he said, looking

disconsolate. 'I didn't want to swamp the fucking place, but there was nothing I could do. They didn't want to take any risks; they ordered the full works, a blanket job.'

I appreciated the fact that Felix had apologised and that he had told me what his bosses had ordered. But the fact that Felix had been overruled by his superior officers, against his advice, made me realise how unimportant I really was to the men in power. I wondered if the top brass always treated the men on the ground, the agents who risked their lives, with such disdain and disinterest. I expected so.

Despite this, the fact that I had been called to another IRA meeting gave me hope that all was still well. It also made me think that I could have overreacted.

I arrived at the cell meeting in a house in Turf Lodge as arranged. But although I could see everyone inside the house, I was told as I waited in the hall that the meeting had been called off. I didn't say a word, didn't question the decision, but as I walked to my car I knew that my days were numbered. I kept my eyes peeled, believing that an IRA squad would pounce at any moment and take me for questioning. My heart was thumping, my hands shaking as I got into the car and locked the door. It seemed an age before I managed to get the key into the ignition switch for my hands were shaking with fear.

I didn't hear a word from the IRA, but I did speak to Felix warning him that the operation was still scheduled for that Saturday.

During the brief conversation I told him, 'You should also know that I was banned from the final planning meeting and told to go away. I don't think that's a good sign.'

That Saturday afternoon, Felix phoned and I called him back from a phone box.

'Marty,' he said, 'that kit's been moved from your friend's house.'

'Impossible,' I said.

'Believe me,' he replied, 'the kit's gone. We've done nothing yet but we're tracking it now. It's in Turf Lodge at the moment. We will see if it travels anywhere else. If we think there's any danger we will pick them up with the kit.'

'Jesus!' I said, realising that if the IRA gun carriers were stopped on their journey to Bangor, then it would spell curtains for me, because the planned attack had now been ordered without my knowledge or presence and I had been a vital, integral part of the original plan.

'Marty,' Felix said, 'You must understand. If they travel towards Bangor we have no option but to pick them up. There are too many lives at risk. Do you realise 20 or 30 people could be killed in this operation, if not more? We have no choice.'

'But these are just the carriers,' I shouted, 'they're not the active service unit. Nothing can happen until the weapons arrive at Bangor. When it does, the lot can be picked up. I told you every detail of the plan.'

'We have no choice,' Felix replied. 'We have to obey orders.'

In my heart, I understood the SB rationale but thought it a grave error. I now had to face the fact that Felix, the man I trusted, no longer had any influence with his senior officers. They, in their wisdom, were prepared to sacrifice me in case, just in case, they fouled up. Although they had full knowledge of all the facts, they did not have the confidence in the Army and its men to intercept and stop an attack at the right moment. They obviously preferred to take the easy way out and simply stop a hijacked car, which they knew contained weapons and a couple of low-grade Provo gun carriers.

I put down the phone feeling sick to the pit of my stomach, and went round to my mother's house to watch television and to decide on a course of action. I knew that if it had been at all possible, the Branch would have targeted and marked the gun-carrier's car.

The Special Branch had discovered a 'magic' spray which they would daub on the roof of a suspect car. The spray, invisible to the naked eye, could be picked up by a device fitted into a helicopter, and the mark would remain visible for a couple of weeks even if the car was washed and polished. It was one of the SB's most successful weapons in tracking IRA suspects and was the reason why so many IRA members were caught travelling around the country in what they thought were safe vehicles.

A few hours later, there was a knock at the front door. My mother went and shouted to me, 'Martin, you're wanted at the door.'

As I walked along the hall I could see no one in the doorway. The man had obviously walked back to his car, because I could see him silhouetted as he sat in the driver's seat. I recognised the man as Stephen, the IRA man who murdered the soldier Tony Harrison with his accomplice, Paul Lynch.

I walked down the path and we chatted through the open car window.

'What do you want?' I asked.

'I've got some bad news for you,' he said.

'Don't tell me you can't pay me the money you owe me,' I said, referring to £200 I had lent him some weeks before.

He didn't laugh. 'No, two of your friends have been arrested,' he said, looking me straight in the eye.

'You're joking,' I said, acting as though shocked at the news. 'What happened?'

He said, 'They were driving into Bangor and for no reason they were stopped by the RUC.'

'Fuck me!' I said. 'I can't believe that. What happened?'

'They were driving along in a hijacked car when they were stopped on the edge of Bangor. They found two AKs and nearly 200 rounds of ammunition and a short.'

'Shit!' I said.

'You can say that again,' he said, 'they'll go down for a long time.'

I could see by the look on Stephen's face that something was wrong. I instinctively knew that he was being completely honest with me, letting me know that I was in danger yet not spelling out what that danger was.

As soon as Stephen drove off, I went to my arms dump in the woman's house nearby.

'Is all that stuff still in your roof space?' I asked her.

'No, its away,' she replied.

'Away, where?'

'Your mate Gary called earlier today and took it.'

'Was he on his own?' I asked.

'Yes,' she said, 'he was alone.'

As soon as I left the woman's house, I walked to Gary's place 50 yards down the road.

'Gary, did you move that stuff today?'

'Yes,' he said.

'Why?' I asked. 'Who told you to get it?'

'Your mate Paul told me to go and get it,' he replied. ' He said it would be alright by you.'

I then knew that my cell did suspect me since they had taken the gear without my knowledge. They had also decided to go ahead with their operation, deliberately leaving me out of the plan.

No one contacted me for several days, and I began to wonder whether I was going mad. I couldn't sleep at night; I was becoming sharp and bad tempered with Angie and the kids. I felt as if I was waiting for an execution but didn't know when or where they would strike. I could not understand why, if they suspected me of being a British agent, they hadn't picked me up for questioning.

Unable to take the strain any more, I decided to attend a cell meeting that I knew would take place the following night. As I walked into the house people looked at me, as though surprised at my presence. No one said a word. I went through to speak to Spud who was in the kitchen and he told me he would be in touch shortly.

I went back into the room and the four people there began joking with me.

'We'll be at your funeral, Marty,' one said laughing, and his mates laughed, too. Another quipped, 'Don't you worry, Marty, we'll be there.'

Another slapped me on the shoulder, 'We'll all send you a wreath, as well, Marty. No fear of that.'

This time no one laughed. I looked at each of them in turn and I could feel the colour drain from my face.

*   *   *

It would be five years later that the truth about the decision to thwart the IRA attempt on Charlie Heggarty's bar finally emerged. The diaries of the late Detective Superintendent Ian Phoenix, Head of the Northern Ireland Police Counter-Surveillance Unit, were published in a book entitled *Phoenix: Policing the Shadows*. Phoenix was one of the 25 anti-terrorist intelligence officers who were killed when a Chinook helicopter crashed into the side of the Mull of Kintyre in June 1994. His wife, Susan Phoenix, wrote the book detailing the secret war against terrorism in Northern Ireland.

Susan Phoenix's book revealed that the most senior RUC officers, above the rank of Superintendent, ordered the IRA gun carriers' car to be stopped against the advice of Ian Phoenix and other SB officers:

> *As a result, the vehicle and weapons were recovered, but only gun couriers were arrested. In Ian Phoenix's own words, "In total, we may have compromised a source and failed to get the real gunmen, thereby allowing them to continue killing. This was passed to [the Chief Superintendent] that the HQ decision was in fact sanctioning further deaths. He and his colleagues were also concerned about the fate of 'Carol'"...*

> Extract from *Phoenix: Policing the Shadows*
> by Susan Phoenix and Jack Holland
> (Hodder & Stoughton)1996

The diary also revealed that the decision to compromise Agent Carol and let the IRA's gunmen go free to kill again caused officers to lose confidence in their Tasking Co-ordination Group, the overall planning and operations group in Northern Ireland, comprising the SAS, MI5, Special Branch and Military Intelligence officers.

The decisions made by the RUC top-brass had indeed left me hideously exposed, and all too aware of the consequences.

CHAPTER THIRTEEN

I DROVE HOME THAT NIGHT not knowing if I would ever see another dawn, convinced that I would be taken by an IRA squad and handed over to the organisation's Civil Administration Team. This was the Provisional IRA's name for their internal security unit, the people responsible for interrogating those whom the IRA believe have been guilty of passing intelligence and information to the Security Forces.

The following few days stretched my emotions to breaking point. I was unable to sleep and waited daily for the dreaded knock at the door. I even took out my frustrations on my beloved Angie, who had shown such remarkable patience and understanding during our years together.

She had not liked the fact that I had become involved with the IRA and yet she had not nagged me to stop or tried to persuade me to look for a proper nine-to-five job. She never had the faintest knowledge that I was in reality working for the Special Branch, doing my damndest to thwart the IRA's bombings and killings.

During the following few days, my temper got the better of me. Under normal circumstances I was a hyperactive young man who enjoyed life, smiled a lot and always liked to crack jokes with people. I would hardly pass anyone in the street where we lived without a smile and a hello.

One night a few days later, I was standing at our front door waiting for Angie to return with the kids. I had forgotten my key and had expected her to be home. The fact that she wasn't there had annoyed me and my nerves were on edge.

Finally she appeared up the street, pushing the pram with Martin and Pódraig half asleep.

'Where the fuck have you been?' I shouted at her. 'I've been waiting here like an idiot for half an hour.'

'Who are you shouting at?', she yelled at me. 'Have I no right to go and see a friend without telling you?'

'Not when I'm fucking waiting for you here, you haven't,' I yelled at her.

'Well you can shut up,' she said, as she went to push past me to open the door.

I saw red and slapped her across the face, pushing her against the doorpost. She tripped and fell, her head hitting the door, cutting her beneath the eye and drawing blood.

'You bastard!' she screamed, trying to scramble to her feet. Our violent argument had woken the boys and they both began to cry.

It must have been the sight of Angie's blood that brought me to my senses. Suddenly I realised what I had done – I'd hit the person I loved most in the world and, worse still, for no good reason. Instantly, I felt ashamed and bent down to help her to her feet, but she didn't want to know.

'Get away from me, you bastard,' she screamed. 'Who

the fuck do you think you are, hitting me? Get out of here and stay out.'

I pushed the pram into the sitting room while Angie went to the kitchen to try and stem the flow of blood. Trying to placate her and help in some small way to make up for my fit of temper, I asked her if she needed any help.

'No,' she said, sounding quieter. 'Leave me and don't come back ... you've been in such foul moods lately ... you're no good for me or the kids because you're never around ... you may as well not be living here.'

I thought it best to leave. I decided to go and stay with my mother, but not only because of what Angie had said. She had given me an idea.

I knew that it would only be a matter of time before IRA thugs came to take me away. I thought of fleeing Northern Ireland but I had nowhere to go. I hadn't done a real day's work in my life, nothing that I could tell prospective employers. And no experience. All these thoughts were racing through my head and they became jumbled – I knew I should get away but had nowhere to go. I went to the one person whom I knew I could trust – my mother.

I told her that Angie and I had had a row and I wanted to stay with her for a few days 'until the air had cleared'. That night, I slept better and recalled that Felix had advised me to find somewhere else to stay for a few nights, away from Angie and the kids. He had also told me to phone him every day.

My mother didn't mind me staying with her. She understood that couples need to stay away from each other occasionally, to let the dust settle. But I never told her that I had hit Angie because if I had, she would have boxed my ears.

For some years my mother had been living with a

man she had known for ages. Alfie Donnelly, a kind, good-natured man in his 40s who people would say deserved a gold medal for living for so many years with my rampaging, strong-willed mother. Alfie liked the occasional pint of lager, a man who would have no more than a couple of pints in his local, before going home. But my mother always preferred him to be at home with her, rather than in the pub.

She became well known in Sloane's, the nearest bar to her house, where she would occasionally go for a drink with Alfie. However, whenever she suspected that the wretched Alfie was having a quiet pint on his own without her, my mother would walk down to the bar to join him. When sober, my mother had earned the well-deserved reputation of being an explosive character; when she had enjoyed one drink too many, she would become highly aggressive. Whenever Alfie saw my mother enter the bar, he would not even finish his pint but would quietly make his way out through the back door. Nevertheless, my mother and Alfie always seemed to have a good relationship.

During the time I stayed at my mother's house, Alfie was worried because he knew from the people he saw me associating with in the Republican clubs and bars that I was a member of the IRA, and he feared that I might want to use their home as an arms dump. He was fully aware that when the RUC found arms in someone's home, the man was always taken away for questioning and held responsible. He feared that he might face the same fate. My mother would say later that during those few nights I stayed at the house, Alfie became a bundle of nerves, never sleeping a wink. The moment I left every morning, Alfie would go into my bedroom, strip the bed, examine the drawers and check under the carpets to see whether the floorboards had been disturbed.

I would sleep fitfully, too, waking at the slightest sound.

I wanted to see Angie and the boys, but knew that I should keep away from them, fearing what could happen and not wanting to put her through such agony. I knew that if she saw me being taken away by two IRA men, she would realise that I was in deep trouble. So, a few times a day, I would drive past our house in the hope that I might catch a brief glimpse of her or Martin and Pódraig.

As I drove along Glenalena Park near my house one day, I noticed a couple of men, whom I recognised to be local IRA members, acting suspiciously on some waste ground behind the houses. I drove out of the area and called Felix.

Before I could say anything, Felix, in a relaxed, friendly voice, said, 'How are you doing? It's nice to hear your voice. Is everything alright?'

'Fine,' I said, 'I'm still here, if that's what you mean.'

'Good,' he replied, trying to sound cheerful.

'I've got a job for your lads to look at Felix, near my own home,' and I gave him the details.

I returned to the area and within an hour saw the streets cordoned off with white tape, the sign that a search was about to take place.

On the BBC news that night I heard, 'An AKM rifle and 30 rounds of ammunition, as well as 4lb of Semtex, a detonator and cable were found on waste ground at the rear of Ballymurphy Crescent. A police spokesman said that the area where the find was made is used by residents as a short-cut, and children often play there.'

I realised then that the IRA had planned to set off the Semtex bomb on the footpath used by RUC foot patrols, and then use the AKM to machine-gun them. As the newsreader read the last few words, I felt tears come to my eyes, knowing that some poor kids could have been caught up in it, hurt, maimed or even worse. I felt so angry that the IRA could put the lives of kids, kids like mine, in such danger that, at that moment, I didn't care what the IRA did to me.

*   *   *

The knock at the door came around 11.00am, on the morning of 7 August, as I sat alone in my mother's sitting room. I had become somewhat complacent, believing that the IRA could not be certain that I was a British agent with no proof and only the flimsiest circumstantial evidence linking me with the operations that had gone wrong. On the other hand, I also knew that the organisation's Civil Administration Team would not arrest and question unless they were 90 per cent certain that I was a traitor to the cause.

Standing at the door was a woman I knew named Carol, a good-looking, young IRA messenger in her 20s whom I had met on previous occasions. Polite, cheerful and efficient, Carol was used to call IRA members to urgent meetings, for she knew not only where everyone lived but most of their favourite haunts. If they weren't at home, Carol knew the pubs and bars they frequented.

As soon as I saw her, I feared the worst.

'How are you, Marty?' she said with a smile.

'I'm OK. What's up?'

'You have to go and see Pódraig Wilson at Connolly House, the Sinn Fein headquarters,' she said, 'at ten tomorrow morning.'

'OK, I'll be there,' I replied and she turned and walked away.

Pódraig Wilson, I thought. He's the head of discipline throughout Belfast, the man who decides who gets kneecapped and who receives beatings by the punishment squads. Months before, I had visited Pódraig Wilson's flat to give him a message from Davy Adams.

I needed to speak to Felix urgently to seek his advice, but the SB radio with the secret button was still at my house. When we had moved to our new home I had hidden the radio in a safe place where I knew Angie and the boys would never find it. I drove to the house hoping that Angie was out. As I turned the key in the lock I couldn't hear any noise from inside and breathed a sigh of relief. I found the radio where I had hidden it and pressed the button. It would be the last time I would ever use the secret device.

From that moment, I made doubly certain that I checked everything I did, for I was certain that the IRA would have ordered a 24-hour watch on my movements. As I drove to the appointed spot, I continually looked in my rear-view mirror and drove in and out of housing estates to make sure no one tailed me.

I was so worried that I began to speak as I climbed into Felix's car. 'Felix, I'm in loads of trouble ...' the words tumbling out of my mouth so fast that he could hardly understand what I was saying.

'Calm down,' he reassured me, 'and speak slowly. What's up?'

I explained that I had been called to a meeting with Pódraig Wilson at 10.00am the next day and I needed his advice.

'OK,' he said, obviously thinking hard. 'Don't worry. I'll have to take advice on this one as to how we're going to play it. But, rest assured, I won't let you down. We'll take care of you.'

Before I left, he told me to phone him at around 3.00pm that afternoon. I decided not to return home but to drive around, keeping well clear of any Republican areas.

When I phoned Felix later, I was surprised and disappointed to hear the plans the Special Branch had decided for me. I had hoped they would whisk me away to safety, put me in a safe house where the IRA couldn't touch me. Now the uncertainty would continue.

During this phone conversation, Felix told me that I should drive to the meeting with Wilson the following day, parking the car at Andersonstown Leisure Centre, near Connolly House. He told me to borrow someone else's car and phone him with the details.

He went on, 'Tell no one that you have driven there by car but say you took a black taxi. We will be watching Connolly House and your car at all times. If your car moves we will know you are OK, but if it doesn't then we will know you are in real danger.'

When I put down the phone I felt a little easier, for I trusted Felix to come to the rescue if the IRA did try to spirit me away from Connolly House to one of their safe houses.

Throughout that night I argued with myself not knowing what I should do. Part of me wanted to steal away in the night, take my car to Larne, catch the ferry to Scotland and disappear. I had about £7,000 in the building society, enough to rent a flat for a few months while I searched for a job. At least, I argued, I would be out of danger, away from the IRA and their punishment squads.

But I convinced myself, during those hours of darkness when I never slept a wink, that perhaps I had become paranoid once more. It seemed extraordinary that the IRA would invite me to a meeting the next day when they could have picked me up at any time with no risk to themselves. And, I persuaded myself, if they suspected me of working with the SB, why would they call me to a meeting at Sinn Fein headquarters where

Gerry Adams, the Sinn Fein President, had his own office, and which they knew would be under constant Special Branch surveillance?

I arranged to borrow a green Nissan hatchback and phoned Felix with the details. I told him I would leave my mother's house just after 9.00am and would park the car as arranged. That morning, my mother ironed me a pair of jeans and as I stood in the kitchen watching her ironing away I felt a great surge of emotion, that I desperately wanted to tell her everything, about the IRA and the Special Branch and my job, and that, if things went wrong, it would be the last time I would ever see her.

But I thought better of it. I didn't want to subject my mother to hours, days or maybe weeks of fear and worry over my safety. I had got myself into this shit and I had to find some way out of it, alone.

I didn't kiss my mother goodbye that morning though I wanted desperately to put my arms around her and say how much I loved her. But I had never been like that with my mother and I knew such behaviour would alarm her. So I let it go.

I took off in the little Nissan and when I saw a phone box at a roundabout, I decided to make one final call to Felix to check that everything was going to plan. I drove around the roundabout three times before stopping at the box, naïvely thinking that such a bizarre manoeuvre would confuse any IRA man tailing me.

'Is that you, Felix?' I asked when I was put through.

'I can tell you, boy, that you are going to cause loads of shit if you keep on turning circle after circle like that. You're sending our heads in a spin with all your antics,' and he laughed.

I felt a wave of relief come over me. The boost to my

confidence was wonderful, knowing that the SB were keeping such a close eye on me they even knew how many times I went round a roundabout. I drove on to my destination my spirits higher than they had been for weeks.

When the woman answered the bell at Connolly House, I told her I had a meeting with Pódraig Wilson.

'Oh, he's away,' she said. 'He hasn't been here all morning.'

'I'll just wait,' I said, 'because it's been arranged.'

'Please yourself,' she said, and showed me to a small waiting room where Republican newspapers were scattered about for visitors to read. On the walls were photographs of IRA hunger-strikers.

Twenty minutes later, two IRA men, both of whom I recognised, walked into the office. One, Paul 'Chico' Hamilton, in his 40s was bearded, overweight and liked to think he was one of the IRA's hard men. Instinctively, I hated this man from the moment I met him, because I knew he was an active member of an IRA punishment squad. Some senior IRA men who had known Chico from the 1970s nicknamed him 'Budgie', because he sang to the RUC when arrested in 1977 for his part in the attempted murder of a Major in the Gordon Highlanders. He was sentenced to 12 years' jail.

Some staunch IRA members believed he should have been dismissed from the organisation with ignominy, because he had breached the IRA's Part 1 orders for accepting the authority of a British court and pleading guilty to attempted murder, wounding an officer and possessing a rifle and ammunition. Most IRA men brought before British courts refuse to accept the court's authority, and do not utter a word.

I also knew his companion, James 'Jim' McCarthy, a slim-built man in his 30s with a moustache, who also had a reputation for organising and taking part in punishment beatings. Some years earlier he had also been disciplined, undergoing a kneecapping by an IRA punishment squad. He was known as one of the men who would interrogate victims before deciding their punishment. He also liked to think he had the reputation of being a ladies' man. In reality, most women despised McCarthy for they believed he would take advantage of his authority to try and seduce them. In 1977, James McCarthy had been found guilty of possessing arms and ammunition and was sentenced to five years jail.

Both Hamilton and McCarthy have since become the most trusted henchmen of Sinn Fein President Gerry Adams, employed as his personal bodyguards. They would accompany Adams to Dublin Airport at the start of his controversial 'peace' trip to the United States in September 1994.

Jim asked me, 'Marty, are you waiting for Pódraig?'

'Aye, I am. Why?'

'Pódraig sent us to tell you that he's sorry he can't see you now. You can either go away and make another appointment or we could take you to see him now?'

For two seconds I thought about the option. I knew that if these two fellas tried to take me away I would beat the shit out of them and walk away with only a few bruises for they were both all mouth and no trousers. I also thought that if Pódraig was happy for me to come back another day then the matter couldn't be that serious.

'OK, I'll go with you,' I said, and walked out of the office and down the steps to the road. On the way out Jim McCarthy asked, casually, 'Marty, did you have a car with you?'

'No,' I replied, 'I took a black taxi.'

But that question alarmed me, for I remembered what Felix had said.

The three of us walked out of Connolly House and around the corner to a white, four-door Ford Fiesta. Jim McCarthy drove, Chico sat in the passenger seat and I clambered in the back.

Jim drove faster than I expected, speeding through traffic lights that had just turned red, making it difficult for a pursuing car to keep up. But I knew that Felix's SB-trained drivers would have no difficulty in keeping track of me. But the fact that Jim drove so furiously worried me. I began to feel I had made a mistake. I should have decided to return another day.

Deliberately, I never looked behind me because that would have given the game away. I kept looking at other vehicles, wondering if any Branch men were in them, expecting a car to ram us at any moment, so that in the confusion I could be separated from Jim and Chico and spirited away. The further we drove, the more lonely, isolated and vulnerable I felt.

Chico never stopped talking throughout the ten-minute journey, pretending to be chatty and friendly, obviously trying to put me at ease. They both knew that I had a reputation for violence if I was ever in a desperate situation.

We drove out of Andersonstown, through Suffolk and into Twinbrook, a mainly residential area south-west of Belfast. We came to a halt outside a small block of four-storey flats in Broom Park, a quiet road which seemed deserted.

Jim McCarthy jumped out of the car, slammed the door and ran into the block of flats.

Chico said, 'Come on Marty, follow him,' and I got out and I walked behind him into the block.

IRA graffitti covered the walls and doors in different

coloured chalks and paints and the block smelt of stale urine. I walked through the brown front door of a flat on the third floor and closed it behind me.

I noticed another man, a stranger, in the kitchen talking in a whisper to Jim McCarthy. Jim came out and said, 'Marty, Pódraig isn't here yet but he won't be too long.'

The three men walked back into the kitchen and I stood there waiting. Then they turned and came out again.

'Listen,' said Jim, 'Provisional IRA. You're under arrest.'

I could see them shaking. Then McCarthy pulled out a hand-gun. 'Lie face down on the floor,' he said, 'and don't try anything,' as I felt the stub of the automatic pushed against my head.

At that moment, I thought they were about to pull the trigger and I was a goner.

Seconds passed and I was still alive. Then I felt one of them pulling off my trainers.

'Empty your pockets,' I was told, and did so with considerable difficulty, as I was lying on my stomach.

'Jesus Christ!' someone shouted, fear in his voice. 'Fucking car keys. I thought you didn't have a car with you.'

'I didn't,' I lied. 'They belong to a lorry.'

In one of my pockets I had a bundle of 50 £10 notes, and my driving licence. They told me to get up, walk over to the settee and lie face down. I could see Chico taking the laces out of my trainers. He could hardly remove the laces he was shaking so much and kept telling me, 'Don't try anything, Marty; don't try anything.'

Chico tied my hands together in front of my body but fumbled when he tried to tie the knot. Then he tied the other laces around my ankles, binding them together. I realised that with very little effort I would be able to release the laces.

At the time, I was amazed how inefficient and disorganised they were, having to use my own laces to tie my hands and feet. I wondered how they would have tied my hands and feet if I had been wearing a pair of casual slip-ons that day.

I suddenly saw the whole ghastly business as a comedy – Jim and Chico shaking and nervous, fiddling with my laces, unable to tie a knot, and Jim, waving the hand-gun about, telling me over and over again not to 'try anything'. I began to laugh at the thought, perhaps from nerves. But I did laugh and I looked at them. They looked at each other in disbelief, not knowing what to think was going on.

'Get a blanket, get a blanket,' Jim said and Chico left the room, collected a blanket and threw it over my head. It seemed to reassure them that they couldn't see my face any more.

Five minutes later, McCarthy disappeared and I presumed he had gone to telephone someone to tell them their mission had been accomplished. Chico, meanwhile, sat on the end of the settee and every few seconds told me, 'Remember, Marty, we've got a gun in the kitchen, so don't try anything.'

The room became stifling and I could hardly breathe under the blanket. After ten minutes or so, Chico got up, went to the kitchen and returned with a newspaper. From under the blanket I could now see most of the room and the young lad who was sitting in a chair opposite me, reading a book. I could hear a radio, tuned to a music station, and I listened to the love songs and melodies and thought of young people leading happy, carefree lives, enjoying life and in love with someone.

And, unbelievably, I found myself smiling at my present predicament, tied and trussed like a turkey, waiting for a bullet in the back of the head.

Chico had fallen silent and, as the time dragged on, I could hear the sound of young children playing in the street below. My thoughts turned to little Martin and Pódraig and I bit my lip, desperate to quell the tears that swelled in my eyes as I became convinced that I would never see them again.

I cursed myself for stepping so pathetically into the trap, agreeing to come to see Wilson. I should have known when McCarthy asked whether I had brought a car to the meeting that my days were numbered.

Three hours later, I asked whether I could have a glass of water. The young lad went and found a glass and brought it to me. Still lying on my stomach, the lad fed me the water which I drank with difficulty, and which tasted stale and tepid. At no time, however, had either of them threatened me or given me a hard time – McCarthy had still not returned.

As the minutes ticked away I began to lose faith in Felix and the Branch. I believed that if they had intended to rescue me, they would have intervened before now. I knew they must have known my whereabouts precisely, and I could not understand why I had heard nothing – no helicopters, no RUC sirens, no army activity.

I could not imagine that Felix would simply throw me to the wolves after all we had been through together. I had trusted him with my life and now that I needed him, he had let me down, doing nothing to rescue me. Only that morning he had promised to keep a watch over me and protect me. He had claimed that no harm would come to me and now when I was desperate for help ... nothing. I had never felt so alone in my life.

At least twice in the hours I lay there, I heard Brian Adams' famous song, *Everything I Do, I Do for You*, the song that Angie and I loved listening to during our drives into the country together. I could feel my chin twitching as I fought to hold back the tears that filled my eyes.

I think it was about four or five hours later that I heard a helicopter hovering over the estate. Outside, I heard an army foot patrol and a dog bark. I heard an English voice shout, 'Shut up,' and my heart leapt with hope, convincing myself that rescue was at hand.

I waited anxiously for someone to come bursting through the door, but nothing happened. The chopper flew off and the sound of the foot patrol disappeared into the distance. My hopes dropped once more.

Thirty minutes later, I heard someone coming up the stairs and a knock at the door. The young lad answered it and I thought my time had come. I expected loads of people to come in, members of the IRA Civil Administration Team, but it was only McCarthy returning. And he was alone.

He said, 'There's fucking Army and DMSUs all over the place. I had to hang about outside before I came in, waiting for the fuckers to go away.'

They all went into the kitchen and I could hear Land Rovers driving around outside the block of flats. I knew then that Felix was doing everything in his power to find me, but I also knew that he would not have known my precise location. It had become a race against time.

I heard the radio announcer say it was 5.30pm and I realised that I had been lying on the settee for nearly seven hours.

I was desperate to go to the toilet and decided to ask them.

The young lad came in, untied my hands and showed

me where it was. My ankles were still tied so I hopped to the lavatory.

As I hopped into the bathroom and approached the toilet, I noticed the bath, full to the brim of crystal-clear water. I knew that one of the IRA's favourite tortures was putting a man's head underwater and keeping it there until the man was barely conscious. Then they would bring him out, question him again and force his head back into the bath, keeping the ritual of torture going until the man passed out completely or gave them the confession they demanded.

I realised then that if I did not escape from that flat, I would be faced with that horrific torture and probably others. I doubted whether I would have the strength to survive, to keep denying that I had ever worked for the Branch. I knew then that it was only a matter of time until the Interrogation unit walked in and began their deadly work, using whatever methods at their disposal to make me talk. They were experts; they didn't care what they did to a man as long as he confessed. It didn't matter if the man was innocent or guilty. By the time they had finished, they would either have a confession or the man was dead.

I told myself that if I stayed in that flat, death was a near certainty and I convinced myself, terrified, that I would be unable to take the beatings, the cigarette burns or the torture without confessing. And I knew that the moment I confessed, I would be shot in the back of the head.

I poked my head out of the bathroom door and looked down the hallway at the sitting-room window, wondering exactly how far I was from the ground. I tried to remember how many floors we had walked up that morning. I had no idea what was below that window – concrete, parked cars, trees, shrubs or grass.

All I could see as I looked out of the window was the horizon, no trees, no houses, not even a block of flats. That screamed at me that I must be 40 or more feet above ground level. It didn't matter. I decided that I would risk all and throw myself through the glass, risking probable death rather than face the torturers who would do all in their power to make my death as long and agonising as possible.

At that moment I thought of my sister, Kathy, who had died when I was just a kid. 'Jesus, Kathy,' I said under my breath, 'if you're looking down, take care of me.'

I glanced in the kitchen and they were still looking out of the window, watching the army activity below. I said to myself, 'This is your only chance, Marty ... take it, take it.'

My feet were still bound together, so I hopped out of the bathroom, across the hallway and into the sitting-room. Before me was the window and I jumped as high as I could, hurling myself head-first at the window pane.

I don't even remember hitting the glass ...

CHAPTER FOURTEEN

I CAN REMEMBER A WOMAN HOLDING MY HEAD IN HER ARMS, saying 'You're going to be OK, love, you're going to be OK.'

I looked around my body and all I could see was blood, blood everywhere – my shirt was covered, my trousers were covered, and I could feel blood pouring down my face, the taste in my mouth and in my throat. My mind was swirling as I struggled to remain conscious. But I knew I had survived.

*   *   *

I awoke in a room to see Felix and Mo standing by my bedside looking down at me. Though concussed, I can remember feeling a great sense of relief that my Special Branch friends had finally arrived and my life would no longer be in danger.

'Are you awake, Marty?' I heard Felix say.

'Aye, just about,' I replied.

'Don't say anything now,' he advised. 'You're OK; you're in hospital; you're safe; we'll see you later.'

I slept again and awoke not knowing how many hours or days had passed. I began to look around me, felt pain and throbbing in my left arm and realised that I had been roughly stitched. My head was stitched and heavily bandaged and I tried to recall what had happened and how I had arrived in hospital.

Nurses and doctors came to see me and talk to me. They told me that I had been found on the ground outside a block of flats, and they had been told that I had fallen from a third-floor window. I listened to what they said, but my mind was fuzzy and I wasn't sure what had happened. They told me that they had had to cut all my clothes from my body.

After consultations with the doctors, I was taken by ambulance from the Royal Victoria Hospital to Musgrave Park, a hospital which I later learned was permanently guarded by the RUC. The doctors who examined me at Musgrave told me I was fortunate to be alive and lucky not to be suffering from any life-threatening injuries. They told me that I was suffering from a deep wound to my left side, caused when I crashed through the window; I had wounds and lacerations to my head, a fractured jaw, broken teeth and severe concussion from the impact of hitting the grass head first after leaping from a height of 40 feet. They also told me I had been unconscious for ten days.

Some hours later, I was again examined by doctors who told me that the Special Branch had asked that if I was well enough they would prefer me to be moved to Palace Barracks, Holywood, a secure army base where British army families live during their tour of duty in the Province.

The doctors gave permission for Mo to take me in his car, because there were armed SB officers in two other vehicles. They were taking no chances. I was wrapped in nothing but a hospital blanket and, as Mo drove, I had no idea where we were going. I would regain consciousness for a couple of minutes and then drift back into sleep throughout the journey. With us in the car were two more armed SB officers.

First I was taken to Castlereagh, and spent two or three hours sitting in an armchair in a Chief Inspector's office while senior officers decided where I should be sent. Still in a daze, I was put in another car and driven to the army barracks where a senior Special Branch officer I had never met before came to see if I was OK. Before he left, he gave instructions that I should be moved once again because he considered my accommodation to be too near the perimeter fence and vulnerable to possible attack.

Throughout the next week or so, Felix and Mo would come to see me and chat, and I felt myself growing stronger and more in control. My brain began to clear and, slowly, I pieced together everything that had happened.

Felix told me what happened that day. During the car journey from Connolly House the Branch pursuit cars had lost me in traffic but knew I was somewhere in the Twinbrook area. He had ordered up two helicopters to hover over the area, and they directed the Army and RUC foot patrols. They were drafted in not only to search for me, but also to ensure that an IRA interrogation team would not be able to infiltrate the area to question me. His plan had worked, for no other IRA personnel had managed to reach the block of flats where I was held.

He told me how the three IRA man holding me had raced down the stairs after I had jumped, and began to drag me across the grass by my legs in an effort to get me back into the flat. Something, however, had alarmed them, and they instantly dropped my limp body, ran to a waiting car and made good their escape. Whether the three men believed me to be dead or whether the arrival of an army patrol had scared them, he could not say, but Special Branch sources later discovered that the men had immediately fled across the border to Dundalk.

Later, I heard what had happened on the day I had been kidnapped. My mother, Angie and other relatives toured hospitals in and around Belfast trying to find me. But the Special Branch had taken away all my hospital records in case the IRA tried to find me and kidnap me again. In the past, IRA squads had sometimes been known to walk into hospitals, threaten the staff with guns and abduct someone they wanted to interview.

My mother knew that something had happened but did not want to frighten Angie and the kids. The fact that there were no records of mine at any of the main casualty hospitals led my mother to think that I may have been kidnapped by the IRA, but she did not want to ask them.

She enquired at local RUC stations, but no one had any record of my being arrested or reported missing and there had been no reports of any bodies having been found. Finding nothing, she began to believe that I was still alive although, inexplicably, it seemed that I had somehow disappeared.

The IRA, though, were also searching for me. They sent a team of Sinn Fein and IRA men to my mother's house to tell her that I seemed to have disappeared, as they had not seen me around for a couple of days. They asked that if she should see me, could she give me a message telling me that the IRA were concerned for me and wanted to know that I was safe and well?

Little did the IRA know, however, that my mother's house had been put under 24-hour Special Branch surveillance and everyone visiting her was secretly photographed and identified.

But my Ma became suspicious when the same men also told her to take no notice of any rumours that might be circulating about me, because they were all untrue. When she asked what rumours they might be, they told her that there was some nonsense suggesting that the IRA had spirited me away. In an effort to reassure her, they told her that if I surfaced, she should tell me that the IRA only wanted to check that I was fit and well, and that I should immediately contact them.

'One thing we can tell you, Mrs McGartland,' one IRA man said to her, 'we have no intention whatsoever of harming your son.'

When my mother pressed them for information, they told her, 'Someone came to speak to Marty and for some reason he jumped out of the window, that's all we know.'

She redoubled her efforts to find me.

It seemed that the IRA were becoming desperate in their search for me. They dispatched one of their prettiest young women to Castlereagh, telling the RUC officer at the front desk that she was my girlfriend, Angie, and she wanted to see me. She said that she had heard rumours that I had been injured in a serious fall, but could find no trace of me in any of the main casualty hospitals. She asked whether the RUC could trace me and let her know where she could see me.

The ruse nearly worked. Felix broke the good news that Angie had heard rumours of my fall and had asked to see me, and a date was fixed for her to return to Castlereagh where she would be able to meet me.

Felix warned me that the IRA could have contacted Angie and threatened her in some way, all but forcing her to come to Castlereagh and, more than likely, give me a message warning me that if I didn't give myself up to the organisation, my friends and family would suffer.

'Would they do that?' I asked Felix.

'They've done it before and they'll do it again,' he said. 'When those bastards want to extract information from someone, they will do anything. Never forget that, Marty.'

On the appointed day, Felix took me by car to Castlereagh and I was longing to see and hold Angie once more. I had been unable to keep her and the boys out of my mind since I had been in hospital and was desperate to see them all once again, to check that they were OK and to show that I loved them all.

Felix had never met Angie but he knew she was young, dark-haired and good looking. And so was the girl waiting to see me. But he took no chances. He had arranged for the girl to be sitting in an interview room with a two-way mirror and told me that, before I could speak to Angie, I would first have to identify her. I looked through the glass at the young woman purporting to be Angie. I had never seen her before in my life.

I was bitterly disappointed, but happy that Felix had not permitted me to talk to the girl for I, too, now felt that I would have been given an appalling choice; give yourself up or your family will suffer the consequences. Now the girl would have to return and tell her IRA masters she had not been permitted to see me.

Once again, however, it would be as a result of the publication of Ian Phoenix's diary in 1996 that I discovered what the security chiefs believed had happened the day I was kidnapped.

A surveillance team was tasked to watch 'Carol's' movements. On 8 August, he was told by the Provisionals to go to Connolly House, a Sinn Fein

*office on the Andersonstown Road in West Belfast.
It was assumed that he was to be 'debriefed' by
the Civil Administration Team, the Provisionals'
much feared internal security unit. The surveillance
team was on the spot and observed him leaving
a short time later. He went across the road to the
Busy Bee shopping complex. The surveillance team
reported back to TCG Belfast that 'Carol' was in the
supermarket. They were mistaken. [He] had been
snatched from the Busy Bee car park, bound and
gagged, and whisked to a flat in nearby Twinbrook.
There he was guarded by two Provisionals who were
awaiting the arrival of the interrogators.*

*Fortunately, and quite fortuitously, a helicopter
was passing over the roof of the block of flats where
'Carol' was being held. Meanwhile, an army foot
patrol was observed outside. According to Phoenix,
"This caused the captors to panic" and they untied
their prisoner, expecting the security forces to arrive
at any moment. 'Carol' did not wait to see if he
would be saved. He flung himself head-first through
the window ... landing on his head ...*

*Sheer good luck had saved him from the fate
of dozens of others who have suffered torture and
brutal death at the hands of the [Provisional] IRA's
security team.'*

Extract from *Phoenix: Policing the Shadows*
by Susan Phoenix and Jack Holland
(Hodder & Stoughton)1996

I read those words from the diary of Ian Phoenix over
and over again, for here was a man of experience, a man
at the top of Northern Ireland's anti-terrorist intelligence
organisation, admitting that very little had been done

to watch me from the moment I had entered Connolly House where they knew I was to be 'debriefed' by the IRA's Civil Administration Team. He admitted that they had not seen me leave with my two well-known IRA henchmen, and that no SB car had tracked me to Twinbrook – he finally accepted that only 'sheer good luck' had saved my life.

Senior Special Branch officers had known what was about to happen to me, that I probably faced gruelling interrogation and appalling torture, and yet nothing had been done to protect me; no officer had authorised for me to have been picked up and taken away to a secure house. Indeed, I had been encouraged to attend the meeting at Connolly House, firm in the knowledge that I would be under constant police surveillance, and that nothing would happen to me. In reality, I had been left to my own devices.

I wondered, as I read that passage in the book, how many of the dozens of other alleged agents had been left to fall into IRA hands, questioned, tortured and shot because no action had been taken by the Special Branch senior officers to protect the men and women who risked their lives daily, providing the information that was so vital in the war against the IRA.

It seemed to me unbelievable that senior officers could treat agents with such disdain. They encouraged the closest relationships and deep trust to develop between agents and their handlers, knowing that, in the end, these relationships would count for nothing. The decision of senior officers would always hold sway, and if that meant sacrificing agents' identities and sometimes their lives, then so be it.

When people such as me were persuaded, for whatever reason, to work for the SB and the Government, nothing like this was ever explained. I was never told that I would be sacrificed like a pawn in a game of chess whenever senior officers decided I was no longer a vital part of their larger game plan.

For many months, I became angry whenever I permitted myself to think deeply of how little I, and all the other agents, had meant to the top-brass in the SAS, MI5, Special Branch and Military Intelligence officers who formed the Tasking Co-ordination Group, the overall planners and decision-makers who conducted the secret war against the IRA. Time would eventually soften my anger, but I still despise them.

I remained in Palace Barracks for two months while I recuperated and, with the help of physiotherapists, regained the use of my left arm and shoulder. New clothes were bought for me and, with Felix and Mo, I would occasionally be taken out for meals in restaurants all over Northern Ireland. We would chat and discuss past events, but always tried to keep the conversation light, never referring to the bombings and killings that had been a part of my daily life for four years.

Both Felix and Mo offered me friendship and seemed keen to spoil me, to build my confidence and help me face my uncertain future. Whenever we left the security of the Barracks, we would always be provided with an armed escort and my two Branch handlers would always carry shoulder-holstered hand-guns. They were taking no further chances.

After a week or more, Felix told me that my days working as an agent for the Special Branch in Northern Ireland were finally over. He also broke the news, which I had suspected, that I would no longer be able to live in the Province, and that he would be arranging a totally new identity for me, accommodation in England, and a lump sum which had been granted by the authorities to help me through the first few months of my new life.

He also told me that I had no option but to forget all my relatives and friends in Northern Ireland, and that I had to realise that because of the IRA's international contacts, I would have to accept that my life would always be at risk. He told me that once I had left the Province I would be on my own, and they would not be able to guarantee my life, nor the lives of Angie and the boys if they should join me.

I did not know what to say. Sitting alone in the Barracks, day after day, I missed them so much. I knew that Angie was very close to her family and would be loathe to leave Belfast, and I asked Felix if he would go and ask her what she wanted to do.

Angie was in a quandary, not knowing whether to stay in Belfast with her family and friends or to move to the mainland with me and see whether she could accept the life of secrecy that she knew we would face. It would mean never trusting friends, having to live a lie, moving from place to place and fearing that, at any moment, an IRA unit might strike.

Felix told me of the possible dangers for Angie and her family if she ever met me in the Province, because if the IRA discovered we were seeing each other, Angie, or perhaps other members of her family, risked being kidnapped or beaten.

In October 1991, I left Northern Ireland with two armed Special Branch officers. We took the ferry from Larne and then drove to my new home, a flat in the north of England which had been bought and furnished for me.

I was provided with telephone numbers and introduced to two Special Branch officers who would become my local contacts. When the men left my flat that night, I was feeling fit and well but very lonely and could barely wait for Angie and the children to join me.

Four weeks later Angie, Martin and Pódraig arrived. I felt like laughing with happiness and crying with the sheer emotion of seeing them once again, fit and well. Angie looked gorgeous with a wonderful smile on her face, but I could tell she was somewhat tense. The boys, then aged nearly two years old and nine months, had no idea what was going on. That first night, I went into their bedroom and watched them sleeping peacefully, oblivious in their innocence.

'Do you think we've done the right thing?' Angie asked as we ate supper that night. 'I've never been out of Belfast before.'

I tried to reassure her, to tell her that all would be well now that our family was together again. I told her that Martin and Pódraig would have a more settled, less dangerous future in England, and that was important.

Christmas 1991 was like magic. We rented a cottage in the middle of the country, roasted a turkey and enjoyed a bottle of wine, and sat around a log fire together opening the presents we had bought for the boys. They didn't, of course, really understand about Fatherr Christmas, but they enjoyed the toys and the sweets and the chocolates.

I sat and watched the family on the floor surrounded by Christmas wrapping paper, their eyes shining in the reflection of the fire, and a wave of happiness and emotion surged through me. Angie now seemed happy and loving and understanding, and every time I heard her laugh I felt relieved, happy that she was back to her old, bubbly self, enjoying her life with the children and with me. And every night, as I held her in my arms and kissed her goodnight, I would thank God.

EPILOGUE

After a few months of life in England, however, Angie became increasingly homesick for Belfast, her family and her friends.

She also feared what might happen to Martin and Pódraig, cut off from their family and forced to lead an itinerant life, moving every year or so from house to house, town to town and city to city, never being able to make permanent friends, stay at the same school, put down roots or live a normal, ordinary life.

And Angie understood that the family would always be running from the IRA, having to keep one step ahead of them, and she felt that was not fair on her or the boys.

The more we discussed the matter the more I came to the same conclusion. I alone had made the decision to work for the Special Branch and had never once asked her or discussed the matter with her. She had known that I had joined the IRA, but had not known why. And she had never known that I had been recruited as a British agent to infiltrate the IRA.

Now, I knew I should let Angie return to Belfast and her family, taking the boys with her so that they could enjoy a settled life. I hated the idea of losing them, but I knew that there was no alternative.

Before leaving Ireland, Felix had advised me that if ever the time came when it might be necessary for me to live apart from Martin and Pódraig, then they should be told, in due course, that their father had died and that they would never see him again.

He told me that from experiences with other people in similar circumstances, it seemed better, especially for young children, to believe that their father had died, as indeed many young Northern Irish children had lost their parents in bombings and shootings since the Troubles began.

In early 1992, Angie boarded the boat which would take her and the boys back to Ireland to begin a new life amongst family and friends.

Within 24 hours I had moved, with Special Branch help, to a new life in another part of England, to a flat I had never seen, in a street I had never known, in a town where I was a stranger. That first night I sat on my new bed in a strange room and thought of my mother and Angie, Martin and Pódraig and the fact that I would never see any of them again. The tears flowed and I could not sleep. Throughout the night, my thoughts were with them, thinking of the good times we had enjoyed together and of my sons asleep in their beds, knowing that I could never be with them.

Three times since then I have changed my identity and have moved not only homes but to different towns and cities. One day, I hope to be able to forget my past and live in peace, buy a house and hold down a steady job. Maybe even meet someone who has no idea of my past and start a new family. But that's for the future.

Three years after leaving Belfast, a letter addressed to me arrived at my mother's home. Inside was a Roman

Catholic mass card, usually sent by relatives and friends when a person they know well has died. This one read:

Sincere sympathy.
Lord, grant eternal rest to the soul of Thy faithful servant and comfort and console those who have been bereaved.

The Holy Sacrifice of the Mass will be offered for the repose of the soul of Marty McGartland, with Sincere Sympathy from your friends in Connelly House, Crumlin Road and Long Kesh.

The mass card was signed by Reverend Patrick Crowley, Celebrant.

Connelly House, of course, is the Sinn Fein headquarters in Belfast; Crumlin Road, was the holding centre where suspected terrorists were remanded in custody; and Long Kesh, the jail where convicted terrorists are imprisoned. It was obvious that my so-called friends were members of the IRA. It was their way of informing me that I had not been forgotten, neither would they forget me until after my death. But the cowardly IRA would not stop there.

*   *   *

In July 1996, nearly five years after I had left the Province, my brother Joseph was at home in Moyard, West Belfast, with his girlfriend, Tracey, and Kirsty, their four-year-old daughter, when there was a knock at the door.

Five men, wearing balaclavas and white gloves, two wielding hand-guns, pushed their way into the house. 'Irish Republican Army,' shouted one and grabbed Joseph. They pinned him to the floor, one man standing on his back while others took off his socks and forced them into his mouth. Two other men taped his arms and legs and bound his face with masking tape so he could hardly breathe.

He was bundled into the back of a van and taken for a short ride. They dragged him from the van, tied a rope around his ankles and hung him upside down from a fence. Then they began beating his shins, his ankles and his thighs with iron bars. They then moved up his body, smashing his arms with a baseball bat and and hitting his body with a plank of wood with nails embedded in it. He thought that the beating lasted a full 15 minutes.

It left Joseph with two shattered legs, four broken ribs and two broken arms. He would be unable to walk for three months. No reason was ever given to Joseph McGartland as to why he had been so severely beaten by an IRA punishment squad. But he knew why; he happened to be my brother and, according to the cowardly code of IRA punishment squads, that was sufficient justification to inflict a terrible beating on a totally innocent young man.

In September 1990, a group of courageous men and women formed FAIT, Families Against Intimidation and Terror, and they take every opportunity to condemn and to highlight lawless beatings, some of which are carried out as personal vendettas. But the so-called punishment squads of the IRA and the Loyalists, groups of mindless, cowardly bastards, continue to terrorise their sectarian communities with impunity.

For four years, I had tried, in some small way, to play a part in bringing some form of security to the people of Northern Ireland, trying to save the lives of innocent people, both Catholic and Protestant alike, in the hope that, one day, the Province would enjoy a future without guns and bombs, and without the unbridled violence of the despicable punishment squads.

Sincere Sympathy

*Lord, grant eternal rest
to the soul of Thy
faithful servant
and comfort and console
those who have been
bereaved.*

---

*The Holy Sacrifice
of the Mass
will be offered
for the repose of the soul of*

HARTY MC GARTLAND

*with Sincere Sympathy
from*

Your Friends in Connelly house
Crumlin Road & Long kesh.

REV. PATRICK CROWLEY

Celebrant